AIR DISASTER

Volume 4

Macarthur Job

Artwork by Juanita Franzi

ACKNOWLEDGEMENTS

It can be no secret that it is impossible to produce a book containing as much historical and technical detail as Air Disaster, Volume 4, without the willing assistance of many people, each of them authorities in their own fields.

As with my previous books on major aircraft accidents, I am indebted to the former Bureau of Air Safety Investigation (BASI) in Canberra for providing access to copies of overseas accident investigation reports – in particular to its former Director Dr Rob Lee, and Data Manager Russell Sibbison, now with the Australian Transport Safety Bureau. Air safety investigators Clive Phillips and John Sonneveld, formerly with BASI's Melbourne Field Office, also provided valuable assistance. And for access to official reports on three of the accidents to UK registered aircraft, I am indebted to Ken Smart CBE, Chief Inspector of Britain's Air Accidents Investigation Branch

Australian Aviation's well known airline fleet contributor Gordon Reid willingly provided a wealth of historical information, as well as obtaining US publisher John Wegg's permission to use photographs from his *Airways* magazine. And air traffic controller Phil Vabre generously provided the background to the US air traffic control system at the time of the Grand Canyon collision, as well as sourcing many of the illustrations used throughout the book.

Other industry colleagues upon whose expertise I have drawn include veteran aviation writer Stanley Brogden OAM, airline pilot and former flight engineer Brian L Hill, aviation historian John Hopton, Captains Sandy Howard, John Laming and Tony Lucas, aviation historian and pilot Keith Meggs DFM, Captain Alan Searle and prolific aviation author Stewart Wilson. My appreciation and thanks go to them all. I also acknowledge the generous assistance of Mrs Marie Fearon, originally from County Kerry, Ireland, for her advice on the geographical aspects of the River Shannon ditching described in Chapter 3.

Talented aviation artist Juanita Franzi, as well as producing the cover design, has been untiring in her efforts to present illustrations that convey the mood, as well as the facts, of the various dramas as they unfolded.

My thanks to Jim Thorn, Managing Editor of Aerospace Publications, and to his highly efficient production manager Gayla Wilson, for their efforts in bringing the book to its conclusion. Thanks too, to *Australian Aviation's* Editor, Gerard Frawley, for his help whenever it was needed.

Finally, I record my appreciation for the exacting literary editorship of all my labours by my wife, Esma, ensuring that the technical content of the investigations remain comprehensible to readers not nurtured in the sometimes obscure language that is peculiar to aviators.

Macarthur Job
Melbourne, Australia
June 2001

★ ★ ★

Published by Aerospace Publications Pty Ltd (ACN: 001 570 458) PO Box 1777, Fyshwick, ACT 2609, Australia.
Phone (02) 6280 0111, fax (02) 6280 0007, e-mail mail@ausaviation.com.au and website
www.ausaviation.com.au – publishers of monthly *Australian Aviation* magazine.
Production Manager: Gayla Wilson

ISBN 1 875671 48 X

CONTENTS

NOTE ON UNITS OF MEASUREMENT USED IN THIS BOOK

Units of measurement used in Australian civil aviation have undergone a number of changes since World War 2. Originally the same as for land transport, distance was in statute miles, speed in miles per hour, and altitude in feet.

The first change came in the early postwar years when expression of distance and speed was changed to nautical miles and knots – a logical move, since air navigation has much in common with navigation at sea, and one nautical mile is one minute of an arc of latitude on the earth's surface.

Major changes (creating great confusion for non-aviation writers and readers!), came when Australia "went metric" in 1970. The committee charged with determining standards for aviation then decreed that horizontal distances less than three nautical miles (runway lengths, visibility in fog, etc), would be expressed in metres and kilometres. But nautical miles and knots would continue to be used for navigation, while altitude would continue to be measured in feet.

The units of measurement quoted in this book conform with current Australian and ICAO aviation practice. Conversions are included when it is necessary to quote other units from overseas accident reports.

INTRODUCTION

In one sense this latest volume in the *Air Disaster* series should have been the first, rather than the fourth to be published. For instead of continuing the theme of Volumes 1, 2 and 3, analysing the way the modern miracle of airline travel is being steadily refined in the harsh world of day-to-day experience, Air Disaster Volume 4 returns to the early postwar years to fill in the aeronautical development story that led to the dawn of the jet age of air travel.

They were years full of expectation and promise. Long distance global flying in large four engine passenger aircraft, although pioneered to a degree by Short, Sikorsky and Boeing flying boats in the late 1930s, had become established only as a result of wartime military and troop transport operations. The imperative of national emergency had spawned, or at least hastened, the development of long range military transport landplanes capable of such assignments.

With the coming of peace, those aircraft types, quickly adapted to civil, passenger carrying specifications, provided a ready source of equipment for the burgeoning postwar airline industry. As well, they formed the basis for further airliner development that would offer higher passenger capacity and aircraft performance. International passenger flying suddenly came of age, challenging for the first time in history, the supremacy and appeal of the ocean going liner. Suddenly the future for swift, safe, comfortable air travel seemed almost limitless.

Many of the problems inherent in operating massive four engined aircraft over long distances and long flight times – problems of fuel management and endurance, loading, engine reliability, asymmetric handling, emergency landings and ocean ditchings, and approaches to land in reduced visibility – were encountered by military crews during the war years. But these operational lessons, though undoubtedly valuable, were cloaked at the time by matters of higher priority generated by the stress of war. As a result, as civil airliners began to ply the new air routes – routes in many instances trail-blazed by wartime military crews – and paying passengers increasingly looked to this new form of world transport, the lessons had to be learnt anew.

This book provides a selection of some of the major operational problems encountered in that developmental era of world airline transport – the era that ushered in the jet age of a global transport system whose overall safety standard today, despite occasional highly publicised setbacks, is beyond that of any other transport mode the world has ever seen.

The inclusion of particular case histories in this book is not intended as criticism of the accident record of any aircraft manufacturer, airline, or nation. Rather, the instances chosen are either notable in their own right, or are representative of problems encountered. And in identifying crew members unfortunate enough to be caught up in these tragic learning experiences, the book seeks only to be authentic. As in the later accidents covered in the *Air Disaster* series, their other qualification for inclusion was that comprehensive, reliable reports on the accidents, their circumstances, and their investigations were available.

If aviation has demonstrated any clear principle since the Wright Flyer first lifted off the ground under its own power in 1903, it is that flying has an inexhaustible supply of unpleasant surprises for those who in any way and for any reason, presume to take it for granted. Examining the way some of those hitherto unexpected aviation hazards came to light through costly experience, is exactly what this book is about.

We should never forget that the sum of this experience, and the resulting safety standards to which civil aviation as a whole operates today, have only been gained over the years at a high price in human lives. It is to be hoped that the contents of this book will bring a fresh realisation that the world air transport system we all now take so much for granted has not just "happened" – it has evolved step by difficult step, nearly always as a result of lessons that were tragic as well as salutary.

*With appreciation for the contribution
of the late John Watkins, OBE,
former Director of Engineering for Trans Australia Airlines,
whose affirmation and advice was a constant source of encouragement.*

GLOSSARY OF AERONAUTICAL TERMS AND ABBREVIATIONS

ADF: Automatic Direction Finder. Previously known as radio compass.

Aileron: Control surfaces on (usually) outer sections of wing trailing edges, controlling bank and roll of aircraft.

Airspeed Indicator (ASI): Instrument measuring speed of aircraft through air, expressed in knots.

Air Traffic Clearance: Approval by Air Traffic Control for aircraft to taxi, takeoff, climb, enter controlled airspace, descend or to land.

Air Traffic Control (ATC): System of directing all aircraft operating within designated airspace by radio. Divided into sectors such as Tower (aerodrome control for takeoffs and landings), Departures, Control (en route aircraft), and Approach.

Altitude: Height of aircraft as shown on altimeter adjusted to local barometric pressure.

Angle of attack (AoA): Angle at which wings meet airflow.

Artificial horizon (AH): Instrument displaying aircraft attitude in relation to real horizon.

Asymmetric flight: Multi engined aircraft flying with one engine inoperative.

ATIS: Automated terminal information service. Continuous, recorded radio transmission of meteorological conditions at airport.

Attitude: Lateral and longitudinal relationship of aircraft to horizon.

Bunt: Sudden nose down manoeuvre of aircraft, usually producing uncomfortable negative G.

"Clean" (aircraft): Aircraft in normal cruising configuration, with high lift devices and undercarriage retracted.

Control Area: Designated area of airspace in which all aircraft movements are under radio direction of Air Traffic Control.

Control Zone: Designated airspace encompassing terminal area of an airport in which all aircraft movements are under radio direction of Tower Controller.

Co-ordinates: Latitude and longitude of a position anywhere on the earth's surface, estimated to one minute of an arc.

CVR (Cockpit Voice Recorder): Sophisticated, "crash proof" tape recording equipment fitted to airline aircraft to record flight crew conversations and radio transmissions. The tape is a 30 minute closed loop which is continuously recycled, providing a complete audio record of the last 30 minutes of any flight.

Directional gyro (DG): Instrument accurately registering direction aircraft is heading. When aligned with compass, provides immediate indication of changes in magnetic heading.

DME: Distance Measuring Equipment. Radio navigation aid providing pilot with constant readout of distance from selected radio beacon.

Elevation: Height of terrain above mean sea level. Abbreviated AMSL.

Elevators: Control surfaces at rear of horizontal tail (tailplane), controlling nose attitude of aircraft.

Endurance: Time (expressed in minutes) aircraft can theoretically remain in air before fuel is exhausted.

ETA: Estimated time of arrival.

ETD: Estimated time of departure.

Fin: The vertical aerofoil member of an aeroplane's tail assembly or empennage. Provides directional stability in flight. Known as the vertical stabiliser in US aviation parlance (see also rudder).

FDR (Flight Data Recorder): Complex "crash proof" instrument fitted to airline aircraft to continuously record operating parameters during flight. Early FDRs using stylus scribing on metallic tape recorded only four parameters – airspeed, altitude, heading and vertical acceleration.

Flaps: Adjustable surfaces on aircraft's wing trailing edge. When lowered, flaps increase lift of wing, thereby reducing stalling speed, and increase drag, steepening aircraft's glide angle.

Flightplan: Document prepared by pilot on official form before departure, providing details of proposed flight – track to be followed, waypoints, computations of wind effects, headings and speeds for each leg, all-up weight at departure, and progressive fuel burn.

Flight Level (FL): Expression of height in hundreds of feet, based on standard barometric altimeter setting of 1013.2 millibars. Eg, 12,000 feet on standard altimeter setting would be FL120. Differs from altitude in that the latter is based on actual barometric altimeter setting for a particular area or airport.

"G" (gravities): Expression of force acting on aircraft and its occupants in flight, measured in multiples of earth's gravitational force.

GMT (Greenwich Mean Time): Standard world time used for navigation regardless of location of ship or aircraft. Now generally referred to as UTC (Co-ordinated Universal Time).

Ground speed: Actual speed of aircraft over ground. May be greater or less than airspeed, according to wind.

HF (High (radio) Frequency): Radio propagation in the frequency band from 3 to 30 MHz. Permits communication over long distances, but reception can be subject to atmospheric and electrical interference. Used by aircraft operating beyond range of VHF and UHF radio propagation.

IFR (Instrument Flight Rules): Stipulated procedures for navigating aircraft by reference to cockpit instruments and radio navigation aids alone. Enables flight regardless of visibility. Normal operating procedure for airline flights.

ILS (Instrument Landing System): Electronic approach aid which enables a pilot to carry out an approach for landing when weather conditions preclude visual contact with the ground.

IMC (Instrument Meteorological Conditions): Weather conditions in which visibility is less than specified for visual flying, and in which flight is legally possible only under IFR.

Knot: One nautical mile per hour. Equivalent to 1.853km/h.

Localiser: Horizontal component of electronic Instrument Landing System. As an on-course or approach aid, provides accurate lateral guidance along a directional electronic path which progressively narrows as the transmitting beacon is approached.

LSA (Lowest Safe Altitude): Designated minimum altitude for particular air route, providing minimum of 1,000 feet clearance above underlying terrain.

MSA (Minimum Safe Altitude): Altitude below which IFR aircraft may not descend unless specifically authorised to do so by ATC. Takes into account high terrain underlying an air route.

Mayday (repeated three times): Radio telephony version of former morse code "SOS" distress call. Derived from the French "m'aidez" – "help me".

Nautical mile (nm): Measure of distance used for navigation in the air and at sea. Equal to one minute of an arc of latitude on the earth's surface. Is 800 feet longer than a statute mile and equivalent to 1.853km.

Navaid: Radio navigation aid.

NDB: Non directional beacon. Ground based medium frequency radio transmitter sending continuous signals in all directions for use by aircraft fitted with ADF (radio compass).

NOTAM (Notice to Airmen): Message concerning changes to serviceability of aerodromes, radio and navigation facilities.

Octas ("eighths"): Expression of cloud amount. Eight octas (or eighths) represents a completely overcast sky; four octas a half clouded sky.

Pitot-static system: System of instruments, connecting tubes and air sensors for measuring altitude, airspeed, and rate of climb or descent.

Precipitation: (Meteorological) Rain, hail, sleet or snow in or falling from cloud.

Preflight (inspection): "Walk around" inspection of aircraft by pilot, usually immediately prior to flight.

QFE: Code expression designating altimeter setting in millibars for particular airport. When set on subscale of altimeter, instrument reads aircraft's height above that airport.

QNH: Code expression designating altimeter setting in millibars – when set on subscale of aircraft's altimeter, instrument reads aircraft's height above mean sea level.

Radial: Bearing to or from VOR radio range.

Radio Compass: See ADF.

Radio Range: Type of radio beacon providing defined aircraft tracks to or from that navigation aid.

Rate One turn: Shallow standard rate turn used in instrument flight conditions.

RPM (rpm): Measure of engine speed expressed in revolutions per minute.

Rudder(s): Control surface(s) at rear of vertical tail (fin) controlling yawing movement of aircraft.

SAR: Search and Rescue.

Sigmet: Warning signal issued by Aviation Meteorological Service when weather conditions suddenly deteriorate.

Spot height: Height noted on chart showing elevation of prominent mountain peak.

Stalling speed: Low airspeed at which aircraft wings suddenly lose lift. No connection with engine "stall". Is absolute minimum airspeed at which aircraft can maintain flight.

Tailplane: Horizontal aerofoil member of an aeroplane's tail assembly or empennage. Provides longitudinal stability in flight. Known as the stabiliser in US aviation parlance (see also elevators).

Transponder: Radio device fitted to aircraft which, when triggered off by certain radar wavelengths, emits a signal visible on ground radar screens.

Trim: (verb) Adjusting flight controls of aircraft so that pilot is not required to maintain continuous pressure on elevators, ailerons or rudder, during climb, level flight or descent etc, or as result of changes in the aircraft's centre of gravity.

Trim: (noun) System of controls that enables the pilot to make the required adjustments to the aircraft's handling, as described above.

Turn and bank indicator: Instrument displaying rate of turn and if turn is "balanced" with correct amount of bank – ie neither skidding outwards nor slipping inwards.

V (code): Schedule of indicated airspeeds stipulated for different phases of flight (see following).

V_1: Decision speed during takeoff. Aircraft is committed to fly when this speed is passed.

V_r: Rotation speed. Speed at which aircraft is "rotated" into liftoff attitude by raising the nosewheel off the runway.

V_2: Takeoff safety speed. Minimum control speed plus safety margin to allow for engine failure and other contingencies.

V_{ne}: Never exceed speed.

V_{ref}: Flap reference speed. Landing speed for stipulated number of degrees of flap extension.

VASIS: Visual approach slope indicator. System of lights located on ground on either side of runway to indicate correct angle of descent to approaching aircraft.

VHF (Very High (radio) Frequency): In general use for inflight radio communications on air routes. Its frequency band from 30 to 300 MHZ is largely free from interference and static, but range is limited to "line of sight".

VFR (Visual Flight Rules): Stipulated flight procedure for navigating aircraft visually, clear of cloud, in Visual Meteorological Conditions.

VMC (Visual Meteorological Conditions): Weather providing specified range of visibility, making it possible for pilots to use visual means to avoid obstructing terrain and other aircraft.

VOR: Very High Frequency Omnidirectional Radio Range.

VSI (Vertical Speed Indicator): Instrument displaying rate of climb or descent in feet per minute.

CHAPTER 1

The unlucky Avro Tudor

Avro Ltd's first postwar transport design began full of promise for airlines of the British Commonwealth. But like De Havilland's revolutionary Comet, the Avro Tudor project was to end in disappointment and failure for both its old-established manufacturer and the British aircraft industry.

There is a legend among seafarers that some ships are "unlucky". One vessel that gained this reputation in the late 19th century was the Scottish clipper ship *Loch Ard*. Dismasted at sea on her maiden voyage, driven from her moorings and stranded while undergoing repairs, dismasted for a second time in the Indian Ocean, she was finally and tragically wrecked on the Victorian coast on her third attempted voyage to Australia, with the loss of 51 lives.

Another case in point from more recent history was the Union Steamship Company's Pacific island liner *Tahiti*. After several maritime mishaps in which crew members were either killed or seriously injured, she made Australian history by running down the steam ferry *Greycliffe* in Sydney harbour in 1927. Sliced in two, the *Greycliffe* sank immediately, drowning at least 40 of her passengers, many of them children returning from school. *Tahiti* herself went down at sea in spectacular fashion four years later, after a propeller shaft broke during a voyage from New Zealand to Rarotonga.

Perhaps a similar "unlucky" status could be accorded some aircraft types. Certainly that would seem to be the case with Britain's early postwar Avro Tudor. One of the first generation of new civil

The prototype Avro Tudor 2, G-AGSU, with Rolls-Royce Merlin 102 engines, taking off from the manufacturer's facility at Woodford aerodrome, Cheshire, during its test flying program. (BAE Systems)

The prototype Avro 2, G-AGSU, in flight over Cheshire after being fitted with modified tail surfaces. (BAE Systems)

transport designs to emerge from Britain's military oriented industry at the end World War 2, the Tudor was the product of the pioneer Cheshire based company that produced the highly successful wartime Avro Lancaster bomber and its passenger carrying derivative, the Avro York.

A pressurised, low wing, tail-wheel airliner powered by four Rolls-Royce Merlin engines, the Tudor was designed in two versions. The Tudor 1, intended for BOAC's transatlantic service, was to carry a small number of first class passengers in luxury sleeper accommodation, while the Tudor 2 was a greatly enlarged and stretched version, carrying 60 seated passengers. The biggest aircraft so far produced in Britain, the Tudor 2 as originally envisaged was to become standard equipment on all postwar British Commonwealth routes operated by BOAC, Qantas, and South African Airways. Plans were even in hand for building the Tudor 1 in Australia as a heavy transport for the RAAF, the Government Aircraft Factory at Fishermens Bend in Melbourne going as far a building a wooden mockup.

In the event, teething troubles affecting the performance of both versions, requiring extensive modifications, delayed their planned introduction. Tudor 2 development then suffered a far more serious setback when the prototype crashed on takeoff at Woodford Aerodrome, Cheshire, in August 1947, killing the entire test crew. The fact that the accident resulted from nothing more than crossed aileron controls, and not to any fault in the basically sound design, did not spare the type's unhappy reputation.

Undue haste

Facing the threat of serious competition from Lockheed's postwar Constellation, Avro Ltd was under great pressure to complete the Tudor 2's certification flying.

The prototype had been undergoing necessary modifications to its flight control system in the company's experimental workshops after an enlarged fin and rudder had been fitted, and an important proving flight was scheduled for the morning of Saturday August 14. Its importance to Avro's future was reflected by the fact that the flight was to be made by the Chief Test Pilot, Bill Thorn, accompanied by the company's renowned Chief Designer and Technical Director, Roy Chadwick CBE, FRSA, FRAeS, and Avro's Managing Director, Sir Roy Dobson.

The modifications to the tail assembly involved the replacement of the flight control system and, in order to have the aircraft ready for the test flight on the Saturday morning, new control cables were installed by the experimental workshop's night shift. The airframe fitter who actually carried out the work was the one who had removed the old cables, but he had to work from memory, no drawings being to hand at the time. The cable layout "looked the same" when he completed it and the aircraft was duly signed out as ready for the test flight.

It is doubtless a measure of the pressure under which Avro was working at the time, as well as a salutary lesson on hasty flight preparation, that before the prototype Tudor 2 began its takeoff in bright sunshine that morning, neither the ground engineers nor the flight test crew detected that the ailerons controls had been inadvertently crossed during assembly. As a result, control of the Tudor 2 was lost almost immediately it became airborne, and just missing a nearby farmhouse, it struck the ground heavily, breaking the fuselage apart and catapulting its hapless crew into trees, with fatal results.

Sir Roy Dobson escaped certain death only by the merest chance, having been called to the telephone from the aircraft just before the engines were started.

The South Atlantic mysteries

Despite this severe setback to Avro Ltd and the Tudor in particular, several Tudor 1s, now configured for 32 seated passengers and designated Tudor 4s, began operations in late 1947 with the British South American Airways

The first production Avro Tudor 2, G-AGRX, which flew for the first time in April 1946. This example was fitted with 1750hp (1082kW) Bristol Hercules engines. (BAE Systems)

Corporation on the London/Bermuda route. But only three months later on January 29 1948, Tudor G-AHNP *Star Tiger* disappeared at night northeast of Bermuda with all 31 on board. No trace of it was ever found.

Slightly less than a year later, history repeated itself when another of the Corporation's Tudors, G-AGRE *Star Ariel*, this time with 20 people on board, vanished in equally mysterious circumstances over the sea between Jamaica and Bermuda on January 17 1949.

Again, no trace of the aircraft or occupants could be found. After this second airline disaster, the Tudors were stripped of their passenger carrying status and relegated to freighting operations.

The founding chief executive of British South American Airways was Air Vice-Marshal D C T Bennett, an Australian and prewar Imperial Airways captain who had become famous as the founder and commanding officer of the wartime RAF's elite Pathfinder Force in Bomber Command. A

man with great confidence in Avro aircraft as a result of his extensive wartime experience with Lancasters, he resigned from British South American to found Airflight Ltd, a charter operation based at Langley Aerodrome near Slough.

With two newly delivered Tudors 2s, G-AGRY and G-AKBY (the latter aircraft was in fact designated a Tudor 5 because of minor modifications originally incorporated for British South American Airways, but the aircraft were otherwise identical), Airflight in

The prototype Avro 2, G-AGSU (foreground), formates for the camera with Tudor 1, G-AGRC, over Cheshire, during the former's test flying program. The Tudor 2 was the biggest aircraft type produced in Britain up to that time. (BAE Systems)

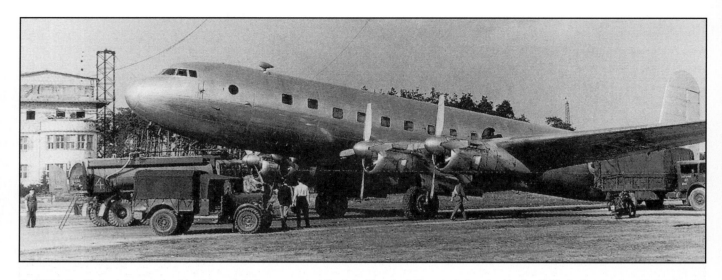

G-AKBY, the Tudor later involved in the accident, snapped at Berlin's Wunstorf Airport during the Berlin Airlift, in September 1948. The big aircraft was amongst the most effective on the airlift.

September 1948 began an intense period of flying on the Berlin Airlift, initially carrying freight of all kinds. G-AKBY was then fitted with fuselage tanks to carry 10 ton loads of diesel fuel. By the time the two Airflight Tudors returned to England at the end of May 1949, they had flown more than 2550 hours on nearly 1000 sorties, the big aircraft proving among the most useful on the entire airlift.

But even though the Tudors had by now more than established their worth, the British Air Registration Board had still not re-cleared them for passenger operations. Modifications were made to both aircraft, in particular to their hydraulic and pressurisation systems, and in August 1949 Air Vice-Marshal Bennett's faith in the Tudors was rewarded when their Certificates of Airworthiness were amended to include passenger operations.

Passengers again

Bennett's company could now undertake passenger charters. Its name was changed to Fairflight Ltd, its headquarters moved to Blackbushe, and throughout the winter of 1949 and the spring of 1950, its two Tudors operated many incident free long distance passenger flights to and from Pakistan, the Middle East and South Africa.

Saturday, March 11 1950, was a notable day on the calendar for Welsh and Irish rugby enthusiasts – the date of the eagerly awaited international match to be played that afternoon in Belfast between Wales and Ireland. Indeed, so keen was the contest that numbers of Welsh supporters were anxious to make the trip to Ireland to watch the match for themselves. Throughout Wales in the weeks preceding the match, supporters serious about travelling to the match clubbed together to charter a large aircraft for the trip.

Fairflight Ltd at Blackbushe could offer what was probably the biggest charter aircraft available in Britain. The company's Tudor G-AKBY could in fact seat 72 passengers, and the organisers, mindful that more than this number were keen to go, arranged for it to make the trip from Wales to Dublin on the Friday morning, remain two nights there while the passengers travelled on to Belfast for the match, and fly the return leg from Dublin early on the Sunday afternoon, March 12.

As it happened, negotiations Fairflight had been making with the Air Registration Board to increase G-AKBY's passenger capacity to 78 came to fruition a few days before the proposed charter flight, and the charter organisers had no difficulty in arranging to fill the additional seats. But although Fairflight was quickly able to reconfigure the cabin seating to provide 13 rows of triple seats on either side of the centre aisle, and submitted revised loading instructions to the Board for approval, this paperwork had not been re-turned by the day of the flight. As a result, no loading instructions were available to the crew except those originally prepared for the aircraft by the manufacturer.

The Tudor's captain for the charter, Captain D J Parsons, was nevertheless mindful of the need to be careful with the load distribution, and during his flight preparation made out a number of trial load sheets, as a result of which he told Air Vice-Marshal Bennett that "he would have to watch the CofG".

Disaster for Welsh rugby

The group chartering the aircraft had asked that the passengers be picked up at RAF Llandow, 17 miles (30km) west of Cardiff, as it was their most convenient aerodrome. Accordingly, on the morning of Friday March 10, the Tudor, with a crew of five, flew to Llandow where the passengers, already assembled and waiting by the RAF control tower, promptly boarded the aircraft. There were no facilities at Llandow for weighing the passengers' luggage, and although some of their heavier items were loaded into the forward hold, most were carrying only light hand luggage for their weekend away.

The flight northwest across the Irish Sea was uneventful, and the Tudor landed normally at Dublin's Collinstown Airport an hour and a half later.

The following day saw Wales beat Ireland at the international

Another picture of G-AKBY, the Tudor later involved in the accident, at Berlin's Gatow Airport during the Berlin Airlift, early in 1949, when it was a tanker transport. Fitted with fuselage tanks, it could carry 10 tonnes of diesel fuel.

match in Belfast, and it was a jubilant load of returning passengers that assembled at Collinstown Airport on the Sunday morning ready for their trip home. All in high spirits, most had made small purchases while in Ireland and some had even bought additional hand luggage, but there was no substantial increase in the total aircraft load for the return flight.

While flight planning for the trip back to Llandow, Captain Parsons obtained a route weather forecast which indicated the surface wind at Llandow on their arrival was likely to be only light from the northwest. To a Cambrian Airways pilot, also flight planning at the time, Parsons remarked that he "wished there was a little more wind at Llandow". The runway at RAF Llandow was only 4800 feet (1463m) long and he felt uneasy about landing the heavy, fully laden Tudor on it in such light wind conditions.

Again a few items of bigger luggage were loaded into the forward hold, but again most passengers carried their hand luggage with them, including their purchases in Ireland. The Irish airline, Aer Lingus, had facilities for weighing luggage at Collinstown, but Captain Parsons apparently did not consider it necessary to use them.

The surface wind at Collinstown when the Tudor's engines were started was from slightly west of north. But instead of using the

into wind 4800 feet (1463m) Runway 35, Captain Parsons elected to taxi to the threshold of Runway 06 because it was 300 feet (91m) longer.

The takeoff was normal, and the flight back to south Wales uneventful. Passengers moved around the cabin during the trip, talking with friends, but as the aircraft approached Llandow, they were all back in their assigned seats with their safety belts fastened, ready for landing.

At 2.50pm the Tudor called RAF Llandow Tower and was instructed to join the circuit at 1000 feet, and that the duty runway was 28. The surface wind, the aircraft was advised, was from 280° at 10 to 15 knots (19-28km/h), and the visibility 15 miles. The aircraft next reported "downwind" and was cleared for both final approach and landing.

Soon afterwards, in fine sunny conditions, the Tudor was seen turning west on to final approach, lining up with the runway about two miles out from the threshold at a height of around 500 feet. The approach seemed perfectly normal, though perhaps a little low, and the undercarriage and flaps were seen to be down. Only one other aircraft was in the vicinity, an Auster, passing directly over the aerodrome at below circuit height, nearly three miles from the Tudor's position.

As its approach continued, the

Tudor appeared to be undershooting on its long shallow final, and when about 2500 feet (800m) short of the threshold, at a height of between 100 and 150 feet, power was increased a little to flatten the glide and reduce the rate of descent. Almost immediately afterwards however, the engines suddenly roared, and the Tudor's nose began to rise. Under the impetus of high power, the change in attitude quickly developed into an increasingly steep climb, and the Tudor rapidly gained about 250 feet in height, its speed falling off at the same time.

Now between 60° and 70° nose up, its engine noise ceased suddenly as the aircraft appeared to stall. The nose and starboard wing dropped, and the Tudor fell away to the right, striking open ground beside the tiny village of Sigingstone a few moments later with great force at an angle of about 60° while still banked 45°. The nose section was crumpled and demolished, both wings were torn off, and the remainder of the fuselage came to rest, broken into two, on its starboard side.

No fire broke out and villagers running to the wreckage saw a survivor, cut about the head, staggering towards them. "Try and help them," he called out. The villagers found another four passengers, injured but still alive, in the rear section of the fuselage. Ambulances that arrived shortly

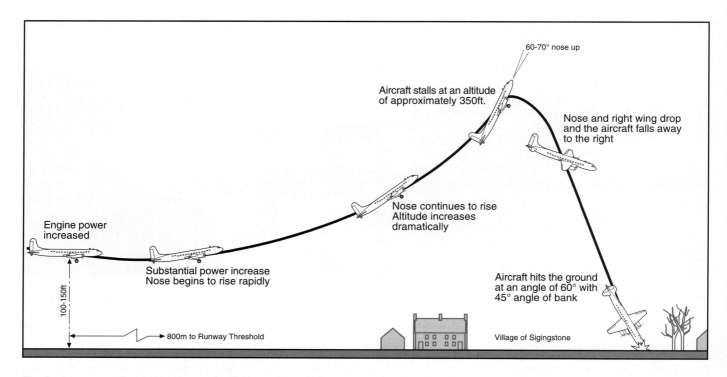

The final sequence that led to the crash. Making a long shallow approach to land at RAF Llandow, with undercarriage and flaps down, the Tudor was undershooting at 100-150 feet when power was heard to increase slightly. A massive increase in power suddenly followed and the Tudor nosed up into an increasingly steep climb. At a height of about 250 feet, the engine noise abruptly ceased as the aircraft stalled. The Tudor fell away to the right, striking the ground beside the village of Sigingstone. (Aero Illustrations)

RAF personnel guard the site as investigators, with firemen and police, sift through the tangled wreckage of the Tudor. (Wide World Photos)

afterwards took the five survivors to the RAF station hospital, but two of them succumbed to their injuries soon afterwards. All other occupants of the aircraft had been killed instantly in the impact. The three remaining survivors were all seated at the rear of the cabin, having been among the last passengers to board the aircraft at Dublin.

Investigation

Examination of the wreckage revealed no sign of any malfunction in the aircraft, its engines, or operating systems. The engines' magneto switches were all in the off position, having evidently been cut by the crew when they realised the accident was imminent.

Two trial load sheets, and one prepared by Captain Parson for the flight from Llandow to Dublin and return, were found amongst the wreckage of the flightdeck. They showed that, with 78 passengers aboard, the aircraft would require around 2000lb (907kg) in its forward hold if its CofG was not to be behind the aft limit. The Tudor's all-up weight of 80,000lb (36,288kg) provided adequately for this amount of luggage or ballast to be carried.

A total of only 1031lb (468kg) of passengers' luggage was accounted for in the wreckage, most of it remnants of small hand luggage and personal clothing. One of the survivors told investigators that, on the return flight from Dublin, his own luggage, including an extra overnight bag he had bought in Ireland, was stowed on the cabin floor at his feet. Before they took off from Collinstown Airport, one of the crew asked passengers if they would like any of their luggage taken forward, but this invitation was declined, the passengers all indicating they were quite comfortable.

No heavy luggage or ballast was recovered from the wreckage, and it was clear to the investigators that nothing like 2000lb (907kg) of personal luggage was stored in the forward hold when the aircraft took off from Collinstown. Calculations to determine the aircraft's load distribution on the flight from Dublin to Llandow showed that the Tudor's CofG would have been at least 109 inches (272.5cm) behind the datum point specified in its Certificate of Airworthiness, and could have been as much as 112 inches (280cm) behind it.

In this configuration the aircraft would have been highly unstable longitudinally, and at low airspeed, such as on its approach to land at Llandow, there would have been little downward elevator control remaining to overcome the powerful noseup tenancy produced by a sudden application of power.

The Royal Aircraft Establishment at Farnborough provided evidence, based on tests carried out at Boscombe Down when the Tudor 2 was undergoing its certification flying, that with the CofG 106 inches (265cm) behind the datum point, no effective down elevator control would remain at an airspeed of 94 knots (174km/h) if full power was applied with the undercarriage and flaps down. With the CofG 112 inches (280cm) behind the datum, the aircraft in a similar configuration would run out of down elevator control at 105 knots.

Captain Parsons, though highly regarded by his principal, Air Vice-Marshal Bennett, who had personally conducted his Tudor training, was not greatly experienced by today's heavy civil aircraft standards, having a total of only a little over 3000 hours. Of this only 300 were in command of Tudor aircraft, with another 600 spent as a first officer on the type.

It was evident that, while making a cautious approach to land at Llandow because of its limited runway length and the size and weight of the aircraft he was flying, Captain Parsons apparently realised too late that he was undershooting substantially. With his initial application of power to correct the glidepath obviously inadequate, he then applied substantial power to reach the runway. Because of the aircraft's excessively aft CofG however, insufficient downward elevator control remained to correct the resulting sudden and substantial change in attitude, and the aircraft entered an increasingly steep climb which culminated in a stall only about 350 feet above the ground.

After a Court Investigation at Cardiff had heard evidence and formally determined the cause of the accident, the Ministry of Civil Aviation took out a summons against Fairflight Ltd, the prosecution alleging that G-AKBY's CofG was between seven and 13 inches (17.5 and 32.5cm) aft of the rear limit. The company was found guilty of "loading the Tudor in such a way that its centre of gravity was beyond the prescribed limits".

Though the highly publicised Welsh accident and its outcome was a further blow to the aircraft type's reputation, international charter flying in Avro Tudors by Fairflight and later, Aviation Traders Ltd at Southend, continued into the late 1950s, by which time most of the remaining aircraft had been scrapped. The last operational Tudor 1, G-AGRH, operated by Aviation Traders, struck a 14,500 foot mountain peak and crashed in Turkey in 1959 while on a charter flight with freight to Woomera, South Australia.

The Tudor 2 design, sound despite the aircraft type's many setbacks, later became the basis for the Avro 706 high altitude research aircraft.

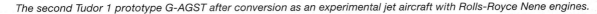

The second Tudor 1 prototype G-AGST after conversion as an experimental jet aircraft with Rolls-Royce Nene engines.

CHAPTER 2

Mystery over the Jungle

The Boeing 377 Stratocruiser was the last word in luxury air travel. But unsolved design problems held a tragedy in store for its airline and passengers alike.

Hailed the "ocean liner of the air" when it first entered airline operations at the end of the 1940s, the Boeing 377 Stratocruiser was a civil derivative the B-29 bomber, developed late in World War 2.

In a sense it evolved in much the same way as the prewar pressurized Boeing 307 Stratoliner did from the earlier B-17 Flying Fortress design. In both cases the aircraft's wings, tail assembly, undercarriage and engine mountings were almost identical with their predecessor's.

Developed first as the Boeing 367, a military transport intended to carry 134 fully armed troops, three small loaded trucks, or two light tanks, the design started with the basic B-29 airframe and engines, with its fuselage becoming the lower lobe of a new double lobe, "figure of eight" fuselage. A larger diameter upper lobe, wide enough to accommodate military transport loads, was married to the lower lobe, with the main cabin floor located on the intersection of the lobes. Rear clamshell doors, similar to those fitted to the later Lockheed Her-

cules, Starlifter and Galaxy military transports, enabled vehicles to be driven aboard via retractable built-in ramps. Bulk cargo could be loaded via an internal overhead hoist which ran the entire length of the main cabin, while the aircraft's two lower cargo holds were accessed through external doors.

A commercial development of the B-367 finally became the Boeing 377 Stratocruiser, which first flew in July 1947, powered by P&W R-4360 Double Wasp 3500hp (2610kW) "corncob" radial engines, each with four rows of seven cylinders. With a gross weight of 67,130kg, it cruised at 295kt (547km/h) and had a range of 3650nm (6765km) with maximum fuel. Its crew comprised captain, first officer, navigator, flight engineer, and radio operator, plus flight attendants, the number of which varied according to the type of route the aircraft was operating.

Like its prewar ancestor, the Stratoliner, a vast, bulbous, tail wheel aeroplane that quickly earned the nickname "Fat Cat", the Stratocruiser looked clumsy

and obese on the ground, but in the air somehow became transformed into a thing of beauty and grace.

Its main upper deck passenger cabin could seat from 55 to 100 passengers, and the most comprehensive galley provided to that time in any airliner was installed at the rear of the cabin. A spiral staircase led to a lounge on the lower deck behind the wing that, usually furnished as a luxury bar, could seat an additional 14 passengers. When fitted out as a sleeper aircraft, the Stratocruiser offered 28 upper and lower berths, plus five seats. Dressing rooms were provided for both men and women.

Airlines which eagerly placed orders for the new luxury airliner were Pan American World Airways, SILA (the Scandinavian forerunner of SAS), American Overseas Airlines, Northwest Airlines, the British Overseas Airways Corporation and United Air Lines. Indeed, such was the regard for the Stratocruiser's standard of comfort, elegance and spaciousness, that in October 1951 the British Ministry of

(above) Boeing's 377 Stratocruiser prototype at the manufacturer's rollout ceremony at Seattle on July 2, 1947. The design's double lobe fuselage is clearly evident in this picture. (below) Stratocruisers in production at Boeing's Seattle plant in 1949. Only 55 Boeing 377 Stratocruisers were sold to airlines, but no less than 888 Boeing 367s, the military transport from which the type was developed, were delivered to the US Air Force (as C-97s and KC-97s) before production finally ceased in 1956. (Boeing)

Stratocruiser ancestor: The world's first pressurised airliner, the prewar Boeing 307 Stratoliner. A massive tailwheel aeroplane, affectionately known as "the Fat Cat", the Stratoliner design was derived from that of the Boeing B-17 Flying Fortress, just as the military Boeing 367 transport and the 377 Stratocruiser were later derived from the B-29 Super Fortress. (Tony Merton Jones)

Civil Aviation chartered BOAC's G-AKGK *Canopus*, commanded by the legendary Captain O P Jones, to take Their Royal Highnesses the Princess Elizabeth (soon to become Queen Elizabeth II) and the Duke of Edinburgh with their entourage to Montreal to begin a State visit to Canada.

Teething problems are likely with any new type of aircraft, but in the case of the Stratocruiser, the deficiencies proved to be much deeper, it quickly becoming obvious that the Stratocruiser was not only an expensive aircraft to buy but, more worryingly for the airlines that had chosen it, exceedingly costly to run.

As with the early B-29 bombers whose engines had a distressing propensity to catch fire, the Stratocruiser's monstrous 28 cylinder radial engines, though a good deal more reliable, were still highly temperamental, appearing to need their cylinders changed almost as often as their 56 spark plugs.

From the five member flightcrews, sharing a flightdeck more spacious than many a suburban bedroom, there was initially great enthusiasm, particularly as it offered visibility far superior to that of any previous airliner. Moreover, despite its great size and bulk, from a pilot's point of

view the Stratocruiser seemed to be a forgiving aeroplane. It was easy to take off, fly and land – while everything was working as intended.

But therein lay the rub, for the Stratocruiser design had some serious drawbacks. Rudder control was inadequate when it was needed to any degree, as in asymmetric flight, and crews had to be to extremely careful of the engines' cowl gill settings. Keeping the huge engines within their cylinder head temperature limitations during climb was a constant challenge to the flight engineer, for if the oversize gills were opened too far, buffeting and a serious loss of lift and lateral stability could result. Fully laden, the Stratocruiser's performance on three engines was in any case marginal, and the wider cowl gill settings needed to cool the remaining live engines made asymmetric flight even more critical. The Stratocruiser's engine-propeller combination was also a particularly unhappy one, with propeller overspeed problems and blade failures occurring all too often.

The flightdeck of the Stratocruiser, though remarkably quiet by the piston engined standards of the day, also had its problems for crews. In the tropics, the extensive nose window panels acted like a greenhouse, making it uncomfortably hot, and in cool weather condensation formed in the top of the fuselage, showering the pilots' seats during descent.

But the majority of Stratocruiser passengers remained blissfully unaware of these operational problems. Indeed, most were highly impressed in every way. The Stratocruiser's creature comforts, size and spaciousness were reminiscent of the standards offered by the great transocean flying boats of the immediate prewar era, and seemed to promise a new way of life for air travellers. Certainly, there was no lack of passenger bookings on routes served by Stratocruisers.

One of these routes was Pan American's regular "El Presidente" service from Buenos Aires, Argentina, to New York, via Montevideo, Uruguay; Rio de Janeiro, Brazil; and Port of Spain, Trinidad.

The new "Ocean Liner of the Air". Pan American's Clipper Flying Cloud *N1028V, provides Europe with its first glimpse of the aircraft that was to bring a new era in passenger comfort in the early postwar era of international air travel. It is seen here at London Heathrow on April 4, 1949. (Flight)*

Royal Stratocruiser: BOAC's G-AKGK Canopus, which the British Ministry of Civil Aviation chartered in October 1951 to take Princess Elizabeth (soon to be Queen Elizabeth II) and the Duke of Edinburgh to Canada. The flight was under the command of the legendary Captain O P Jones. (BOAC via Tony Merton Jones)

On the evening of Monday, April 28 1952, Stratocruiser N1039V, *Clipper Good Hope*, one of 29 now being operated by the company, (and one of two Stratocruisers Boeing had used for the type's certification flying), took off from Buenos Aires at 6.25pm on the first leg of the long international flight to New York. Its call at Montevideo was uneventful, and it landed at Rio de Janeiro just after 1am.

There was a change of crew at Rio de Janeiro, the Stratocruiser was refuelled, and at 3am, with a loaded weight 1610kg below the maximum allowable, the aircraft taxied from the terminal for its next leg to Port of Spain under the command of Captain Albert Grossarth, 37, a pilot of nearly 8500 hours experience. In addition to the normal flightcrew of five, there were four flight attendants caring for the 41 passengers on board. They included nationals from the US, Canada, Britain, France, Germany and Rumania, as well as 25 South American citizens.

At the runway holding point, the Stratocruiser was cleared for an off-airways route, direct to Port of Spain, a track which would take it across the vast unexplored Amazonian forests to the northeastern coast of Venezuela and Trinidad. With an estimated flight time of 10 hours 30 minutes to Port of Spain, the aircraft took off at 3.06am.

The flight progressed normally for at least the next three and a half hours, reporting on time at Belo Horizonte and Monte Claros, flying VFR at 12,500 feet. At

Stratocruiser NX1039V, originally one of two used by Boeing for certification of the type, was later delivered to Pan American as Clipper Good Hope, N1039V. It was to be the first Stratocruiser lost in a fatal accident. It is seen here in flight in its former Boeing livery. The "X" in the earlier registration lettering denotes its pre-certification flying status. (Boeing)

This photograph of sister Stratocruiser N1024V, Clipper Bald Eagle, *about to taxi from the old International Terminal at Sydney Kingsford Smith Airport in the early 1950s, shows Pan American's livery for the type at the time of the accident over the Brazilian jungle. (Jim Harrison)*

6.16am, three hours and 10 minutes after its departure, with some of its passengers probably still comfortably asleep in their berths and the flight attendants beginning to prepare breakfast, the aircraft reported abeam the town of Barreiras, cruising at 14,500 feet, again in VFR conditions. The radio officer passed the Stratocruiser's next estimate for abeam Carolina, Brazil, at 7.45am.

But the aircraft did not report abeam Carolina at 7.45am, nor later at Santarem on the Amazon River, its next check point. When no further reports were received from the Stratocruiser, despite numerous transmissions to it, missing aircraft procedures were begun. USAF, US Navy and Brazilian Air Force aircraft began searching, while both airline and cargo aircraft were despatched from Miami to join the search effort. To the east, Brazilian Navy vessels began scouring coastal waters.

The Stratocruiser had been seen passing over the villages of Formosa and Sao Francisco, near the position of its final report abeam Barreiras, and appeared to be flying normally.

Barreiras, population 4000, 655nm (1215km) north of Rio de Janeiro and situated amid thick jungle, is surrounded by mountains and cut off from the outside world by rivers. Much of the area was unexplored at the time, and inhabited by often savage Indians and venomous snakes. But three of the river valleys had long straight stretches containing sandbars, some of them miles long, where even a large aircraft could make an emergency landing. The search effort was initially given to this area, but without success.

The following day, Tuesday April 29, the search was concentrated on the 327km area between the towns of Barreiras and Carolina, which encompassed the route the Stratocruiser was flying. This territory to the north of Barreiras included some of the world's densest jungle of the vast Amazon River valley, but there were also wide stretches of open prairie where there were some mining camps and trading posts, and where native Indians were more friendly.

Bad weather in the afternoon necessitated postponing the

Interior layout of a Pan American Stratocruiser. On international night flights, facing pairs of seats folded down to form double berths, while single overhead berths folded down from the luggage rack area. (Propliner)

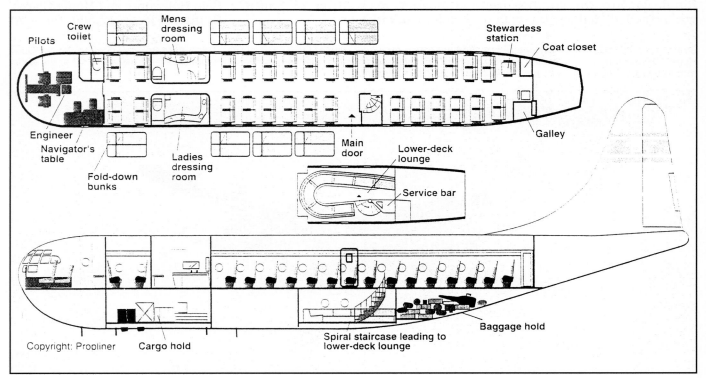

search for the day, but that night some aircraft went out to criss-cross the Stratocruiser's track in the hope that any survivors might have lit signal fires.

The search effort continued fruitlessly with up to 21 Brazilian and American aircraft throughout the Wednesday, but on Thursday, May 1, a searching Curtiss C-46 Commando freighter operated by Pan American, reported finding the disintegrated wreckage of the missing Stratocruiser in densely forested Caraja Indian country, about 220nm (405km) southwest of Carolina. The Stratocruiser, its fuselage lying on the ground inside a 25 metre hole that had been burnt in the thick jungle canopy, appeared to have broken in two, with charred remains scattered on both sides of a 1500 foot hill.

(right) The main upper deck cabin of a Stratocruiser, configured for an international night flight. Curtains could be pulled around each berth for privacy. (below) Spacious dressing rooms were provided for both men and women at the front of the main upper deck cabin. The women's dressing room depicted was on the port side of the aircraft. (Airline Quarterly)

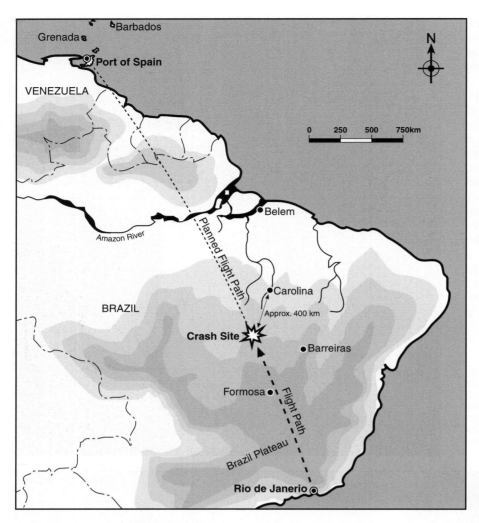

Map of Brazil showing the route Clipper Good Hope *was flying at the time of the accident, and the crash site. The aircraft took off from Rio de Janeiro just after 3am and was estimating abeam Carolina at 7.45am. (Aero Illustrations)*

The captain of a Panair de Brazil (Pan Am's Brazilian subsidiary) airliner that circled the wreckage soon afterwards added that he saw extensive evidence of fire, and that two of the Stratocruiser's engines were lying 500 metres apart in the hilly, heavily timbered country. The location of the wreckage was confirmed soon afterwards by a USAF Search and Rescue aircraft which reported its position as on track, 282nm (523km) north-north-west of its last abeam Barreiras reporting point, and 30nm (56km) south-south-east of its estimated position abeam Carolina reporting point.

A Pan American airliner, specially equipped for the purpose at the company's regional base at Belem on the northern coast of Brazil, picked up a USAF seven man parachute rescue team, including an air force flight surgeon,

from the USAF base at San Juan on the island of Puerto Rico in the West Indies. But after flying the team to the crash site and circling the wreckage for some time at low level without being able to sight any sign of survivors, the rescue team decided it would be inadvisable to jump, because of the hostile and extremely remote nature of the country. The aircraft therefore returned to land at Belem.

Investigation

Aerial photographs, taken by the USAF Search and Rescue Unit that confirmed the position of the crash site, showed the wreckage of the Stratocruiser was scattered in dense hilly jungle over an area about a kilometre and a half square. A further survey from the air indicated that the accident would certainly not have been survivable and that any attempts to

reach the scene by parachute teams would be enormously difficult as well as dangerous, because of the dense jungle in which the wreckage lay.

In accordance with International Civil Aviation Organisation agreements, the Brazilian Government opened an official inquiry into the loss of the aircraft, inviting the US Civil Aeronautics Board (the predecessor of today's National Transportation Safety Board) to participate and send representatives to the investigation.

To examine the wreckage and seek to determine the cause of the disaster, elaborate plans had to made to reach the site overland. After being assembled at Belem, an official investigation team, led by Pan Am's Latin America manager and a Brazilian Air Force Major, boarded a USAF Fairchild C-82 Packet and a C-47 for a three and a half hour flight to a bush airstrip at Araguacema, 450nm (835km) south of Belem and 174nm (322km) southwest of Carolina. From here a Panair de Brazil Consolidated PBY Catalina amphibian flew them on to Lago Grange, a tiny Indian village of mud huts 75nm (139km) south of Araguaceme on the Araguaia River, where a stretch of its water made it possible for the amphibian to alight safely. The team established their base camp at Lago Grange.

The 27-man investigation team was now only 56km southeast of the wreckage site, but more than 40 of those kilometres lay through dense jungle, and across deep gorges with near vertical cliffs. After 17 days of trekking, enduring extreme privations which progressively forced 20 members of the team to turn back to Lago Grange, seven of the men finally reached the wreckage on May 16, 17 days after the accident.

As best they could, the remaining members of the party began an examination of the widely scattered wreckage. But, with their limited resources and manpower, they soon found the task overwhelming in the inhospitable and rugged jungle-covered hills. Despite now being supported as far as possible by a USAF Sikorsky S-51 helicopter, flown into Araguacema aboard the Fairchild

The Panair de Brazil Catalina amphibian which flew the initial 27 man investigation team to Lago Grande, a tiny village on the Araguaia River, 56km southeast of the wreckage site, where the team established its base camp. (Charles Boaz)

Flown in to Araguacema aboard a Fairchild Packet, this USAF Sikorsky S-51 helicopter supported the investigation team during its days of arduous trekking through dense jungle and across deep gorges to reach the accident site. (Charles Boaz)

Sketch map showing relationship of the wreckage site to the Araguaia River and the village of Lago Grande, with the route followed by the investigation team. (Airways magazine)

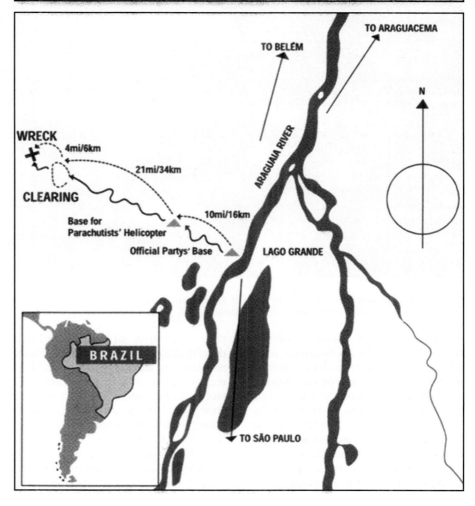

The No 1 engine, with the burnt out remains of the port wing, as investigators found them when they finally reached the inaccessible jungle crash site, 17 days after the accident. (UPI-Bettmann)

Packet, a severe shortage of water, difficulties in maintaining food supplies and deteriorating health in the distressing jungle conditions, quickly convinced the remaining team members that a thorough investigation would require a far more carefully organised and much better equipped expedition.

Although the remaining team members were able to make accu-rate sketches of the wreckage distribution, as well as to take numerous photographs, further examination of the wreckage had to be abandoned after four days at the site. Evacuated to Lago Grange by helicopter, the team returned to Belem.

With the agreement and co-op-eration of the Brazilian Govern-ment, the US Civil Aeronautics Board then organised a fully equipped second expedition which reached the crash site on August 15. An airstrip long enough for transport aircraft was cleared at Lago Grange and a 40km track to an additional advanced camp, much closer to the accident site, was cut through the jungle. Though narrow and difficult to negotiate, Jeeps were able to traverse it in only six hours. Thoroughly prepared and fitted out for all eventualities in this way, this second investigation team was able to remain at the scene for nearly four weeks.

Findings at the scene

The wreckage of the Stratocruiser was found in three main sections, strewn across the jungle covered slopes of three adjacent hills, each separated from the other by around half a kilometre.

The main wreckage included the complete fuselage with the exception of the tail section, the undercarriage, the starboard wing with its nacelles, engines and propellers, and the stub of the port wing from the fuselage to slightly outboard of the No 2 nacelle, but without the No 2 engine and propeller. The wrecked aircraft was upside down and it was evident from the condition of the surrounding trees that it had fallen to the ground almost vertically while in a horizontal attitude.

The remainder of the port wing was found about 700 metres northwest of the main wreckage, complete with the No 1 nacelle, engine, and propeller. The port aileron and the outer section of the port flap lay with the wing.

The wreckage of the tail assembly, comprising the fin, starboard elevator, the tailplane from its starboard tip to about the midspan of the port tailplane, and the rear end of the fuselage, lay some 760 metres northeast from the port wing. Numerous other smaller pieces of wreckage were found within the area marked out by the main three sections, but there was no sign of the missing No 2 engine and propeller.

The various pieces of the aircraft had sustained extreme disintegration as a result of the impact and subsequent fires. Local Indians had burnt the wreckage for sanitary reasons before it could be professionally examined, and as well, a forest fire had swept the wreckage before the arrival of the second investigating team.

Melted by the heat of these fires, many pieces of the aircraft's aluminium alloy structure had resolidified into unrecognisable globules and masses of metal. As well, the many structural parts

(above) For the second, better equipped expedition to the crash site, an airstrip was cleared at Lago Grande and a 40km track to an advanced camp cut through the jungle. At the Lago Grande strip, a Pan American Curtiss Commando unloads a Jeep for the investigation team. (below) One of the investigator's Jeeps on the narrow jungle track to the advanced camp. Though the difficult 40km journey took six hours, it vastly improved access to the crash site. (Charles Boaz)

which remained identifiable had their fractured edges melted or burned away, making any study of them worthless.

The team was nevertheless able to carry out a reasonably complete investigation of the crash site until 10 September, when the onset of the Brazilian wet season forced their withdrawal, even though they were still unable to find the missing No 2 engine and propeller.

Analysis

Despite the extensive destruction of the Stratocruiser's wreck-age, a good deal of evidence came to light as to the nature and cause of the structural failures of various components of the aircraft. From this evidence, in conjunction with the way the wreckage was distributed, it was possible to establish with a reasonable degree of certainty the sequence of failures that brought the accident about.

It was apparent that some failure occurred in either the No 2 propeller or engine which resulted in these units being violently torn from the aircraft during its cruising

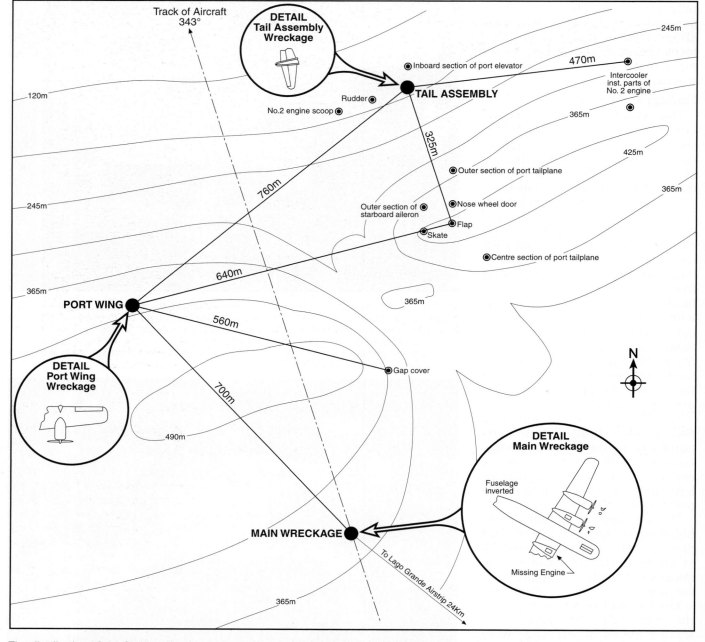

Track of Aircraft 343°

DETAIL Tail Assembly Wreckage

245m

●Inboard section of port elevator

470m

Intercooler inst. parts of No. 2 engine

●TAIL ASSEMBLY

Rudder◉

No.2 engine scoop◉

120m

365m

◉

325m

425m

◎Outer section of port tailplane

760m

365m

Outer section of starboard aileron◎

◉Nose wheel door

245m

◉Flap

◉Skate

◎Centre section of port tailplane

640m

365m

365m

PORT WING ●

560m

DETAIL Port Wing Wreckage

700m

◉Gap cover

N

490m

DETAIL Main Wreckage

Fuselage inverted

MAIN WRECKAGE ●

365m

To Lago Grande Airstrip 24Km

Missing Engine

The distribution of the Stratocruiser's widely scattered wreckage, as painstakingly determined by the investigation team under extremely difficult conditions. The wreckage not only lay in remote, inaccessible jungle, but amongst rugged, steep-sided hills and deep gorges, as indicated by the contour lines. (Aero Illustrations)

flight at relatively high altitude. Shortly after the loss of the No 2 engine, the port wing failed and, almost simultaneously, as a result of the violent pitching of the aircraft which would have occurred, the entire tail section broke from the fuselage in a downward direction just aft of the dorsal fin.

Because the No 2 engine and propeller were not recovered, they could not be examined to determine the cause of their separation from their mountings on the aircraft. Nevertheless, it could be concluded from the investigators'

examination of the No 2 engine mountings, which remained with the main wreckage, that the separation resulted from out of balance forces far greater than those for which it was designed. Similar separations of engines from Boeing 367 and 377 aircraft in flight, as a result of excessive loads being applied to the engine mounting, had occurred a number of times since the types had entered service. In all cases, when the engine and propeller combinations were recovered, examination disclosed that the separation had resulted from a propeller blade

failure and the consequent extreme out-of-balance loads produced by the broken propeller.

Cause

In the absence of more complete evidence, the US Civil Aeronautics Board's finding was that the probable cause of the accident was the separation of the No 2 engine and propeller from the aircraft as a result of highly unbalanced forces, followed by uncontrollability and disintegration of the aircraft structure for reasons that could not be determined.

CHAPTER 3

Ditching after takeoff – but nobody knew!

Mystery surrounded the ditching of a Super Constellation in the Shannon River estuary in the early hours of the morning. But the long delay in Search and Rescue that followed was almost as hard to understand.

Forty-six passengers, most of them American, and a crew of 10, were aboard the KLM Lockheed Super Constellation, PH-LKY, as it taxied for a night takeoff from Shannon International Airport in the early hours of September 5 1954.

Situated in low lying country on the south-west coast of Ireland. 20km west of the city of Limerick, Shannon Airport in the prejet era of international flying was a busy transit hub for trans Atlantic flights. Adjoining the northern shore of the great tidal estuary of the River Shannon, with an elevation of only 1.5 metres AMSL, the airport is protected on its southeastern boundary from the waters of the estuary by a dyke rising four metres above the airport level. At high tide, the waters of the estuary lap the base of this embankment, but low water exposes an extensive area of estuary mudflats.

In 1954, Shannon Airport had four paved runways. Runway 14, from which the Super Constellation was to take off, was 1720m

long and bounded beyond its southwestern end by the airport perimeter road and the dyke. In line with the end of Runway 14, the top of the dyke was marked by red obstruction lights.

As well as its Control Tower and Area and Oceanic ATC services, the airport at the time was equipped with Ground Controlled Approach (GCA) radar. The airport's own Protection Service, responsible for fire fighting and rescue, ambulance services, and overall security, was equipped with an assortment of fire fighting vehicles and ambulances, plus amphibious units and rescue launches. The launches were based at the port of Foynes, across the estuary from the airport, some seven nautical miles (13km) distant.

The Super Constellation was operating Flight 633, one of the Dutch national airline's regular transatlantic services to New York, which had originated at Schiphol Airport, Amsterdam, nearly three hours earlier. Scheduled to depart Schiphol at 9.45pm,

the aircraft had been held on the ground for an hour and a half so that through passengers aboard a delayed European flight from Zurich could make their connection with the New York service. The night flight, when the Super Constellation finally got away, was almost uneventful, the aircraft cruising above 12,000 feet. During its final approach to Shannon Airport, the aircraft's VHF transmitter failed, but it touched down normally. The unit was changed at Shannon while the aircraft was refuelled.

Now about to depart for the longest leg of the trip under the command of Captain Adriaan Viruly, 49, an experienced international airline pilot who had been flying with KLM since 1931, the Super Constellation was bound for its next refuelling stop at Gander near the east coast of Newfoundland. The long transocean flight was expected to take nearly 10 hours, and the aircraft was carrying a heavy load of fuel.

The weather forecast for the Atlantic crossing was favourable,

Map of the Shannon region in County Clare, on Ireland's west coast. The location of Shannon International Airport, on the northern side of the Shannon estuary to the west of the city of Limerick, is indicated. The port of Foynes lies to the southwest, on the southern side of the estuary.

and on the southwest coast of Ireland, the clear autumn night, though dark with no moon, was almost perfect. With practically unlimited visibility, there was only broken cloud at 8000 feet. A wind of 12 knots was blowing from the southwest, and the QNH was 1009 millibars.

At 2.30am, now ready for departure in front of the passenger terminal with all engines running, the Super Constellation called the Tower for taxi instructions. Only one airport controller was on duty at this time of night, and he promptly cleared the aircraft to taxi to the threshold of Runway 14. Lining up on Runway 14, the Super Constellation crew carried out their takeoff checks and engine runup, and at 2.38am the Tower cleared the aircraft for takeoff.

To the tower controller watching the departure, the takeoff appeared normal, the aircraft becoming airborne about 1200m from the threshold and passing over the remaining third of the

runway in a shallow climb as its undercarriage retracted. Crossing low over the obstruction lights on the dyke 260m further on, it assumed a somewhat steeper climb. The controller continued to watch the lights of the aircraft until it reached a height of about 200 feet, then informed Area Control on the ATC intercom that the flight was airborne, and logged the takeoff time. A minute later, in accordance with the current practice, he called the aircraft on VHF to confirm its departure time. There was no acknowledgement.

When two or three further calls were also unanswered, he contacted the Area Control Officer and requested that Oceanic Control try calling the Super Constellation on one of their H/F frequencies. At 2.44am Area Control reported back that they too were unable to contact PH-LKY.

Four minutes later, about the time the aircraft was due to report outbound over Kilkee on the Irish coast, the tower and area controllers were discussing the situation

on the intercom. When the area controller asked whether GCA had seen the aircraft on radar, the GCA Director cut in on the conversation to say it was "23 and a half (nm) west now", confirming that the radar blip was outbound. Satisfied the aircraft was maintaining track and that its lack of contact was the result of radio failure, the controllers agreed the runway lights should be left switched on in case the aircraft should return.

The Super Constellation's takeoff was also watched by four fire crew at the Airport Fire Station. One was on lookout duty in the glass sided watchroom on the roof of the station, while the others were standing by their vehicles. The lookout saw the aircraft lift off the runway, watched it passing over the obstruction lights on the dyke, then also turned away to log its takeoff time. When he looked out again a moment later, he was unable to pick up its lights. This did not unduly concern him however, because reflections from the airport buildings on the windows

An artist's impression of a Super Constellation refuelling at Shannon Airport at night while enroute to the USA. (F Wooton/Esso)

of the watchroom frequently made it difficult to pick out fainter, more distant lights.

Meanwhile a Customs officer watching the Super Constellation's takeoff had become concerned for its safety. He too had seen its shallow climb over the lights of the dyke, but after it began to climb more steeply, this appeared to change into a shallow descent – what he later described as "a gradual glide". His line of sight was interrupted when the lights of the aircraft passed behind the Fire Station.

He had been watching from just inside the terminal building. But concerned that the aircraft was descending into the estuary, he hurried outside with a colleague to see if its lights would reappear. When they did not, the men spoke to the senior security officer in the terminal, asking him to check with the Airport Fire Station that all was well.

The security officer telephoned the Fire Station Section Leader. "There's some talk up here about that last aircraft – PH-LKY – that just took off." he said. "They say they did not see her any more after she went over the dyke – I think it would be advisable for you to have a look and see."

Running up the stairs to the watchroom, the Section Leader went out on to its balcony and looked towards the estuary. But as he could see nothing out of the ordinary, he did no more about it. Back at the terminal a few minutes later, when the Customs officer saw the Fire Station was taking no emergency action, he assumed he had been mistaken.

Meanwhile, Area Control was continuing its efforts to contact the aircraft. When all further calls proved unsuccessful, other aircraft flying in the vicinity, as well as a weather ship on station in the Atlantic, were requested to call PH-LKY on all frequencies. But despite the fact that there was no response from the aircraft to any of these calls, ATC declared no emergency and no further measures were taken to investigate the reason for the aircraft's failure to report setting course.

Nearly two hours later at 4.15am, the tower controller saw red flares and faint lights out on the darkened estuary, well beyond the airport dyke. Telephoning the Fire Crew, he asked them to try and identify the lights. More flares appeared, so two amphibious rescue vehicles were ordered out to the estuary mudflats to investi-

gate. A short time later the rescue launch base at Foynes was told to alert its crew. Because the crew were off duty and at home in bed, however, this took some time.

At 5.12am, an hour after the flares were first sighted, and before the amphibious vehicles had reported finding anything, a bedraggled young Dutchman, wearing the remains of a KLM crew uniform, covered in mud and slime from the estuary, and in a distressed condition, staggered into the Airport Fire Station. Gasping for breath, he conveyed to an incredulous fire crew that he was the third pilot of the KLM Super Constellation – they had come down in the estuary after takeoff. He had swum from one of the aircraft's inflatable dinghies to a mudbank, then picked his way through the mud to the shore, scaled the dyke and finally run across the airport to the Fire Station, the nearest building he could reach. He was Third Officer J M Tieman, 25, who had joined KLM only a short time before and was on board the aircraft for flight familiarisation.

Springing into action, the Fire Crew sounded the airport alarm, contacted the Tower, and instructed the Airport Rescue Section to rush

Amsterdam's Schipol Airport in the 1950s. The triple tail of a KLM Super Constellation frames a company DC-3 and a DC-6 on the busy apron. (KLM)

all available rescue equipment, vehicles and personnel to the dyke. At about this time the launch base also telephoned the Tower to report the crew were now on their way to the vessel. And a third call to the Tower in as many minutes informed the controller another survivor from the KLM aircraft had reached the passenger terminal, also in a distressed condition.

At 5.30am the rescue launch finally got under way from Foynes, calling Shannon Tower on its H/F radio for instructions. But although the launch crew could hear the Tower, it was obvious the Tower was not receiving transmissions from the launch. With no alternative but to put back to Foynes, the coxswain telephoned the controller who then found the Tower's H/F receiver off frequency. The launch left again at 5.50am.

Meanwhile, the rescue party, scouring the exposed mudflats beyond the dyke towards the waters edge, came across 28 dishevelled people struggling through the mud. All were covered in slime and barely recognisable. The survivors, 22 passengers and the re-

maining six members of the flight crew, had paddled ashore in two inflatable dinghies. The aircraft itself, far out in the estuary channel, was by this time was almost covered by the rising tide.

At 6.20am, as day was breaking, the rescue launch finally reached the nearly submerged aircraft, its crew sighting two more survivors clinging to the empennage. But as the launch approached to take them off, one let go his hold and fell into the water. Attempts to rescue him failed and he was lost. The other survivor, safely taken aboard, told his rescuers they had escaped through an overwing emergency hatch, and swum to the tail. The aircraft's inflatable dinghies had been unable to reach them, and they had been clinging there for 3 hours 40 minutes.

Altogether 28 of the aircraft's 56 occupants were rescued, one of whom, an American woman passenger, had sustained serious injuries. She was admitted to the airport hospital. The survivors included all seven flightcrew, but none of the three cabin crew. Apart from the passenger lost

from the tailplane, 26 occupants remained unaccounted for.

Investigation

The accident investigation, conducted by the Irish Department of Industry and Commerce, wanted answers to three principal questions:

• The reason for the aircraft's descent.

• The reasons for the long delay in rescue efforts.

• The cause of the loss of 28 lives.

At the time of its departure, the loaded weight of the Super Constellation was 131,930lb (59,843kg), more than 1000lb (454kg) under its maximum takeoff weight, and its load distribution was within specified limits. The takeoff from Runway 14 into the southwest appeared to have been normal, but 35 to 40 seconds later the aircraft made a survivable ditching into the waters of the Shannon estuary, 2.5km from the departure end of the runway. The night was completely dark at the time.

The Super Constellation ditched about 200 metres to the left of the

Passengers board a trans Atlantic flight at Amsterdam's Schipol Airport in the 1950s. The aircraft in this case is KLM DC-6 PH-TPP. (KLM)

extended centreline of Runway 14. Yet it hit the water with some starboard bank, shedding its No 3 and 4 propellers, followed by their engines. It came to rest partly floating, with its nose resting on a shallow mud bank. Although it appeared substantially intact, the ditching had in fact inflicted major damage.

The final impact had broken the back of the fuselage in front of the wing main spar. The break extended around the fuselage with compression damage at its top. On the underside of the fuselage, the break had opened up a gap of more than a metre across the full width of the fuselage, exposing the main spar of the wing centre section, and opening No 5 fuel tank to atmosphere in the floor of the cabin. It was evident the fuselage fractured as the nose grounded on a mudbank, forcing it upwards, before the aircraft came to rest.

The port wing was relatively undamaged, but the starboard wing sustained substantial impact damage. Both its engines were torn off and both propellers broken from their hubs. Aft of the wing's rear spar and in line with the engines, the trailing sections of the wing were torn away, resulting in the loss of No 3 inflatable dinghy in its wing stowage. The outer wing section exhibited impact damage on its leading edge.

The flap actuating mechanism, as well as the flap selector on the flightdeck, indicated the flaps were up when the aircraft struck the water. The starboard flaps were torn off but the port flaps were intact in the retracted position.

The propeller blades of all four engines were severely damaged. All engines were under power at impact and there was no evidence of pre-crash failure or malfunction. No 1 propeller was probably the last to strike the water.

The outboard portion of the starboard tailplane, together with the starboard fin and rudder, were broken off. It was not possible to examine the flying control linkages, their attachments or any of the control surfaces themselves, as they were under water. Their inspection was rendered still more difficult by a storm four days after the accident, which turned the nose section forward of the break in the fuselage through about 90°, separating it from the rest of the aircraft. The starboard outer wing also broke away, and the rear fuselage and tail was severed at the rear pressure bulkhead. Further damage occurred during salvage operations.

After the wreckage was recovered, it was found that, although the flightdeck undercarriage selector was in the up position and the port main undercarriage leg up and locked, the nose leg and

A Lockheed Super Constellation in flight, similar to the KLM aircraft that crashed in the River Shannon.

The ditched KLM Super Constellation, PH-LKY, in the Shannon estuary, several hours after the accident. Note how the nose, resting on a mudbank, is well out of water, while the rear fuselage is nearly submerged. Most of the 27 fatalities occurred in this part of the aircraft. (Popperfoto)

Descending at a shallow angle in a nose up, slightly starboard wing low attitude, the Super Constellation's first contact with the water, probably by its No 4 propeller, was fleeting. Skipping several times before ditching, the aircraft was almost immediately plunged into darkness when the flight engineer cut the master switch. The emergency lighting system came on, but quickly failed as the battery "drowned". From the time the Super Constellation crossed the end of the runway until it contacted the water, the flight lasted only 31 seconds.

Captain Viruly said that, as they were climbing, he observed the altimeter passing through 250 feet. But just before the crash, he saw it reading only 100 feet, with the rate of climb indicator showing a descent of 1000 fpm. First Officer Parfitt added that, when he glanced at the instrument panel before moving the undercarriage selector lever from its up position to neutral, the initial climb seemed normal. He was in the process of picking up his checklist to call the after takeoff check when the aircraft hit the water.

With the aircraft now in darkness, crew members armed with torches, left the flightdeck at once to assist the passengers. Opening the door into the forward cabin,

starboard main leg, though retracted, were not in the locked position. Examination of the wreckage also revealed that fuel tanks No 3, 3A, 4 and 5 were breached, allowing their contents to escape, some of it into the passenger cabin.

Captain Viruly and his first officer, Edward Parfitt, a highly experienced British pilot and the only non-Dutch member of the crew, said the takeoff, with the captain handling the controls, began at 2.38am and was normal, the aircraft reaching V_1 speed 1100 metres down the runway, and lifting off at just over V_2 at 125 knots (232km/h), another 150 metres from the threshold. The undercar-

riage was retracted, the first power reduction to METO made at 140 knots (259km/h), the flaps selected up at 150 knots (278km/h), and climb power set at 160 knots (298km/h). Immediately afterwards the captain, sensing something was wrong, pulled back firmly on the control column, but the elevator control seemed stiff and there was no apparent response.

Moments later, a "shudder", lasting three to five seconds, ran through the aircraft, the first indication of trouble to the crew, apart from the captain. This was followed by several major bumps, then the aircraft ploughed heavily into the water.

The flightdeck of a Super Constellation. The flight engineer's station, with its duplicated engine power levers, is at right. On the dark night takeoff, after the first officer selected the flaps up and the flight engineer set climb power, the captain sensed "something was wrong". Moments later, as the first officer was about to call the after takeoff checks, there was a shudder and the aircraft ploughed into the water. (Fallon Photographs)

Second Officer Evert Webbink saw No 1 and 2 inflatable dinghies already afloat by the port wing. The break in the fuselage had stretched the cables that release the dinghies from their stowages in the wings, and the dinghies had inflated automatically. Water and aviation fuel was flooding into the cabin, mainly from its lower starboard side above the wing, and pouring aft, filling the cabin with strong fumes. Opening the forward door and over wing exits, the crew made urgent efforts to evacuate the passengers, but were hampered in the dark by the overpowering smell of fuel.

One woman passenger, seated near the fracture in the fuselage, had sustained multiple injuries. Other passengers had already opened one of the emergency exits on to the port wing and escaped through it. A distraught male passenger, still in his seat and not thinking what he was do-

ing, pulled out a cigarette. But the woman passenger beside him knocked the matches out of his hand before he could to light it, her quick witted reaction probably saving the survivors' lives.

The three flight attendants, Willem van Buren, Robert Westergaard and Helga Lowenstein, trying to open the main cabin door at the rear of the cabin, were soon overcome by the fumes, as were a number of passengers seated in this part of the fuselage. Though unaffected at first and able to assist passengers to escape from the forward and main cabins, the flightcrew found the fumes so nauseous and overpowering that they could only stay in the main cabin for short periods of time, and were frequently forced to gulp fresh air at the forward door or wing exits.

When eleven passengers were safely aboard No 1 dinghy, Captain Viruly told First Officer Parfitt, with Flight Engineer

Hendrik Rademaker and Second Flight Engineer C J Kievits, to make for shore to seek assistance. Through the sinking aircraft's windows as the dinghy drew away in the dark, they could see the remaining members of the crew still desperately searching with torches for surviving passengers.

By the time the water inside the fuselage had almost reached neck height, another nine passengers had been loaded into No 2 inflatable dinghy, together with Second Officer Webbink and Third Officer Tieman. Captain Viruly and Radio Officer H E Oudshoorn, satisfied then that all possible rescue in the sinking aircraft had been accomplished, boarded the dinghy also.

As this second dinghy pulled away, those on board heard calls from the tailplane. But because the wind and the ebbing tide were carrying the dinghy away from the aircraft, they were unable to reach it. It took the dinghies nearly two hours to paddle to the shore,

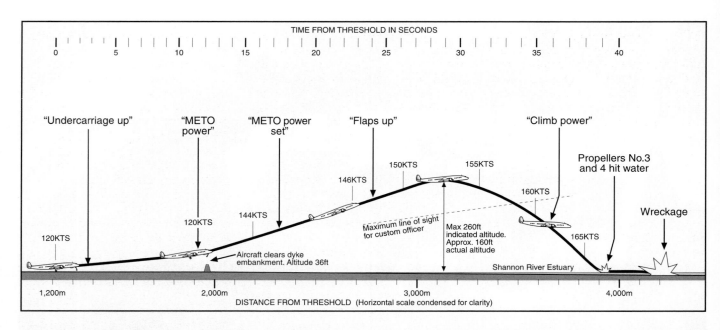

TIME FROM THRESHOLD IN SECONDS

0 5 10 15 20 25 30 35 40

"Undercarriage up"   "METO power"   "METO power set"   "Flaps up"   "Climb power"

Propellers No.3 and 4 hit water

150KTS   155KTS

146KTS

160KTS

144KTS

Wreckage

120KTS   120KTS

Maximum line of sight for custom officer

Max 260ft indicated altitude. Approx. 160ft actual altitude

165KTS

Aircraft clears dyke embankment. Altitude 36ft

Shannon River Estuary

1,200m   2,000m   3,000m   4,000m

DISTANCE FROM THRESHOLD (Horizontal scale condensed for clarity)

Diagrammatic profile of the Super Constellation's takeoff, brief climb, and descent into the estuary, as determined by the investigation. The dotted line indicates where the customs officer's view of the aircraft's descending flightpath was obstructed by the intervening airport fire station. (Aero Illustrations)

Third Officer Tieman finally deciding to swim the remaining distance to the mudbank and make his way to the airport to raise the alarm.

The crew were unable to take the aircraft's portable emergency radio in one of the dinghies because it was stowed at the rear of the cabin and, with this part of fuselage filling quickly after the ditching, it could not be reached. Because of fuel spillage on the water in the vicinity of the aircraft and in the dinghies, it was not possible to fire the dinghys' signal flares until the survivors reached the shore. Earlier attempts to attract attention from the dinghies with the crew's electric torches were unsuccessful.

Nearly two hours elapsed from the time the aircraft crashed into the estuary until rescue operations began. When the aircraft failed to respond to numerous radio calls after its departure, both the Tower controller, who was alone in the Tower at the time, and ATC Area Control assumed it had experienced radio failure, an impression strengthened by the erroneous report from the GCA Director. So ATC's main preoccupation became one of attempting to re-establish radio communication.

The tower controller was unaware of the message received by the Fire Crew Section Leader, while the Section Leader was unaware ATC had lost radio contact with the aircraft. If the information received by the Fire Crew had been passed to the Control Tower, the Rescue Services would have been alerted at once.

The failure of the rescue launch to establish H/F communication with the Tower when the vessel first set out caused a further delay of about 40 minutes before it reached the scene of the ditching. The type of radio equipment in use, liable as it was to the possibility of its receiver being knocked off tune, was inadequate and unsatisfactory for its purpose.

The woman who received multiple injuries in the crash died in hospital several hours after being admitted. After the tide had receded, rescuers found 26 bodies still in the fuselage. Post-mortem examination found all had died as a result asphyxiation by avgas fumes. The body of the passenger who, after waiting on the tail for rescue, cold and wet, for nearly four hours, fell into the water as the launch was approaching, was recovered about a week later. His death was not the result of drowning but of a loss of consciousness following shock.

Analysis

The investigation ruled out any possibility that structural failure, loss of engine power, or substantial instrument malfunction had caused the accident.

Although the captain said the aircraft reached a height of 250 feet after takeoff, performance calculations showed it could not have exceeded about 160 feet in the time available before the unintentional descent began. However, examination of the altimeters and pitot static system indicated that a combination of minor factors – position error, instrument calibration and altimeter setting – might have combined to result in the captain's altimeter over-reading by 90 to 100 feet.

The calculations indicated an initial climb of 150 fpm, the aircraft crossing the dyke at a height of 36 feet and accelerating to 140 knots (260km/h) 12-13 seconds after liftoff. The undercarriage was retracted, a steeper climb set up with METO power selected and, with speed gradually increasing, the aircraft would have climbed at 530 fpm, reaching 140 feet at an airspeed of 149 knots (276km/h). Unnoticed by any crew member, there was then a gradual transition to a descent at an airspeed of between 150 and 160 knots (278-296km/h).

The flaps were up at the time of the ditching. Super Constellation handling procedures require the undercarriage to be up and locked before the flaps are retracted, and the fact that the aircraft was not in this configuration appeared to be the most telling clue to the unintentional descent. Although the investigation found the nose and starboard main undercarriage legs were retracted, neither had reached the locked position when the No 3 and 4 engines, driving their hydraulics, were torn off in the water.

The investigators considered whether the flaps could have been inadvertently selected up before the undercarriage retraction cycle was complete. Giving weight to this theory was the fact that the instrument panel lamp which indicates the undercarriage is in transit, was burnt out. The resulting false indication could have led the crew to retract the flaps before the undercarriage had completed its retraction cycle.

Flight test data showed that if a Super Constellation's flaps are selected up while the undercarriage is still retracting, the flaps will come up first, delaying the undercarriage retraction and, in some cases, allowing it re-extend temporarily. The combined operation – flaps up, undercarriage up – takes 34-38 seconds. This could have caused unexpected drag which, while not actually causing the accident, could have contributed to it. The investigators therefore sought to "reconstruct" the flightpath the aircraft was likely to have followed in these circumstances, together with its flight instrument indications.

A gradual increase in airspeed is not uncommon during flap retraction and would not have appeared abnormal at first. And the altimeter would have continued to indicate around 250 feet for about nine seconds, before showing a gradual loss of height.

For the first nine seconds also, the vertical speed indicator would have indicated a climb of around 500 fpm, then decreased gradually. About 11 seconds after the flaps were selected up, it would have shown level flight, then a de-

scent at an increasing rate. To the captain, who had no reason to suspect a descent had begun, this could have conveyed the erroneous impression of a gradually flattening flightpath, to be followed by more or less horizontal flight by the end of flap retraction.

As the flaps began to retract, the artificial horizon would have shown a noseup attitude conforming with the climb taking place. But six seconds afterwards, it would have begun to indicate a slightly lower nose position, settling about four degrees lower than the climb attitude, even though still slightly noseup.

Power would probably have been reduced from METO to Climb about 11 seconds after the flaps were selected up. At this stage, the altimeter would have been indicating around 200 feet and the rate of climb about zero. But within the next one or two seconds, the vertical speed indicator would have displayed an appreciable rate of descent and the altimeter a loss of height at an increasing rate.

The descent was by then fully developed and it was evidently at this moment that the captain, suddenly realising something was wrong, pulled back hard on the control column. This could have given him the impression of stiffened elevator controls. Apart from the noseup movement of his artificial horizon, in the few seconds that remained before the aircraft flew into the water, none of the other flight instruments had time to indicate a response. Although too late to avert the accident, the captain's action undoubtedly prevented a heavier impact with the water.

★   ★   ★

Rescue operations were delayed because no one suspected the need for rescue. The crew were unable to transmit a distress call after the accident because there was no electric power, and no Verey pistols were carried in the aircraft. Fuel on the water, and in the vicinity of the aircraft and dinghies, precluded the firing of the dinghys' distress flares at the scene of the accident.

Any fears aroused by the alarm given by the Customs officers were allayed by the absence of fire or other indication of danger on the darkened estuary, while the Customs officers' own minds were set at rest by seeing no unusual activity from the Fire Station. If either of the airport Protection Service officers contacted had communicated the Customs officers' concern to the Tower, and the controller learnt one observer thought the aircraft was in danger after takeoff, he undoubtedly would have investigated further. The false impression that the trouble with the aircraft was no more than radio failure might then have been averted.

The GCA Director committed a grave error of judgment in identifying the blip he saw on his radar screen as PH-LKY without adding that he had not followed it from the vicinity of the airport and had only seen the blip for about 10 seconds.

There were no casualties to the crew on the flightdeck, among the passengers in the forward passenger cabin, or in the first eight seats of the main cabin. Death from asphyxiation occurred in the rear portion of the main cabin and in the rear cabin because the aircraft was in a noseup attitude, causing the heaviest fuel vapour concentration – heavier than air – to flow rearwards.

The flight attendants were quickly overcome by these fumes. Their apparent lack of awareness of the toxic effect of the fumes meant that valuable time was lost as they unsuccessfully tried to open the main cabin door. The flightcrew found they could only stay in the main cabin for short periods at a time. With no lights in the cabin, their rescue work was also hampered by having to hold electric torches.

Though face masks and a portable bottle of oxygen were standard equipment on the aircraft, by the time the need for them became obvious, it was probably too late.

Author's comment

The investigators, while postulating their well researched theory

Part of the rear passenger cabin of a Lockheed Super Constellation. Most of those who died in the accident were seated in this part of the fuselage. Though uninjured, before they could escape from the aircraft they were asphyxiated by a high concentration of avgas fumes flowing aft from ruptured fuel tanks in the wing centre section. (Lockheed California)

for the accident, prescribed no definite cause. But another possible explanation, not apparently considered at the time, is that of the "false climb" illusion.

In Britain during World War 2, an investigation carried out into a series of accidents in which RAF aircraft, taking off on dark nights, flew into the ground shortly after leaving the runway, concluded that pilots were deluded into thinking their aircraft were climbing when they were actually descending.

The villain in this scenario was found to be the otolith, an organ in the inner ear and vestibular apparatus, whose function is to sense the position of the head relative to the vertical. In the absence of visual cues, it becomes a powerful influence on the balance and orientation of the body. Without the otolith, it would be impossible to maintain our balance with our eyes closed.

The structure and function of the otolith can be represented as a hair standing vertically with a small stone at its tip. At the base of the hair is a sensory cell that conveys information about the angle of the hair to the brain. When the head is tilted back-

wards, the weight of the stone bends the hair, the message is relayed to the brain, and is interpreted as a backward tilt. If the head is held vertical while being accelerated forwards, the hair will bend in a similar fashion. But although both tilt and acceleration produce the same response, the brain is unable to differentiate between the two and so acceleration is sensed as tilt.

If tilt and acceleration are experienced together, the sensation is that of a much steeper tilt. So when a pilot, deprived of external visual cues, is subjected to climb and forward acceleration at the same time, he experiences a sensation of a steeper than actual climb. This tempts him to lower the nose of the aircraft, increasing the forward acceleration further and increasing the illusion of climbing. Because of lag in the aircraft's pitot static instruments, the loss of height can go unnoticed until it is too late to avoid flying into the ground.

Even a relatively low acceleration of 0.2g, if sustained for a period, can produce the illusion, and all pilots, irrespective of experi-

ence or skill, are susceptible to it. The illusion is subtle, an apparently positive climb being sensed by the body, even though the aircraft may be descending. Eventually, the aircraft's pitot static instruments will show the descent, but perhaps not in time to avoid an accident. The only remedy is to anticipate the illusion and ignore it, to establish a positive climbing attitude on the artificial horizon, and then to hold that attitude while checking other flight instruments for confirmation of the climb.

Could this have been the explanation for the Super Constellation's mysterious descent into the Shannon estuary? It certainly seems possible. Over the years since the effect was identified, many aircraft, both heavy and light, have fallen victim to it. And the circumstances of this particular takeoff, from the lighted airport directly towards the wide, totally dark Shannon estuary, would certainly have been conducive to creating a "false climb" illusion.

The most that could be said is that, like the undercarriage's failure to retract promptly, it might have been a contributing factor.

CHAPTER 4

"Do not descend any lower!"

The DC-6B crew's long overnight transatlantic flight from Europe was fatiguing enough. But their fourth attempted instrument approach in nearly three hours additional holding was to prove the last straw.

Visibility around New York's Jamaica Bay was poor when Flight 451 of the Italian airline, Linee Aeree Italiane, from Rome and Milan, finally arrived over Idlewild International Airport on a murky midwinter morning on December 18 1954.

The DC-6B's long transatlantic night flight, under the command of Captain Guglielmo Algarotti, 52, was uneventful and at 9.30am local time, it made its initial American landing at Boston's Logan International Airport. Nine of the aircraft's 31 passengers from Rome left the aircraft there, and it was refuelled, remaining on the ground for about an hour before the crew of 10 resumed the flight to the final destination at New York.

The brief 155nm (278km) leg from Boston was also uneventful, and at 11.20am the aircraft reported to Idlewild Approach that it was over the Radio Range transmitter at 7000 feet.

The DC-6B was then cleared to join other inbound New York traffic in the Scotland holding pattern, 13nm (24km) southwest of Idlewild Airport, and was progressively stepped down in the stack as other aircraft landed. By 11.45am, the DC-6B had reached the No 1 position in the stack, but because the weather on the ground had now deteriorated below the ceiling minimum of 400 feet for landing on Runway 22, the runway in use, the aircraft continued to hold.

After half an hour, visibility improved and the aircraft was cleared for an approach to Runway 22, using the back course of the ILS. But at 12.18pm the DC-6B reported discontinuing the approach because conditions had again deteriorated below the minima for Runway 22. Idlewild Tower then issued the crew with missed approach instructions and the aircraft returned to the Scotland holding pattern. Weather observations recorded at Idlewild at this time were: "Ceiling 300 feet, broken, 2500 feet, overcast; visibility two and a half miles (4km), light rain and fog; wind southsouthwest at 20 knots (37km)."

Nearly an hour later, while the DC-6B was still holding, the approach controller asked the captain if, despite the strong tailwind component, he would consider trying an approach to Runway 04, the reciprocal of Runway 22, as this was the ILS runway. The final approach to Runway 04 lay over the waters of Jamaica Bay, crossing a narrow neck of land and then an island swamp before reaching the approach lights for the runway which are carried on two parallel piers jutting 600m out into the bay. Linee Aeree Italiane's company minima for ILS approaches to Runway 04 at Idlewild were a ceiling of 200 feet and a visibility of 800m.

Captain Algarotti accepted the controller's offer and at 1.07pm the aircraft was cleared for the ILS approach. But six minutes later the aircraft called the Tower to report it had been forced to make another missed approach.

The Tower then offered the captain a Ground Controlled Approach (GCA) to the same runway, but at 1.24pm he was forced to break this off too, because of

A DC-6B similar to the aircraft operating Linee Aeree Italiane's Flight 451 from Rome and Milan on December 18 1954. After four attempted approaches in poor visibility, the aircraft crashed into an approach light pier short of the threshold of La Guardia's Runway 04. (APN/B Stainer)

near impossible visibility near the ground. Again the aircraft followed the prescribed missed approach procedure, and again it returned to the Scotland holding pattern, maintaining contact with Idlewild Approach Control.

Twenty-five minutes later, the controller informed the aircraft that conditions at the airport appeared to be improving, and again offered the Captain an ILS approach. As the DC-6B, inbound from the holding pattern, neared the airport yet again, it was transferred to the Tower frequency and cleared for an ILS approach to Runway 04. This was now its third approach to this runway and its fourth attempt to land at the airport.

But as the aircraft continued inbound on the ILS, monitored by the GCA radar controller, its flight became somewhat erratic. Now 60m to the right of the localiser course, the aircraft began sinking below the electronic glidepath shortly before reaching the outer marker.

"Do not descend any lower," the radar controller warned, "Do not descend any lower."

Although the controller saw the aircraft's deviation from the localiser was being corrected, its glidepath was not and the aircraft continued to lose height.

"Level off – altitude 200 feet," instructed the controller, as the aircraft re-intercepted the localiser. The aircraft responded, climbing quickly back towards the glidepath, but swinging several hundred feet to the left of the localiser course.

"You're about to intercept the glidepath – 150 feet below it," advised the controller. But again the aircraft descended, at the same time failing to correct its deviation from the localiser.

"Your altitude is very very low," the controller warned urgently. "Pull up! – pull up!" Again there was an immediate response, the aircraft climbing quickly to the level of the glidepath, but deviating further to the right.

"I see you're pulling up – 500 feet (150m) to the left of course,"

transmitted the controller, noting a moment later that the aircraft was also moving back towards the localiser course.

But just on 2pm, as the DC-6B approached the position of the inner marker, only 10 minutes after this last attempt to land began, but two hours forty minutes since it arrived over Idlewild, it again abruptly descended.

Before the radar controller transmitted again, the tower controller, watching intently for the aircraft's breakout from the low overcast, saw a violent explosion, followed by an intense fire, as the DC-6B struck the pier supporting the left hand row of the approach lights, bursting into flames. Tower staff immediately sounded the crash alarm and the airport's emergency services leapt into action.

As it happened, the first man to reach the scene of the crash was Idlewild's airport manager, George McSherry. Sitting in his car on the apron in front of the customs office, he had felt a

slight tremor then saw a column of black smoke coming from the direction of the bay. Driving off at once around the perimeter road, he switched his car's VHF transceiver to the tower frequency in time to hear the controller announcing to the emergency services that a DC-6 had crashed into one of the approach light piers.

Reaching the pier, he quickly parked the car and ran out towards where fire was blazing. At the shattered, wreckage strewn end of the pier, flames belching thick black smoke were shooting more than 12m into the air. As he neared the fire, two bedraggled survivors, helped by a man in an outboard motor boat, were clambering on to one of the pier's ladders. Leaning over the railing, McSherry helped them up. "Are there any others?" he demanded urgently.

"There's an old man under the pier!" they shouted.

The heavy smoke was making visibility difficult, but before the flames forced him back, McSherry untied a line from a lifeboat on the pier, and threw it through the smoke to the elderly man in the icy water. With another man in the water now yelling for help as well, McSherry then grabbed a lifebuoy from the pier railing and hurled it to him.

A Sikorsky helicopter from the nearby Coast Guard station at Floyd Bennett Field, flying low through fog and light rain, now reached the accident site, hovering below the worst of the smoke to one side of the pier. The intense fire was spreading on the water, and McSherry pointed out the man in the lifebuoy. The helicopter lowered a metal basket and, as the survivor scrambled in, the second man appeared and clung to the basket. The helicopter towed

the basket to the pier, where McSherry, joined by an airport doctor, climbed down the ladder and hauled the elderly man from the water. Apart from shock, he seemed relatively unhurt. Airport rescue personnel helped them all back to the decking, while the

helicopter lifted the survivor in the basket to shore.

Meanwhile, a smaller Coast Guard Bell helicopter had also arrived, but although its crew recovered three more bodies from the water, they were all dead. Two other survivors, young American

DC-6s belonging to the airline, Linee Aeree Italiane, parked at Rome's Ciampino Airport in 1951. Their Italian registrations were I-LOVE and I-LUCK! The company later became part of today's Alitalia. (John Stroud)

medical students returning home for Christmas, who were seated in the rear of the DC-6B's cabin, had found themselves being hurled through the air when the aircraft crashed, still strapped to their seats. Landing in the water, they released their seatbelts and made their own way to shore.

Investigation

At the time of the accident the airport's weather was recorded as: "ceiling 200 feet overcast; visibility two miles (3.2km), light rain and fog; wind south-southeast at 16 knots (30km/h)."

Descending very low, the aircraft had struck the pier carrying the approach lights on the left or northern side of the inbound localiser course. Built of heavy wooden piles, its decking 4m above water at low tide, the narrow pier's offshore end was 770m from the runway threshold.

Flying parallel and to the right of the pier, only a few feet above the water, the aircraft had shattered half the end of the pier as it hit, breaking and splintering the tops of the piles over a distance of 300 metres before the DC-6B's wreckage fell in pieces along the pier's side and sank. The damage to the pier, and the fact that little wreckage came to rest near the point of impact, indicated the aircraft struck with no appreciable rate of descent.

A propeller slash made by the No 1 propeller on the centre pile at the end of the pier showed that the No 1 engine was centred on that position at impact, with the aircraft in a slightly noseup atti-

tude. Other damage across the end of the pier showed it was flying level laterally.

On impact, the port outer wing wrapped around the piling and broke up, while its centre section continued above the pier deck, smashing several light installations before veering off to the right into the water. The fuselage itself, further to the right, continued on, making glancing impacts against the pier as it did so. The starboard outer wing and forward fuselage were demolished and Nos 3 and 4 engines torn out, the remainder of the fuselage finally pivoting through 180° and sliding backwards before sinking beside the pier.

★   ★   ★

Salvage operations, undertaken by divers in the cold waters of the bay in extremely difficult conditions, recovered about 80% of the aircraft's structure. The wreckage was laid out for detailed examination by investigators from the Civil Aeronautics Board, but disclosed no evidence of fatigue cracking, structural failure, or malfunctioning of the controls before the crash.

The condition of the recovered undercarriage and flap components showed that the undercarriage was retracted and the flaps were extended about 18°. Examination of the aircraft's severely damaged ILS receiver and its indicators revealed no evidence of malfunction before the crash.

Of the aircraft's 32 occupants, the entire crew of 10 and 16 of the 22 passengers were all killed in-

stantly. In addition to the captain, the crew for the long transatlantic flight consisted of first officer, two second pilots, two flight engineers, a radio operator, and three flight attendants. Most of the passengers were Italians, coming to spend Christmas with relatives and friends in the United States.

The aircraft was also carrying a large cargo of Christmas parcels. The six survivors were seated in various positions in the passenger cabin. Two were able to extricate themselves from the wreckage and climb up onto the burning pier, but the others were thrown into the bay, to be rescued as already described.

The Italian crew were all well qualified and highly experienced. Captain Algarotti himself had made 150 flights across the Atlantic, half of which had terminated at New York's Idlewild International Airport.

The Idlewild radar controller, located in the tower building but several floors below the tower cab, gave radar advisories to all aircraft making ILS approaches. Their purpose was to give pilots their positions on radar relative to the glideslope, the localiser course, and the distance to touchdown.

Before the DC-6B's last instrument approach began, voice communication was established between the aircraft and the radar controller, and the aircraft crew were informed of the latest weather and altimeter setting.

Analysis

The fluctuating weather conditions throughout the time the DC-6B was in the Scotland holding pattern and making its four attempted approaches to land, were greatly influenced by the velocity of the surface wind. The resultant turbulent mixing of the air probably kept the ceiling and visibility in the vicinity of the airport from deteriorating to near zero.

During the DC-6B's first three approaches, the crew adhered to the prescribed minimum altitude for instrument letdowns at the airport, evidently maintaining some margin above it. The decisions to discontinue these approaches were entirely a matter for the captain's judgment.

The pronounced tailwind component and windshift the aircraft encountered during the approaches to Runway 04 were probably important factors influencing his decisions. These landings were being made downwind only because no other runway was equipped with an ILS, and the marginal visibility was not conducive to the use of the reciprocal, into wind Runway 22. This downwind component was probably also a factor influencing the captain to fly the last approach at a lower than normal airspeed.

Radar evidence showed that, on the last approach, the captain began descent before intersecting the glidepath and, although repeatedly advised by the radar controller to level off, continued to descend. The altitudes flown suggest the aircraft's ILS glideslope indicators would have been displaying full scale "fly-up" indications throughout the approach.

This strongly suggested to the investigators that the captain was not attempting to follow the glidepath, but rather had decided beforehand to descend, with the undercarriage lowered and some flap extended, until he could establish visual reference with the approaches to the airport.

Reconstructing the final path of the aircraft from the observations of the radar controller and unambiguous evidence of surviving passengers, the investigators believed the captain descended below the overcast somewhere between the outer and middle markers, probably in an attempt to continue visually below the overcast to the runway.

While trying to do so however, the aircraft might have encountered drifting fog, and as they broke clear of it, still descending, in the vicinity of the outer marker, the captain probably sighted the surface of the bay only about 200 feet below, but without catching sight of the approach lights. Reacting quickly, probably with alarm, he pulled the aircraft up again into the overcast. Then, in an attempt to re-establish visual contact, the captain evidently eased his control column forward, with the result that the aircraft descended very low, probably below 200 feet.

Reacting again as he suddenly sighted only the swamp, he apparently pulled the nose up sharply, the aircraft drifting slightly left at the same time. During the resulting brief climb, the aircraft lost airspeed and began diverging to the right. With the outcome of the approach still doubtful, even though the aircraft was almost visual, its undercarriage appears to have been retracted again at about this time in case this fourth attempt to land at Idlewild also had to be abandoned.

But with success now seemingly almost within his reach, the captain persisted, apparently lowering the nose of the aircraft once more in a third effort to become fully visual and complete the landing, at the same time applying some power to maintain airspeed. This final descent was obviously allowed to continue until the aircraft was only a short distance from the pier – too close to avoid it when its structure suddenly loomed out of the fog.

The investigators considered whether the pilots could have misinterpreted the appearance of the approach lights or been subject to an illusion associated with them. But as the entire crew were killed, this line of enquiry could not be pursued. While recognising this possibility, the investigators were unable to determine whether or not the lights were a factor.

Although the entire crew was lost and their rest periods remained unknown, the investigators believed fatigue to be a factor in the accident, not only as a result of the $22\frac{1}{2}$ hours they had spent enroute from Rome, but more likely because of the additional two hours forty minutes they were forced to devote to the four approach attempts, with the high mental and physical demands this would have made upon the pilots. The element of fatigue was especially evident during the final approach – as portrayed by the captain's consistently poor adherence to the localiser course, his descent to a very low altitude before a sharp pullup, and his abrupt control inputs.

Fatigue was also evident to some degree in the captain's slow response to the effect of windshift and the probable loss of airspeed

Survivors, seated in the rear of the aircraft and thrown into the bay when the DC-6B struck the pier, are assisted from the water. The parallel northside approach light pier can be seen in the background. (Associated Press)

that caused the aircraft to continue sinking before it struck the pier. It could only be concluded that fatigue had seriously impaired the highly experienced captain's ability and efficiency.

Deliberately descending through set minimum altitudes during instrument approaches to land is known to be a hazardous procedure at the best of times. Although the captain was reasonably familiar with Idlewild Airport, the actual reasons for his doing so in this instance could not be determined.

Cause

The Civil Aeronautics Board determined that the probable cause of the accident was an erratic approach, resulting in a descent to too low an altitude to avoid striking the pier. A contributing factor was pilot fatigue in the particularly difficult circumstances.

Newspaper picture of the badly damaged southern side approach light pier, taken from a helicopter during attempts to recover the wreckage of the DC-6B. A US Navy salvage barge lies alongside the pier. The threshold of Runway 22 on which the aircraft was attempting to land, can be seen in the right background. (The New York Times)

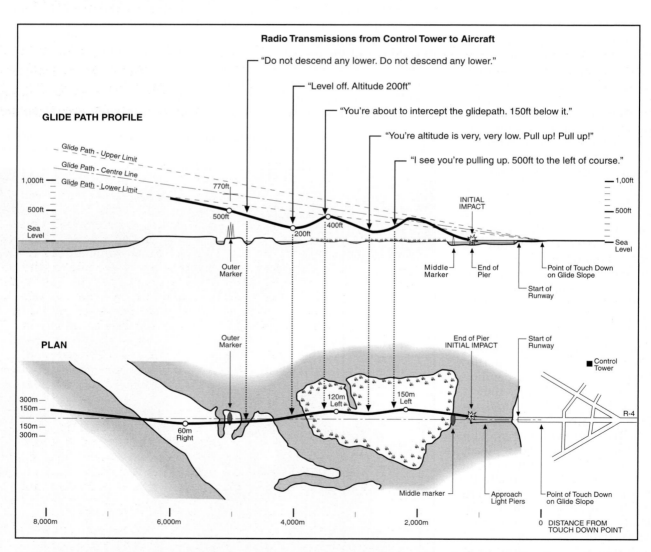

Radio Transmissions from Control Tower to Aircraft

"Do not descend any lower. Do not descend any lower."

"Level off. Altitude 200ft"

"You're about to intercept the glidepath. 150ft below it."

"You're altitude is very, very low. Pull up! Pull up!"

"I see you're pulling up. 500ft to the left of course."

GLIDE PATH PROFILE

PLAN

Profile and plan of the ILS glidepath over Jamaica Bay to Idlewild Airport's Runway 04, with the approach path actually followed by the DC-6B superimposed. The aircraft's approach became increasingly erratic as it descended.

CHAPTER 5

A fatal propeller reversal

In the early postwar years, when piston engines reigned supreme, there were probably more accidents to multi-engined aircraft as a result of simulated engine failures than those resulting from the real thing. But this was hardly considered a danger to a DC-6 training flight with three experienced airline captains on board.

On the afternoon of April 4 1955, a United Airlines check captain was carrying out instrument rating checks with two of the company's line pilots at McArthur Field, Islip, in New York State. The day was fine and clear, but the wind from the southwest was strong, blowing at about 20 knots (37km/h), gusting at times to as much as 30 knots (56km/h).

The aircraft engaged on the flying training session was one of the company's DC-6s, N37512. Loaded to only a little over 61,000 pounds (27,700kg), it was well below its maximum permissible weight, with its centre-of-gravity within prescribed limits.

At about 3.50pm, in the course of a number of circuits, the DC-6 was seen to be making another takeoff on the into-wind runway. Becoming airborne 1500 to 1800 feet down the runway, it initially climbed normally on the runway heading, and the undercarriage began to retract. But as it climbed

through about 50 feet, the DC-6 began banking and turning to the right.

The angle of bank and rate of turn progressively increased as the climbing turn continued, soon reaching alarming proportions, and by the time the DC-6 had turned through about 90°, the bank had increased to the point where the wings were almost vertical. Now at a height of about 150 feet, with the engines still at high power, the DC-6 stalled, its nose dropping violently. Moments later the aircraft, diving steeply, struck the ground on its nose and starboard wing. Cartwheeling, it fell right side up and exploded into flames.

Despite the prompt arrival of the airport fire service tenders, fire consumed most of the wreckage before it could be brought under control. The three pilots on board, the only occupants of the DC-6, had died instantly in the impact.

Investigation

The check captain, 45, who was in the right hand control seat, had a total of nearly 10,000 hours experience, including 550 hours on DC-6s. He had been a check captain with the company for two and a half years. The pilot in the command seat at the time of the fatal takeoff was 40 years of age, and had 9000 hours, including more than 1100 hours on DC-6s. The third pilot, with similar flying experience, was acting as flight engineer when the accident occurred.

Bystanders who saw the DC-6 taking off on the fatal flight, said that everything appeared normal until the aircraft began banking to the right at such a low altitude. Although all four engines were severely damaged by impact and fire, it was evident from the damage sustained by their twisted and bent propeller blades that each was developing power at impact. To what extent could not be determined, but no evidence of

The prototype DC-6, seen over Santa Monica during certification flying in the middle of 1946. A stretched, fully pressurised development of the highly successful DC-4 Skymaster and C-54, the aircraft was powered initially by four 2100hp (1567kW) Pratt & Whitney Double Wasp radial engines. It seated 52 passengers in its normal configuration, but could carry up to 86 in high density cabin layouts. The DC-6 retained the DC-4 wing, but had a 2.06m longer fuselage, with a gross weight increased from 33,113kg to 44,089kg. The type entered service with both United Air Lines and American Airlines in late 1946. (Boeing)

operational failure could be found in any of the engine wreckage.

Early in the investigation, the integrity of the fuselage, wing, tail assembly, control surfaces and the flight control systems, was subjected to detailed examination to determine if any problem could have developed in the airframe during takeoff. No indication of any malfunction could be found. All control surfaces and trim tabs were in place on their hinges, and both the gust lock and the autopilot were disengaged. The flaps were extended between 15 and 20°, the usual setting for takeoff, and the undercarriage was retracted. The mixture controls were in the auto rich position, also the normal setting for takeoff.

Examination of all four propellers disclosed no evidence of faulty operation. The propeller governors were all positioned for takeoff rpm, but while Nos 1, 2, and 3 propellers were all at 34° positive pitch, the full fine setting for takeoff, the No 4 propeller was in full reverse pitch at minus 8°. None of the electrical switches and relays affecting the operation and control of the No 4 propeller disclosed any evidence of malfunction, and it was evident that all damage had been caused by the impact or the fire that followed.

The propellers of a DC-6 are designed to provide reverse thrust for braking, once the aircraft is on the ground after landing. The propellers are reversed after touchdown by retarding the throttle levers rearward of their forward idle positions. This movement activates electrically powered mechanisms in the hub of each propeller, which rotate the blades into a position where they develop thrust in the opposite direction to normal.

The degree of engine power and reverse thrust developed is proportional to the amount of rearward throttle movement applied by the pilot. Forward thrust can be restored by returning the throttle levers to the forward idle position in the throttle quadrant, or beyond.

While the aircraft is in flight, an automatic latching mechanism prevents inadvertent throttle lever movement rearward of the forward idle position, thus preventing unwanted propeller reversals. The throttle latch is controlled by switches on the main undercarriage struts. The switches close when the aircraft's weight is transferred to the undercarriage on landing, energising a solenoid which releases the latch. At the same time, a reverse warning flag swings up into view on the control pedestal to show that the throttles

are unlatched. Mechanically linked to the solenoid, this red metal flag may be raised manually by the crew to release the latch should the solenoid fail to do so.

When the aircraft becomes airborne on takeoff, the undercarriage strut switches open and the solenoid is de-energised, allowing the latch to return to the locked position. As this occurs, the flag swings down out of sight.

Reverse thrust indicator warning lamps were not installed on the aircraft involved in the accident. When fitted, the lights, one for each propeller, illuminate to warn the crew that the propeller is reversing as its blades pass the zero degree blade angle. At the time of the accident, United Airlines was progressively installing the indicator lamps on its DC-6 and DC-6B aircraft.

Three years before the accident, United Airlines, concerned that an inflight propeller reversal could possibly occur as a result of an electrical malfunction, modified the propeller reversing control circuits on its DC-6 fleet to automatically remove electrical power from them while the aircraft were in flight. This was accomplished by the addition of a relay, controlled by switches actuated by the throttle latch solenoid. Electrical power was restored to the propeller control circuits when the throttle latch release solenoid was energised as the aircraft touched down.

During the investigation of the accident, tests established that if a DC-6 propeller, modified in this way, was reversed by rearward movement of the throttle lever while the aircraft was still firmly on the ground during takeoff, and the aircraft then lifted off in this configuration, the blades would remain in reverse pitch, regardless of the positioning of the throttle lever.

The amount of reverse thrust it developed would depend upon the amount of throttle applied, either in a forward or rearward direction. In this situation, the propeller could only be returned to forward thrust by lifting the reverse warning flag and advancing the throttle.

Lifting the flag had the same function as the closing of the undercarriage switch when the aircraft's weight was transferred to the undercarriage legs on touchdown, i.e. it again energised the propeller's electric reversing system, enabling forward thrust to be restored. But if the flag was not lifted when the throttle lever was moved forward, the reverse thrust being developed would simply increase in proportion to the amount of throttle opening applied.

United Airlines also conducted a series of flight tests at a safe altitude to investigate the effects of a reversed outboard propeller on the handling characteristics of a DC-6 at low airspeeds. These tests indicated that in the takeoff configuration, with METO (maximum except takeoff) power or higher on Nos 1, 2 and 3 engines, the aircraft almost immediately becomes uncontrollable when full reverse power is applied on No 4 engine and the airspeed is 100 knots (185km/h) or less. During the tests, it was found that the roll to the right could be delayed for a short time by applying full left aileron, but a violent yawing to the right continued, resulting in a loss in airspeed and, within a few seconds, a violently roll and pitch down. The aircraft attitudes that resulted during the flight tests closely resembled the manoeuvres of the DC-6 that witnesses described immediately before the accident.

A United Air Lines DC-6, snapped at San Francisco Airport. (Airline Publications)

scribed immediately before the accident.

The flight tests also confirmed the investigation's findings concerning the positioning of a throttle lever after unintentionally displacing it into the reverse range during takeoff while the weight of the aircraft was still on the undercarriage. The flight tests showed conclusively that moving the throttle lever back into the forward thrust range after the aircraft became airborne would not bring the propeller out of reverse, but result only in increased reverse thrust.

Some time before the accident, United Airlines, in the course of updating its fleet, acquired a number of DC-7 aircraft which, instead of having the DC-6 type electrically operated throttle reverse latch, were fitted with a manually operated sequence gate latch, known as the Martin bar. This latch in principle consists of a bar across the throttle quadrant behind the forward idle position which can be moved clear on landing to enable the throttle levers to be pulled back into reverse. But when in position during flight, the latch prevents the levers being inadvertently placed in reverse.

As a result of favourable operating experience with the Martin bar latch on its new DC-7s, United Airlines decided to equip all its DC-6 and DC-6B aircraft with the latch as well. Although the DC-6s' electrically operated throttle latches had functioned satisfactorily, the pilot actuated mechanical lock on the Martin bar was considered

safer and more reliable than the automatic, electrical installation, with all its switches and relays. United Airlines had ordered the required Martin bar modification kits several months before the accident, and the company's first DC-6 was fitted with the new latching system only a week before the accident occurred.

Analysis

The flight tests showed conclusively that, at takeoff configuration and airspeed, a DC-6 becomes uncontrollable with an outboard engine at full power with its propeller in reverse pitch. Control is lost so quickly that there is little the crew can do at low altitude. In the case of this accident, it was doubtful if there would have been time for forward thrust to be restored before control was lost. For the same reason, it was doubtful that reversing warning lamps could have made any difference to the outcome.

The tests also showed that, while airborne, the engine driving the reversed propeller will stall if its throttle setting is at either forward or reverse idle. There was evidence that the No 4 engine was running at impact, and the tests established that, to achieve a flightpath similar to that of the accident aircraft, full reverse power was required on No 4 engine, with the other three engines developing METO power in forward thrust.

There were only two ways in which the No 4 propeller could have been reversed during takeoff. Either there was a malfunction in the propeller control

Layout of controls and instruments as fitted to the flightdeck of a DC-6. The flight engineer's station is out of the picture. A separate set of throttle levers was provided for captain and first officer. This flightdeck incorporates the later, manually operated sequence gate latch to prevent the levers being inadvertently placed in reverse. The pilot actuated mechanical latch was considered more reliable than the automatic, electrical installation. (Smith's Industries)

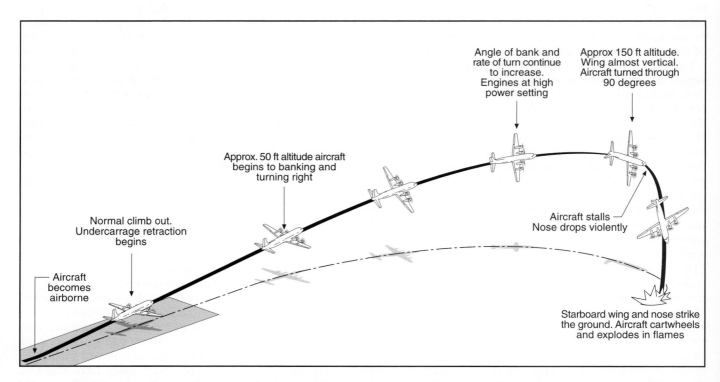

Angle of bank and
rate of turn continue
to increase.
Engines at high
power setting

Approx 150 ft altitude.
Wing almost vertical.
Aircraft turned through
90 degrees

Approx. 50 ft altitude aircraft
begins to banking and
turning right

Normal climb out.
Undercarriage retraction
begins

Aircraft stalls
Nose drops violently

Aircraft
becomes
airborne

Starboard wing and nose strike
the ground. Aircraft cartwheels
and explodes in flames

Artist's impression of the DC-6's all too brief flightpath. Becoming airborne normally, the DC-6 initially climbed straight ahead. But at about 50 feet, it began turning to the right, the bank and rate of turn increasing. Finally, with the wings near vertical, the DC-6 stalled, dived into the ground and exploded. (Aero Illustrations)

system, or the No 4 throttle lever was retarded past the forward idle position before the DC-6 became airborne. Because the detailed examination of the electrical system of the No 4 propeller eliminated the possibility of malfunction, it had to be concluded that the propeller reversal was an unintentional crew action.

Several aspects of the DC-6's takeoff indicate that an instrument takeoff, followed by a simulation of engine failure, was being conducted at the time. This particular takeoff was the logical point in the check flight to carry out these exercises and, according to company requirements, No 4 was the correct engine to select for the simulated failure. Furthermore, the aircraft's short delay at the beginning of the runway before its final takeoff began was consistent with the practice of making a last cockpit check before an instrument takeoff. This would normally be followed by a simulated engine failure as part of the checking procedure.

To the investigators, it seemed highly probable that the accident sequence began when the check pilot, simulating a failure of the No 4 engine by reducing its thrust to idle during the instrument takeoff exercise just before the DC-6 became airborne, unintentionally brought the No 4 throttle lever too far back and into the reverse range.

When this emergency developed, it would have been a natural reaction for the check pilot to immediately push the No 4 throttle lever fully forward from the reverse range again in a frantic effort to restore forward thrust. But, as the flight tests proved, because the reverse warning flag was not lifted as well, this had the fatal effect of applying full reverse power instead.

Conclusions

The Civil Aeronautics Board, as a result of its investigation of the DC-6 accident, found that:
• As power was reduced to zero thrust during an instrument take-off to simulate an engine failure, the No 4 propeller was unintentionally reversed just before the aircraft became airborne.
• There was evidence that, in an attempt to correct the error, the No 4 throttle lever was moved out of reverse into the full forward thrust position. But because the reverse warning flag was not lifted, full reverse thrust resulted.
• An outboard propeller reversing as a DC-6 becomes airborne at takeoff configuration and airspeed, in conjunction with high power on the other three engines, results in the aircraft becoming almost immediately uncontrollable.
• There was insufficient time and altitude for the crew to take effective corrective action.
• The probable cause of the accident was the unintentional movement of the No 4 throttle lever into the reverse range just before the aircraft lifted off. With the other three engines operating at high power, the aircraft, once airborne, quickly became uncontrollable.

CHAPTER 6

Grossly inadequate maintenance claims 28 lives

When the crew of a C-54 asked an aircraft workshop to investigate some oil leaks, they never suspected this would lead directly to a disasterous accident.

The midwinter night of November 16, 1955 was clear but cold as 65 non-commissioned US Army personnel boarded a chartered civilian Douglas C-54 parked in front of the passenger terminal at Boeing Field, Seattle. The former US Air Force C-54, a military version of the Douglas DC-4, now with the civil registration N88852, belonged to the Peninsula Air Transport Company, a privately owned non-scheduled operator based in Miami, Florida.

Peninsula Air Transport undertook frequent military contracts, and on this occasion the Army had chartered the C-54 to fly the soldiers, granted leave for Thanksgiving Day, to their homes in Chicago, New York and Newark. Thanksgiving, a national holiday throughout the United States, is traditionally celebrated on the fourth Thursday of November. Also on board the aircraft as passengers were a newly appointed company pilot, Captain Edward McGrath, with his wife and three children, who were on their way to Boston.

It was nearly midnight by the time the sole flight attendant had

settled all her passengers in their seats, First Officer Frederick Hall had closed the C-54's doors and taken his position on the flightdeck, and Captain William McDougall had started the engines.

Loaded to just under its maximum permissible weight, and with the airfield all to itself at this time of night, the C-54 taxied for a takeoff from the main runway into the south. At the runway holding point, the crew conducted their pre-takeoff checks, running up the engines in pairs so as not to delay the takeoff, the aircraft having just undergone engine and propeller maintenance at an independent aircraft workshop facility based at Boeing Field.

Lining up on the runway with 15° of flap extended, the crew began their takeoff at two minutes to midnight. The C-54 became airborne normally, the first officer retracted the undercarriage and the captain tracked south over the Duwamish River, gaining height before beginning a left turn on to the heading for their first refuelling stop at Billings, Montana, nearly 600nm (1110km) distant on

the eastern side of the Rocky Mountains.

As the aircraft climbed normally through 300 feet, he eased back the throttle and pitch controls from their takeoff settings to normal rated power, and the first officer reduced the flap setting to five degrees. But suddenly, with an unnerving high pitched howl, the No 4 propeller surged, rapidly increasing in rpm to about 2800. The captain immediately retarded the No 4 throttle and pitch levers, but the surging propeller remained unaffected. He then pressed the feathering button for the No 4 propeller, but again there was no response, the loudly whining propeller continuing to register a steady 2800 rpm.

With the greatly increased drag of the runaway propeller now taking effect, the C-54 began to lose both airspeed and height. The crew countered by reapplying takeoff power on Nos 1, 2 and 3 engines and further reduced the power settings for No 4 engine, but this action only resulted in the No 4 propeller surging again, the engine rpm increasing to more than 3000.

The C-54 transport, as used in large numbers by the US Army Air Force and other allied forces from 1942. At the end of WW2, the civil version became the superb DC-4 Skymaster, widely used by airlines throughout the world to make inter-continental flying a reality. (Boeing)

Unable to reduce the rpm of No 4 engine in any way, or even to hold the aircraft straight against the drag of its overspeeding propeller, the crew knew they were in serious trouble. The aircraft was now veering to the right as it continued to descend and, realising a crash landing in the dark was inevitable, the captain raised the nose to reduce the airspeed until the aircraft was almost in a stalled condition, then applied full power to all four engines.

The aircraft continued to settle in a noseup attitude towards a hillside in Riverton, a collection of modest homes just south of the outskirts of Seattle. Striking a telephone pole with its starboard wing, the aircraft grazed across the roof of a nearby house, demolished the garage at its rear, and struck the ground in the backyard of a neighbouring two-storey home, spraying it with fuel as the impact sheared off the wings and engines and tore open the fuel tanks. The fuselage was broken open as it struck other buildings and trees.

Fire broke out, but occupants who had survived the crash and

The reliable and versatile DC-4 continues in freighting operations in developing nations even today. This Tanzanian registered DC-4, engaged on a cargo flight, was photographed at Harare. (Julian Green)

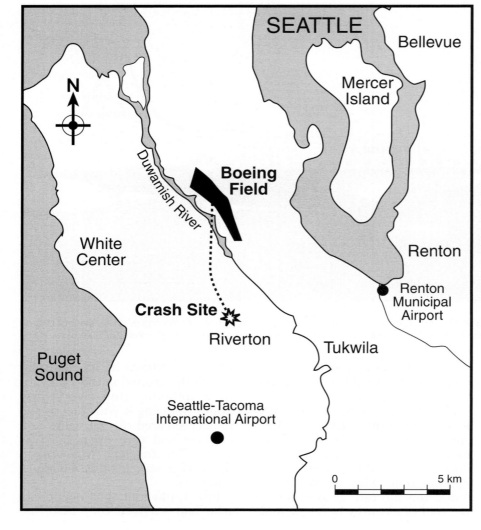

Map showing relationship of Seattle, Boeing Field and accident site. (Aero Illustrations)

were not seriously injured, escaped through the break in the fuselage before a sudden flare up of the fire that quickly consumed much of the wreckage. Fire engines, ambulances and rescue equipment rushed to the scene over icy roads and arrived soon afterwards.

The fire was extinguished, but not before it had done extensive property damage, as well as destroying most of what remained of the aircraft. Ambulance officers provided first aid to the dazed survivors, some of whom were by this time being cared for in nearby houses. Forty-six of the aircraft's 74 occupants, including the three members of the crew, survived the crash and fire, but all sustained injuries of varying degrees. The surviving passengers included the newly appointed pilot's family, but the man himself, trapped in the

wreckage, died in the fire, together with the aircraft's 27 other occupants.

First Officer Hall told rescuers that when the wrecked aircraft lurched to a stop, Captain McDougall "seemed to be sitting there in a sort of a daze." He continued: "My own chest was hurting pretty badly, and I didn't know if I could carry him out. So I called, 'Hey, get up and walk.' And he did!"

Investigation

The site of the accident was just over five kilometres from Boeing Field and 300 feet above its elevation. When it struck the telephone pole, the C-54 was on a heading of 210°, banking to the right. Shattered wreckage extended for 200m from the pole. At the end of the wreckage trail, the separated but unburnt tail section, with fin and tailplane still attached, rested

against a line of small fir trees on the boundary of the property in which the aircraft struck the ground. An engine, with only a single twisted blade left on the hub of the propeller, had fallen into the front garden of the two storey house, while portion of one wing lay against a large tree at its rear.

Examination of the remaining portions of the wings, fuselage, and tail disclosed no evidence to indicate any structural failure or malfunction before the impact. Captain McDougall told investigators from his hospital bed that there had been no engine failure, and they had experienced no difficulty with the aircraft except that associated with the runaway No 4 propeller. First Officer Hall made a similar statement, corroborating the captain's evidence.

The No 4 hydromatic propeller, still attached to the engine's reduction gear casing, was found eight metres from the main wreckage. Its hub and reduction gear casing, and the forward face of all three propeller blades, were heavily coated with engine oil. Inspection disclosed that the propeller dome retaining nut, although fitted with a locked safety cap screw, had not been adequately tightened, allowing oil to leak out from around the base of the dome, even though the dome seal was in sound condition.

On Hamilton Standard fully feathering hydromatic propellers, used on many types of large piston engined transport aircraft, the dome carried on the front of the propeller hub houses the hydraulically operated pitch change and feathering mechanisms. Oil pressure acting against either side of a piston within the dome is transmitted via a mechanical linkage in the hub to helical gears on each blade root, providing the means for a change of pitch. Because of the centrifugal twisting movement of the blades, the natural tendency of the pitch change mechanism, when not restrained by oil pressure acting against the piston, is to move to full fine pitch.

As well as the fact that the dome of the No 4 propeller had not been properly tightened, it was found, when the propeller hub mechanism was dismantled, that the

No 1 and 2 blades were incorrectly positioned in the hub by one helical gear tooth, or 8° of blade pitch. As a result, when the propeller was in its fine pitch setting, the No 3 blade was in the normal fine pitch position of 24°, but the No 1 and 2 blades were at only 16°, 8° less than normal.

To determine the degree of oil leakage that would have occurred because of the loose dome, investigators reassembled the propeller using replacement parts only where necessary. The exact dome looseness was duplicated on a propeller test stand and oil pumped into the propeller assembly at various pressures. The tests revealed there was oil leakage at all pressures and that the maximum oil pressure obtainable in the propeller dome was 200 psi – because about 19 litres of oil a minute was leaking from around its base. The pump would normally have produced a dome pressure of about 600 psi.

The oil capacity of each of the C-54's engines engine was 100 litres, so it was evident from the test results that, if the flight had been able to continue for much longer, the No 4 engine's entire oil supply would have become exhausted.

Investigators therefore dismantled the No 4 engine itself and examined it in detail. This revealed that its rear master rod bearing was in the process of failing, and that the front master rod bearing was also beginning to fail. Although neither failure had progressed to the extent of appreciably affecting the operation of the engine or its power output, the bearing failures were characteristic of oil starvation. The engine examination disclosed no other evidence of malfunction.

Peninsular Air Transport's company records showed that the No 4 propeller had been overhauled two months before the accident, then installed on another company aircraft, a DC-4. But on November 11, five days before the crash, the propeller was removed from this aircraft because a pilot had complained that it was "rough".

A DC-4, the civilian version of the C-54, snapped soon after takeoff. Note the flap still partially extended. (Photograph via Harry Gann)

The propeller was inspected, reassembled using a new dome seal, and tested, after which company maintenance engineers installed it in the No 4 position on C-54 N88852, the aircraft involved in the accident. At the time of the accident this propeller had accumulated 475 hours since its major overhaul, and 20 hours since its installation on N88852.

In the course of this 20 hours flying on charter operations, N88852 flew to Kansas City where, on November 13, Captain McDougall took command of it to continue a military contract flight to McChord Air Force Base at Tacoma, only a short distance south of Seattle. The flight to McChord was largely uneventful, except that the C-54's No 4 engine's starter solenoid failed after the aircraft was refuelled enroute at Billings, Montana.

No aircraft maintenance facilities capable of replacing the solenoid were available at Billings, and the crew considered attempting to airstart the engine while rolling fast on the runway. But with snow on the ground, they believed it inadvisable, because it might not be possible to stop safely in the remaining runway distance.

The crew solved the problem at Billings by offloading the passengers, taking the aircraft into the air on three engines, and airstarting the No 4 engine in flight. They then landed the C-54 again,

reboarded the passengers, and continued on their way to McChord.

After arriving at McChord Air Force Base and discharging their passengers while leaving No 4 engine idling, the crew took off again almost straight away to ferry the aircraft the short distance north to Boeing Field where civilian maintenance facilities were available. Here Captain McDougall placed the C-54 in the hands of an independent aircraft workshop, instructing its engineering director to have the No 4 starter solenoid replaced, and to correct several other minor discrepancies that had developed during the charter flight.

The captain also asked the workshop staff to inspect the No 4 engine to ensure it had not been damaged in any way by the airstart. Both pilots pointed out an accumulation of engine oil on the starboard wing around the No 3 and 4 engines, asking that it be investigated and corrected.

But the workshop's maintenance engineers, without first cleaning up the oil on the wings and then running the engines to watch for the source of leakage, simply carried out a visual inspection of the aircraft as it was, and concluded that the leakage was coming from the Nos 3 and 4 propeller dome seals.

Some of the maintenance engineers and their unlicensed assist-

Wire photograph published in The New York Times, *for Saturday November 19, 1955, showing the tail assembly of the burnt out C-54 – the only part of the aircraft still recognisable. (Associated Press)*

ants who worked on the aircraft were employed by the workshop only on a part time basis. Moreover, the licensed engineer who was assigned to carry out the work on the No 4 propeller had not replaced dome seals for three years, and his unlicensed assistant was only recently employed.

Neither was familiar with the experience and capability of the other, nor with the prescribed procedure for replacing hydromatic propeller dome seals. No reference manuals for the C-54, DC-4 or Hamilton Standard propellers were available to them, and the workshop's management had defined no clear line of responsibility within the organisation for the supervision of work to be done.

Analysis

Captain McDougall and First Officer Hall told investigators that, after returning to Boeing Field to take delivery of the serviced aircraft, they spoke to the engineering director of the workshop and

were assured the C-54 was ready for flight. They examined the documents detailing the maintenance work they had requested, and it all appeared to have been done. Taking over the aircraft, they then started the engines and taxied the C-54 to the passenger terminal, ready to load their military passengers later in the day.

Questions addressed to the maintenance engineers to whom the work was assigned showed clearly that at no time after the C-54 was received into the workshop after its arrival from Tacoma on November 14 were the engines run up to determine if the dome seals were properly installed, or if any oil leaks remained. Such a runup was essential to the vital work performed on the No 3 and 4 propellers, and a clear responsibility of the maintenance workshop.

It was even more necessary in this case, because the maintenance engineers had concluded, when they first inspected the air-

craft, that the oil leaks pointed out by the pilots came from the propeller dome seals. Yet they did not even first clean the oil from around the engines to be sure of their diagnosis. Had the engines been run up and the propellers exercised when their work was completed, the excessively loose propeller dome on No 4 engine would have been immediately evident from the amount of oil leaking from around it.

Numerous expert witnesses, including a representative of Hamilton Standard, the propeller manufacturer, said it was standard procedure, as detailed in the propeller's workshop manual, to change dome seals with the propeller blades in the feathered position. This was not done in this case because the engineers working on the propeller were unfamiliar with what they were doing, and had no workshop manual to guide them.

The investigators believed that if the correct workshop procedure had been followed during the

"Captain McDougall (had) placed the C-54 in the hands of an independent aircraft workshop...to correct several minor discrepancies that had developed..."

changing of the propeller dome seal, the incorrect positioning of the propeller blades would not have occurred. Again, a thorough engine runup when the work was completed would have revealed this error. Good maintenance practices and procedures certainly dictated an engine runup, and it was the responsibility of the workshop company to ensure this was done. Poor overall supervision, an excessive workload, and generally poor workshop procedures were responsible for the omission.

Tests during the investigation of the accident also showed that considerable roughness would have been evident in the incorrectly assembled No 4 propeller, especially when the pilots warmed up

the engines before taxying the aircraft to the passenger terminal and while it was holding before takeoff. But in view of the fact that all four engines were used during taxying and the engines were run up in pairs before takeoff, it is possible that the roughness would not have been noticeable.

When the crew made their first power reduction after takeoff, the No 4 propeller did not respond. This was undoubtedly the result of an insufficient oil supply to the propeller governor to actuate the propeller mechanism towards a coarser blade angle. Sufficient feathering oil still existed to start the process, but soon after the blades began to move the supply became exhausted.

Exhaustion of the feathering oil resulted in the blades returning to the fine pitch setting, causing the engine and propeller to overspeed. Engineering data for the C-54 and the DC-4, as well the excessive drag from the runaway propeller described by the captain, showed that it would have been extremely difficult, if not impossible, to sustain flight under these conditions.

Although the No 4 engine's total supply of 100 litres of oil was not entirely exhausted during the brief flight, a substantial proportion of it probably would have been lost before takeoff. It is probable this occurred during the No 4 engine's pre-takeoff runup, when its propeller was exercised,

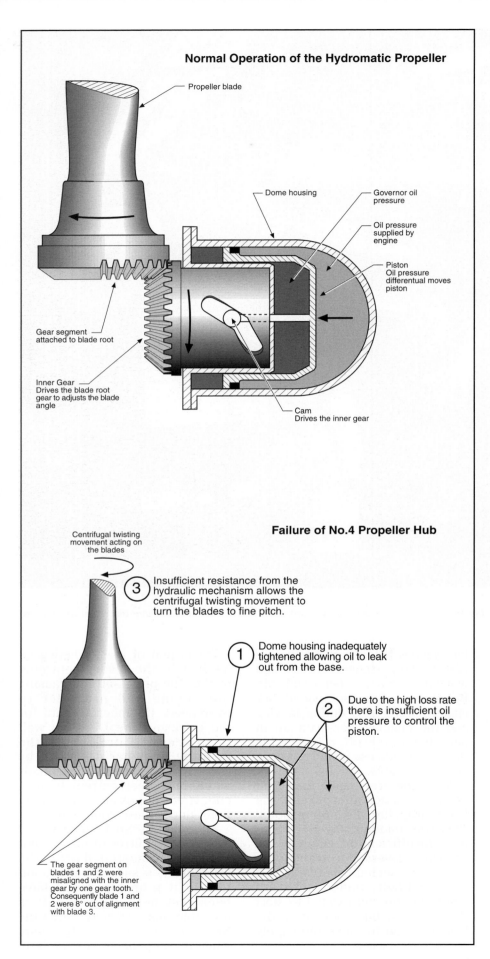

Schematic diagram of hydromatic propeller, showing how loss of oil from propeller dome affected control of pitch mechanism. (Aero Illustrations)

Normal Operation of the Hydromatic Propeller

Propeller blade

Dome housing

Governor oil pressure

Oil pressure supplied by engine

Piston
Oil pressure differentual moves piston

Gear segment attached to blade root

Inner Gear
Drives the blade root gear to adjusts the blade angle

Cam
Drives the inner gear

Failure of No.4 Propeller Hub

Centrifugal twisting movement acting on the blades

③ Insufficient resistance from the hydraulic mechanism allows the centrifugal twisting movement to turn the blades to fine pitch.

① Dome housing inadequately tightened allowing oil to leak out from the base.

② Due to the high loss rate there is insufficient oil pressure to control the piston.

The gear segment on blades 1 and 2 were misaligned with the inner gear by one gear tooth. Consequently blade 1 and 2 were 8° out of alignment with blade 3.

The Pratt & Whitney Twin Wasp R-2000 14 cylinder engine of a DC-4 showing its Hamilton Standard fully feathering hydromatic propeller. The propeller dome retaining nut, with its safety cap lock screw, is clearly visible. Because the retaining nut had not been adequately tightened, oil was able to leak freely from around the base of the dome, the reduced oil pressure in the dome allowing the propeller mechanism to move automatically into the full fine pitch position. (Brian L Hill)

and its feathering operation checked. It could not be determined whether the leak could have been seen from the flight-deck in the circumstances of the night takeoff.

It was unfortunate for the victims of the accident that the C-54's first departure after its propeller maintenance happened to take place at night. If the take-off had been made during day-light hours, the crew would surely have noticed the excessive oil leak around the No 4 propeller dome while exercising that propeller during their pre-takeoff checks.

Cause

The probable cause of this accident was excessively high drag resulting from the No 4 engine's improperly assembled propeller blades and their inability to feather. These conditions were the result of a series of maintenance errors and omissions.

CHAPTER 7

Misjudged approach in fog

The night sky was clear with unlimited visibility – except for shallow fog in the vicinity of the airport. Yet it was enough to fatally mislead a Constellation crew attempting an ILS approach.

It was probably fortunate that there were only 12 passengers, in addition to the normal crew of five, aboard the first leg of Eastern Air Lines' early morning mail flight from Miami, Florida, to Boston, Massachusetts, via Jacksonville and New York, on Wednesday, December 21 1955.

The Lockheed Constellation 749, N112A, allocated to the five hour trip, one of seven long range Constellations Eastern had been operating for the past seven years, could well have been carrying up to 69 people. Doubtless the very early departure time of 2.30am from Miami was one of the reasons for the light passenger loading.

The terminal forecast for Jacksonville which the crew received while flight planning at Miami indicated that the sky would be clear of cloud with unlimited visibility. But the weather forecaster also told the crew that, because weather stations from Miami as far north as Savannah, 105nm (195km) beyond Jacksonville, were reporting only a small spread between ground temperature and dewpoint, patchy ground fog could be expected in the Jacksonville area.

Eastern Air Lines' weather minima for ILS approaches to Jacksonville by Constellation aircraft, required a ceiling of 200 feet and a visibility of half a mile (.8km) by day or night. The crew completed an IFR flightplan, nominating Orlando, Florida, as their alternate for Jacksonville.

Under the command of Captain Tom O'Brien, 43, an Eastern Air Lines pilot since 1942, the Constellation took off normally, cruising northwards from Miami in clear weather towards the thriving industrial city of Jacksonville, the aircraft making routine radio transmissions at designated airway reporting points.

At 3.15am, 45 minutes after leaving Miami, the Constellation called Jacksonville, reporting it was now over Daytona Beach, 87nm (161km) south of the city at 11,000 feet, and passed an estimate for Jacksonville of 3.36am. Jacksonville's Imeson Airport at the time was enveloped in a light fog which had reduced horizontal visibility to only three kilometres, and the only wind was a light breeze from the north-northwest at five knots (9km/h). Air Traffic Control passed the current weather observations to the Constellation and with traffic in the area light at that hour of the day, the aircraft was instructed to continue its descent towards Jacksonville to 2500 feet, maintaining this altitude until further advised. When it reached the "Sunbeam" Intersection, 16nm (30km) south-southwest of the airport, the aircraft was to change frequency and call Jacksonville Approach Control.

Fifteen minutes later at 3.31am, the Constellation called Approach Control as instructed, reporting it was now over the Sunbeam Intersection at 2500 feet. The approach controller then cleared it to join an ILS approach to Imeson Airport's Runway 05, informing the aircraft that visibility was now reduced to half a mile in fog, and that the QNH was 1023 millibars. A moment later, the controller added that the ceiling was an "indefinite 300 feet".

A graceful Eastern Air Lines Lockheed Constellation 749 identical to the one operating the company's early morning mail flight from Miami, Florida, to Boston, Massachusetts, via Jacksonville and New York, on Wednesday, December 21 1955. It was fortunate that the aircraft was carrying only 12 passengers. Note the "Speedpak" cargo container attached to the underside of the fuselage. (Lockheed)

The crew acknowledged this terminal weather information and reported they were leaving Sunbeam at 2500 feet. Moments later they queried whether there was any other traffic. Replying, the approach controller advised that there was no other known traffic in the area, and requested the crew to call Jacksonville Tower when over the outer marker, inbound to Runway 05. Five minutes later the Constellation called the tower, reporting it was now over the outer marker, and was cleared to land.

Shortly afterwards the tower controller, watching for the lights of the aircraft as it approached through the fog, saw a huge flash of flame erupt close to the ground in the vicinity of the ILS middle marker for Runway 05. Alarmed, he immediately called the Constellation again, but there was no reply. At once he pressed the tower's emergency button.

Airport emergency and fire service vehicles sped through the darkness and fog to the scene of the accident in response to the tower controller's call and found the Constellation had crashed to destruction a kilometre southwest of the threshold of Runway 05. Narrowly missing houses in the semi-suburban area, it had demol-

ished a parked caravan and a chicken coop in the extensive grounds of the semi-rural properties. The wreckage was burning fiercely and it was obvious that there could be no survivors.

Investigation

Investigators from the US Civil Aeronautics Board who arrived in Jacksonville later that morning found the main wreckage of the Constellation lay just over 1000 metres short of the Runway 05 threshold, and 70 metres past the ILS middle marker transmitter.

A wreckage trail 200 metres long and 30 metres wide clearly showed the path of the aircraft's descent to destruction. The outer sections of both wings were separated from the main wreckage, and the under belly "Speedpak" cargo container was torn from the bottom of the fuselage. The starboard main undercarriage and part of the nose leg had also been torn off when the aircraft struck the ground, but the port main undercarriage leg was intact and in the extended and locked down position.

The aircraft had first struck the top of a small pine tree about 200 feet below the ILS glide path, 80 metres to the left of the extended centreline of the runway, and 1220

metres short of the threshold of Runway 05. It then flew through the upper branches of a 50-foot oak, shearing off the topmost 20 feet. As the aircraft continued its descent, it struck a clump of other big trees which tore off both wings and part of the tail assembly. The Constellation finally struck the ground on a heading of 55° magnetic, exploded, and burnt fiercely.

Because of the early morning hour, there were few witnesses to the accident, but one householder who happened to be out in his yard at the time and was attracted to the Constellation's approach by the sound of its engines, said "it sounded like it was in good mechanical condition and running good, but appeared to come in too low." Another nearby local resident, still inside his house at the time who heard the aircraft approaching, said he saw its landing lights come on, then heard the sounds of impact as the Constellation sheared off the tree tops. "The big ship hit the ground, but there was no fire until it hit," he continued. He thought it "appeared to be about the normal height for a landing".

Most of the fuselage, including the flightdeck and passenger cabin, were completely consumed

Frontal and profile views of an Eastern Air Lines Lockheed Constellation 749 fitted with the ventral all-metal "Speedpak". With a cargo capacity of 11.3 cubic metres, the container incorporated an electric hoist, enabling it to be lowered to ground level for loading and unloading

by the fire, with the exception of the underside and some of the cabin flooring. The fuselage aft of the rear pressure bulkhead, with the centre fin and part of the tail-plane, remained intact, but were scorched by heat. The Constellation was carrying 83 bags of mail and, although much of it was destroyed in the fire, postal inspectors were able to recover some of it, including a quantity of bank

Lockheed Constellations for Eastern Airlines nearing completion on Lockheed's production line at Burbank, California, in the late 1940s. (Lockheed)

notes, in fire and water damaged condition.

The tail cone was relatively undamaged, with the control booster mechanisms still in position. The wing flaps were extended to 60% of their travel, and were symmetrical at the time of the impact. There was no evidence of any control system failure before impact, and the flightdeck undercarriage lever was in the down position.

The flightdeck instruments were largely destroyed, but the readings that were decipherable indicated the approach had been a routine operation. The radio equipment was set for a normal ILS approach to Jacksonville.

Checks of Imeson Airport's ground-based radio navigational facilities after the accident showed their operation to be normal. Simulated ILS approaches were also made to determine the effect on flightdeck instruments of vehicles parked below the glidepath on the highway which crossed the approach path only 35 metres east of the middle marker.

On one approach, with a mobile crane parked at the side of the highway beneath the glidepath, the glideslope needle on the test aircraft's ILS dial showed a spurious "fly-down" indication before reaching the middle marker, and it was found necessary to descend 60 feet below the actual glidepath to bring the needle back into the centre of the dial. However, at the middle marker itself, which was where the accident occurred, the glidepath indication was found to be normal.

Both Captain O'Brien and his first officer, 39 year old John Rinyu, a former World War 2 military pilot of considerable experience, were quite familiar with Imeson Airport, having made numerous recent landings there in the course of their Eastern Air Lines operations.

About 15 minutes before the accident occurred, an aircraft of another airline was conducting instrument training in the vicinity of Jacksonville. Completing an ILS approach to Imeson Airport's Runway 05, it landed there at 2.38am.

The captain of that aircraft, giving evidence on weather conditions and the operation of the airport's radio navigation aids at the time, told investigators that the top of the low lying deck of broken stratus cloud that covered the airport was at a height of only about 450 feet, with its base at 300 to 250 feet, and that all radio navigational facilities were operating normally.

He also said the cloud condition seemed to be caused, at least partly, by smoke from adjacent mills and factories. Although his aircraft entered this cloud near the middle marker, elsewhere the weather was "spotty to clear".

Analysis

All components of Runway 05's ILS system were operating normally at the time of the accident.

The Eastern Air Lines Lockheed Constellation did not encounter cloud or reduced visibility until it was nearing Jacksonville. From the evidence of other pilots flying in the vicinity a short time before the accident, there was a layer of cloud, which included smoke and fog, capping the airport with a general foggy condition, and extending a few kilometres to the southwest. All other areas were apparently clear. It therefore seemed likely that the Constellation was flying clear of cloud from the Sunbeam intersection to the middle marker, then outbound to the outer marker, and that it probably did not encounter reduced visibility until in the vicinity of the middle marker inbound.

Other pilots who made approaches to Imeson Airport not long beforehand reported that horizontal visibility was reduced

The industrial city of Jacksonville as it was at the time of the accident. The Lockheed was preparing to land at the city's Imeson Airport when it crashed during an ILS approach in fog. The major Florida city is an important world port, as well as a commercial centre. (Florida News Bureau)

to less than 1000 metres, but that vertical visibility generally remained good throughout the area.

Witnesses to the accident itself described ground visibility at and near the accident site at the time as "poor". There was no way of accurately determining the ceiling height or horizontal visibility there at the time, but the weather information reported to the crew when the Constellation was cleared for its ILS approach was actually observed from the control tower, about 1600 metres north-northeast of the accident site.

But a wind of about six knots (11km/h) was blowing from the north-northwest, so the weather observed at the tower would have moved to the general area of the accident by the time the aircraft crashed. Conditions at the accident site would therefore have been essentially as reported.

Consideration also had to be given to a decrease of horizontal visibility with elevation and, at 300 feet above the ground, visibility could have been near zero. For the same reason, slant visibility down the glide path should have

Newspaper wire photograph published the day after the accident. Investigators (right, and left background), are examining the fragmented, burnt out wreckage of the Constellation. (The New York Times)

been gradually increasing as the aircraft descended.

The radar operator's screen at Jacksonville did not display altitude. However, because the radar operator "saw" the Constellation cross the outer marker outbound as it began the ILS instrument approach pattern for Runway 05 before making the prescribed procedure turn and returning inbound, it was reasonable to believe this would have been flown at the normal altitude of 1200 feet.

Eastern Air Lines' operational instructions for Constellation aircraft recommended that an ILS approach from the outer marker inbound to the minimum authorised altitude be flown at an airspeed of 115 knots (213km/h). Yet slash marks made by the Constellation's propellers at the scene of the accident indicated the speed of the aircraft at impact was nearer 140 knots (260km/h).

The aircraft was evidently flying normally immediately before it hit the trees and there was no evidence to suggest any malfunction had occurred. The flaps were extended to a position for manoeuvring at reduced airspeed, and this amount of flap was customarily used during an ILS approach until reaching the middle marker, when full flap would be lowered. Although the Constellation was 70 metres to the left of the localiser course when it struck the trees, this was only a minor deviation at that stage of the approach, requiring only a slight correction to again line up with the runway. The fact that the aircraft was in a slight right turn and almost level at impact would suggest the pilot flying was in fact turning towards the localiser course at the time, indicating the aircraft was under control.

The results of the investigation pointed to the accident having been caused by one or more of three possibilities:

• The crew's adherence to the electronic ILS glidepath was somehow affected by an aberration in the glidepath signal because of interference from vehicles on the highway below it, inadvertently setting up an increased rate of descent which was not subsequently checked.

• The crew were visually deceived by the fluctuating horizontal and slant visibility conditions.

• The pilot actually handling the controls simply made a manipulative error of judgement in positioning the aircraft, as he evidently had with its approach speed, perhaps because of fatigue at that early hour of the day.

But the degree to which any of these three possibilities had actually contributed to the accident could not be finally determined.

Cause

The Civil Aeronautics Board determined that the probable cause of the accident was that, during the final portion of the Constellation's ILS approach, the crew, for reasons that could not be determined, either permitted or caused the aircraft to descend below the glidepath to an altitude too low to clear ground obstructions in its path.

The flightplanned route of Eastern Air Lines' Lockheed Constellation 749, N112A, early on the morning of Wednesday, December 21 1955. (Aero Illustrations)

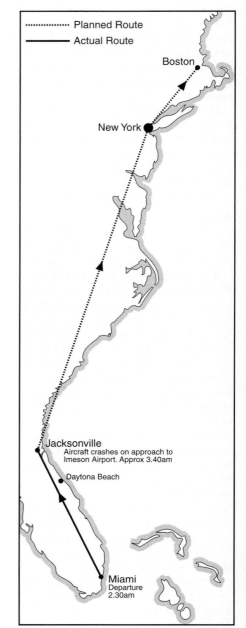

Advertisement for Eastern Air Lines flights, as published in 'The New York Times' in the mid 1950s.

CHAPTER 8

Minor error – major result

It is not often that a major accident can be attributed to a single error on the part of the crew. But in this case a seemingly minor mistake by the flight engineer had totally unforeseen and drastic consequences.

Morning departure

The autumn morning was cold and overcast as Northwest Orient Airlines' Boeing Stratocruiser, N74608, taxied out for takeoff at Seattle Tacoma International Airport just after 8.00am on Monday, April 2 1956.

With a crew of six and 32 passengers on board, it was operating the company's daily eastbound transcontinental Flight 2 to New York via Portland and Chicago.

The crew went through their pretakeoff checks and extensive runup of the four massive radial engines at the runway holding point and, as usual, just before the aircraft turned on to the runway to line up, the wing flaps were extended to 25°. The takeoff into the prevailing light southwesterly wind itself seemed normal in every way, the power being reduced to METO after liftoff and the aircraft climbing out at 145kt (269km/h).

As the Stratocruiser reached a height of about 1500 feet, now in and out of the overcast cloud, the captain called for the flight engi-

neer to make the second power reduction to climbing power, and for the first officer to retract the flaps. But almost immediately, the aircraft began to buffet severely, adopting at the same time a strong tendency to roll to the left.

Believing an asymmetric flap condition had developed, with the flaps retracting on only one side, the captain reduced power momentarily in an attempt to alleviate the buffeting, but to no avail. He then ordered METO power to

Northwest Orient Airlines first Stratocruiser, N74601 Stratocruiser Manilla, operating a transcontinental domestic flight in the 1950s. The aircraft's outsized engine cooling cowl gills (in the closed or "trail" position), are visible on the Nos 3 and 4 engine nacelles just ahead of the trailing edge of the wing. Buffeting caused by the gills in the fully open position was known to cause some loss of lift and lateral stability.

(left) US press advertisement lauding the glories of Northwest Airlines' domestic Stratocruiser services.

be applied again and, with the aircraft now over the waters of Puget Sound on which the city of Seattle is situated, called Seattle Tacoma Tower, requesting an immediate return to the airport.

The Tower cleared the Stratocruiser to return and land, but in view of the aircraft's obvious instability, and the extreme control difficulties he and the first officer were now experiencing, the captain decided that attempting a 180° turn to land back at the airport could be hazardous. Instead he told the tower controller they would try to divert to McChord Air Force Base, a short distance to the south near Tacoma, as this would require only a comparatively shallow turn.

But the buffeting continued to worsen, and the captain feared they could lose control completely. As well, the Stratocruiser was losing height and, as the terrain bordering Puget Sound offered no place for an emergency landing for an aircraft of the Stratocruiser's size, the captain felt he was left with no alternative but to ditch the aircraft straight ahead in the waters of the Sound.

Cutaway view of the Boeing Stratocruiser. In its day, the Stratocruiser, with its upper and lower decks, was considered the ultimate in luxury airline travel. Note the large cooling gills in their retracted position, immediately behind the engine cowlings. (Take Off magazine)

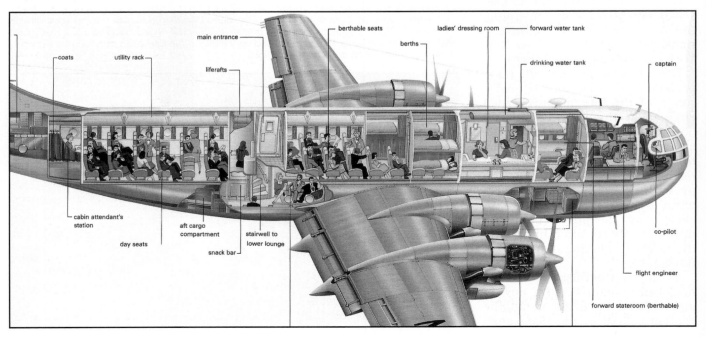

(below) Stratocruisers abounding: This early picture of Northwest Orient Airlines' N74604, Stratocruiser New York, on the ground at the base for which it was named, shows no less than four other Stratocruisers in the background – another of Northwest Orient's, one of BOAC's, and two of Pan Am's. (Air Enthusiast No 18)

The Stratocruiser's Mayday transmission, only four minutes after takeoff, announcing its intention to ditch, was heard by both a nearby Coast Guard vessel, and a small twin engined Grumman SA-16 Albatross amphibian, operated by the USAF's Military Air Transport Service, in the air at the time in the vicinity of McChord.

The surface of the Sound was calm, and because the captain's touchdown on the water was smooth, there was no violent deceleration and the aircraft remained afloat after it came to rest, though taking water fairly rapidly. All 38 on board, none of whom were injured, escaped through the overwing hatches, many of them standing, partly awash, on the wings during the few minutes that the Stratocruiser remained afloat.

Because the intended flight to New York across the North American continent was a domestic operation, the Stratocruiser carried no lifejackets or dinghies, and crew members grabbed seat cushions from the cabin to hand to passengers as makeshift flotation equipment.

The MATS amphibian which had heard the Mayday call alighted in the water within about 10 minutes of the ditching and launched inflatable liferafts, but not all the survivors were able to reach them before the Stratocruiser sank five minutes afterwards. Many of the survivors were left struggling in the water, clinging to floating cushions until rescued by lifeboat crews from the Coast Guard cutter a few minutes later.

When all the survivors were later accounted for, it was found that four passengers, including a six year old boy and his mother were missing, together with a male flight attendant. Those who lost their lives had apparently been overcome by hypothermia in the icy waters of the Sound and lost their hold on the buoyant cushions.

Investigation

The Stratocruiser sank in 132m (72 fathoms of water), but by carefully using underwater grappling equipment, salvage crews succeeded in moving it to a much shallower part of the Sound where the water was no more than 12m (40ft) deep. Divers then made an initial underwater inspection of the wreckage, before it was raised for detailed examination by CAB investigators.

The investigators found there was no asymmetric flap condition and that the flaps on both wings were fully retracted. The No 1 engine had been torn off, but sig-nificantly, the cowl gills of all three remaining engines were fully open. Metallurgical examination of the No 1 engine's mounting revealed no evidence of fatigue failure, and marks on the shank of a bolt in its upper outboard section indicated a loading in an upward inboard direction, quite unlike previous Stratocruiser engine mount failures in flight.

The investigators established there had been no malfunctioning of the engines before impact, and it was evident that the No 1 engine mount failure had occurred either during the ditching, or more likely on the seabed during the grappling operation. The No 1 engine itself could not be found in the deep water.

The captain, who had a total of 14,000 hours experience, 1500 of which he had flown in Boeing 377 aircraft, told investigators that because of the excessive buffeting, the aircraft's inability to maintain altitude and its tendency to roll to the left, requiring almost full opposite aileron to maintain lateral control, he believed a total loss of control was imminent.

But a study undertaken during the investigation on the effect of fully open engine cooling gills on the performance and controllability of Boeing 377 Stratocruiser

aircraft generally, showed that they exhibited no abnormal characteristics during takeoff with the customary 25° of wing flaps extended. On retraction of the flaps after takeoff with the cowl gills still fully open however, vibration and buffeting of the aircraft began as the flaps reached about 10° from the fully retracted position.

Then, as the flaps continued to retract, the vibration and buffeting built up rapidly, becoming severe as the flaps reached their fully up position. The vibration was not as violent as the buffeting experienced when the aircraft was approaching a full aerodynamic stall, but was more regular.

The turbulence created over the wings by the open engine cowl gills that was the source of the buffeting, also reduced the lateral stability of the aircraft, giving the pilot the feeling that it was balanced on a stanchion, something like a model aircraft mounted on a stand. As a result, an abnormal amount of aileron control and trim were required to keep the aircraft level laterally.

The performance of the aircraft in level flight with undercarriage and flaps retracted, but with all cowl gills wide open and all engines operating at maximum continuous power, would be similar to that of a Stratocruiser with one engine shut down and the cowl gills in the normal closed "trail" setting. Rates of climb in excess of 600ft/min should be possible, and the aircraft should be capable

Simplified diagram indicating how Stratocruiser engine cowl gills in the open position created turbulence affecting lift generated by the wing. (Aero Illustrations)

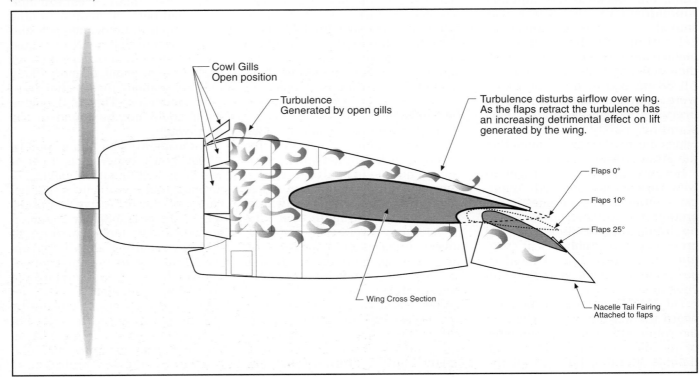

of making moderate turns in either direction without great difficulty.

The Boeing 377 data further indicated that, with the wing flaps retracted, the buffeting, although apparently severe, was not likely to cause immediate structural damage. Rather, its most pronounced effect was on the lateral control and stability of the aircraft, and a good deal of aileron trim in one direction, usually to the right, would probably be required to keep the aircraft level, even though all four cowl gills were opened to the same extent.

Analysis

The final pretakeoff checks on a Stratocruiser flightdeck required the flight engineer to close the engine cowl gills, which were usually fully open while taxiing, before the takeoff began. In the case of the takeoff from Seattle Tacoma, the flight engineer certainly called the pretakeoff check list as usual. Indeed, the captain told investigators that he heard

him call the item "Cowl flaps set for takeoff", with the flight engineer making his own verbal response, "Set for takeoff". But the flight engineer himself later admitted to investigators that he could not be certain he closed the cowl gills at the time.

Although the captain and first officer in particular, could have quite easily seen the settings of the engine cowl gills from the side windows of the flightdeck, no one

on the flightdeck made a visual check of their positions. Instead the crew were content to accept the flight engineer's assurance that they were properly set for takeoff.

Immediately after takeoff, as the Stratocruiser was transitioning to a normal climb, the captain was unexpectedly faced with what he thought was an extreme emergency that threatened to deprive him of all control of the aircraft.

Press picture taken from the air, showing the Coast Guard cutter and the MATS Grumman Albatross amphibian rescuing the Stratocruiser's survivors. The inflatable liferafts seen on the right have been deployed by the crew of the amphibian. (Associated Press Wirephoto)

In the situation in which he suddenly found himself, beneath a low overcast and surrounded by impossible terrain for any sort of emergency landing, the captain was under great and urgent pressure to make a decision.

Convinced that an asymmetric flap condition existed, and that any attempt to continue the flight would result in a complete loss of control and a disastrous accident, the captain elected to ditch the aircraft in the waters of the Sound beneath them, believing it to be the safest action in the circumstances.

Cause

The Civil Aeronautics Board officially determined that the accident had arisen from "incorrect analysis of control difficulty which occurred on retraction of the wing flaps as a result of the flight engineer's failure to close the engine cowl flaps – the analysis having been made under conditions of great urgency and within an extremely short period of time available for decision."

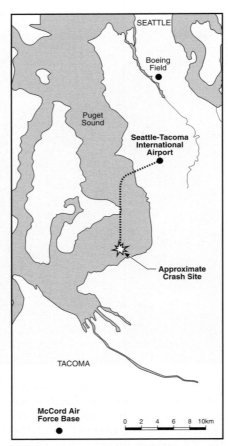

Map showing relationship of Seattle-Tacoma International Airport to Puget Sound, and approximate flightpath of Stratocruiser to point of ditching. (Aero Illustrations)

Author's comment

Although the CAB did not include the matter as a contributory factor in the development of the accident, it seems possible that the flight engineer might have unconsciously reverted to previous conditioning when he failed to close the cowl gills during the pretakeoff checks.

The engine cowl gill control levers on the Boeing 377 Stratocruiser move in opposite sense to those on the Lockheed L-1049 Super Constellation for opening and closing the cowl gills. Although the flight engineer had 236 hours experience on Stratocruisers, much of his total flying time of a little less than 1400 hours had been on Super Constellations.

The CAB investigators could apparently offer no explanation as to why the Stratocruiser continued to lose height during the emergency, when theoretically at least, it should have been capable of a shallow climb.

CHAPTER 9

A black day in the US

A midsummer's morning in 1956 will long be remembered in the history of civil aviation in the United States. Ninety minutes after two major airliners departed on near parallel domestic flights on June 30, they collided in midair. The tragedy, with its toll of 128 lives, would be known as the Grand Canyon Collision.

Flights to the east

Saturday at Los Angeles International Airport was busy, with both domestic and international traffic departing and arriving as usual.

The city was uncharacteristically overcast by a layer of morning stratus, but this was expected to burn off under the effect of the hot sun. Although the coastal weather would then remain clear, inland to the east it was cloudy, with a possibility of scattered thunderstorms.

Amongst the numerous airliners in various company liveries on the terminal's extensive concrete aprons, were two big four engined types being readied for domestic flights to the midwest and the east coast. Lockheed Super Constellation, N6902C *Star of the Seine*, now boarding its 63 passengers, was to operate TWA's Flight 2 to New York via Kansas City. Scheduled to depart at 8.30am, the service was running late. The aircraft had undergone maintenance at Los Angeles overnight, and some

last minute minor adjustments, discovered while the two flight engineers assigned to the trip were making their preflight inspection, had become necessary.

Not far away on the airport, United Air Lines' DC-7, N6324C, *Mainliner Vancouver*, was also boarding for Flight 718 to Chicago, Newark and Philadelphia, departing at 8.45am. Fifty-eight passengers were being shown to their seats and the aircraft was expected to get away on time. This was the second eastbound United Air Lines flight from Los Angeles that morning, a sister DC-7 operating Flight 708 having left an hour earlier.

The weather the crews could expect enroute was influenced by a cold front extending from a low pressure area in Nebraska, southwest into northern Colorado, then westwards through central Utah and Nevada. Producing a southeasterly flow of moist air into northern Arizona, it was resulting in considerable cloud and show-

ers in the desolate Grand Canyon area with some thunderstorms, though the winds at higher levels were more westerly. Freezing level was 15,000 feet with light icing and turbulence in cloud. Moderate to severe turbulence was likely in the thunderstorms, expected to develop to 30,000 feet or higher. Apart from the thunderstorms, the tops of the lower clouds would be at about 15,000 feet, with good visibility above them.

The TWA Super Constellation's IFR flightplan to Kansas City specified the first leg would be in controlled airspace to Daggett, 101nm (187km) northeast of Los Angeles. The second and third legs would then be flown outside controlled airspace, direct to Trinidad in southern Colorado on a heading of 059°M, thence to Dodge City, Kansas. At Dodge City the flight would re-enter controlled airspace for the final leg to Kansas City. The nominated cruising altitude was 19,000 feet at a TAS of 270kt (500km/h).

The TWA livery: A new TWA Boeing 707 with one of the company's Lockheed Constellations at Oakland, California, in about 1960. The TWA aircraft were painted white, with bright red cheat-lines and lettering. The aircraft in the centre background is a Japan Air Lines Douglas DC-6.

Reporting points for the first and second legs would be Daggett itself; Lake Mohave (abeam the Las Vegas VOR) 99nm (183km) on from Daggett; and the Painted Desert line of position, a further distance of 172nm (319km). This latter position was on a line linking the VORs at Bryce Canyon to the north of the aircraft's track and Winslow to the south, and lay about 20nm (37km) beyond the Grand Canyon.

Because of the delay for minor maintenance, Flight TWA 2 was nearly half an hour behind schedule by the time the doors were closed and the engines started. Under the command of Captain J S Gandy, the crew comprised First Officer James Ritner, Flight Engineers Forrest Breyfogle and Harry Allen, and Flight Attendants Tracine Armbruster and Beth Davis. Cleared to taxi promptly for the duty runway when it was finally ready, the Super Constellation lifted off from Los Angeles' Runway 25 Left at 9.01am.

Calling Los Angeles Departures after takeoff, the Super Constellation was radar vectored as it climbed through the low overcast. Reporting on top at 2400 feet, the aircraft was then transferred to Los Angeles Control for its enroute clearance, the controller specifying the aircraft's climb to cruising altitude should be made in visual conditions.

Nearly 20 minutes later, now on TWA's company frequency, the Su-

per Constellation reported approaching Daggett and, in accordance with company practice, asked the TWA radio operator to request Los Angeles Control for a change in cruising altitude to 21,000 feet instead of 19,000 feet. This was refused – 21,000 feet was not available "because of traffic". The Super Constellation then requested, again through the TWA operator, a clearance for "1000 feet on top" (ie 1000 feet above cloud level). This was entirely in accordance with US airways procedures at the time, and not an unusual request.

The Los Angeles controller, after obtaining the TWA operator's assurance the Super Constellation was by that time at least 1000 feet above cloud level, cleared it as requested. To the TWA radio operator the controller added, "Advise TWA 2 traffic is United 718, direct Durango, estimating Needles at 0957." The TWA operator transmitted the amended clearance and the traffic information to the Super Constellation, adding that the United aircraft was also at 21,000 feet. Captain Gandy himself read back the clearance, acknowledging "traffic received".

At 9.59am the Super Constellation called the TWA operator at Las Vegas, reporting it had passed Lake Mohave four minutes before at 9.55am and, now cruising "1000 on top", was estimating the Painted Desert line at 10.31am. Because of the height of the cloud level, the

Lockheed's "1000 on top" clearance happened to put it at an actual altitude of 21,000 feet also.

Conflicting traffic

The conflicting traffic at 21,000 feet, United Air Lines Flight 718, under the command of Captain R F Shirley, and crewed by First Officer Robert Harms, Flight Engineer Gerard Fiore, and Flight Attendants Nancy Kemnitz and Margaret Shoudt, had taken off from Los Angeles' Runway 25L at 9.04am, only three minutes after the TWA Super Constellation.

The first leg of the DC-7's IFR flight to Chicago was in controlled airspace as far as Palm Springs, 106nm (196km) almost due east of Los Angeles, thence outside controlled airspace on a heading of 046°M direct to St Joseph, 50nm (93km) north of Kansas City on the Missouri River. Here it would again enter controlled airspace for the 345nm (639km) leg to Chicago's Midway Airport. The DC-7's flightplan nominated a cruising altitude of 21,000 feet at a TAS of 288kt (534km/h). It would report at Palm Springs; Needles on the Colorado River; the Painted Desert line of position; the towns of Durango and Pueblo in Colorado; and St Joseph, Missouri.

As with the Super Constellation before it, Los Angeles Departures vectored the DC-7 through the low overcast, and when it reported "on top", transferred it to Los Angeles Control for onward

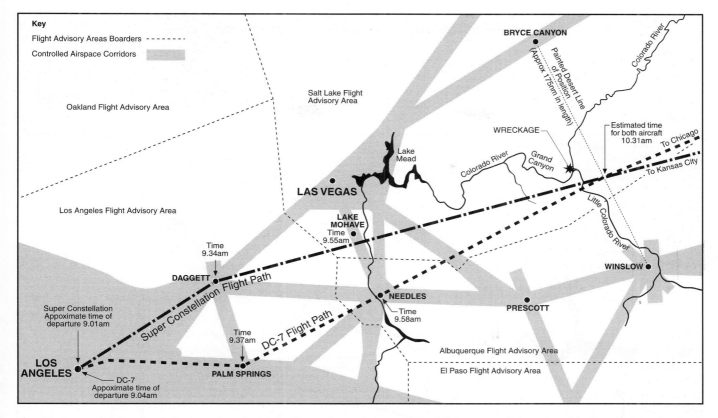

Key

Flight Advisory Areas Boarders --------

Controlled Airspace Corridors

Simplified map showing the flightplanned tracks of the Super Constellation and the DC-7 eastwards from Los Angeles, and the times and places of their position reports. The two aircraft took off from Los Angeles within three minutes of each other and their planned tracks intersected at the Painted Desert Line of Position. Unknown to their respective captains, both aircraft were estimating this line at the same time. The stippled sections of the diagram define corridors of controlled airspace existing at the time. (Aero Illustrations)

clearance. Again the aircraft was cleared in accordance with its flightplan, and again the controller specified it was to climb in visual conditions.

At 9.17am the DC-7 reported on the United company frequency that it was passing over Palm Springs at 18,000 feet, still climb-ing, and gave estimates for Needles on the hour, and the Painted Desert line at 10.34am. Forty min-utes later at 9.58am the DC-7 called the Civil Aeronautics Ad-ministration's (CAA's) Flight Serv-ice station at Needles to report it was now over Needles at 21,000 feet. It also amended its estimate for the Painted Desert line to 10.31am – precisely the time the TWA Super Constellation also ex-pected to reach this line.

At 10.31am United radio opera-tors in both Salt Lake City and San Francisco heard a brief garbled transmission on the company fre-quency that they were unable to

The United Air Lines' paint scheme: This inflight photograph of a United DC-7 (identical to the DC-7 involved in the collision), shows the airline's standard livery at the time of the accident. The nose, flightdeck roof and broad fuselage cheat-line at window level were dark blue, while the fuselage top, fin and rudder were white. The two bands of colour immediately below the company lettering on the fin were red and blue respectively, and all four propellers had similar red and blue bands at their tips.

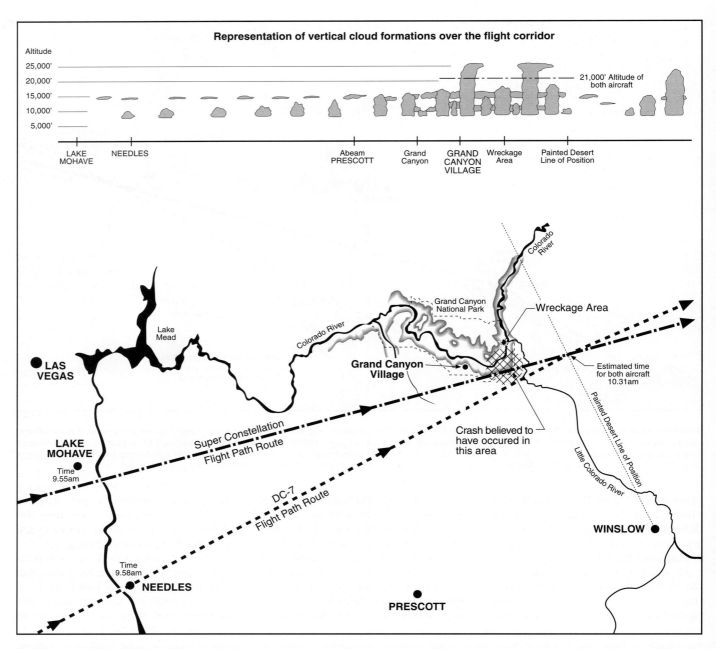

Representation of vertical cloud formations over the flight corridor

Altitude
25,000'
20,000'
15,000'
10,000'
5,000'

21,000' Altitude of both aircraft

LAKE MOHAVE   NEEDLES   Abeam PRESCOTT   Grand Canyon   GRAND CANYON VILLAGE   Wreckage Area   Painted Desert Line of Position

Colorado River

LAS VEGAS

Lake Mead

Grand Canyon National Park

Wreckage Area

Super Constellation Flight Path Route

Grand Canyon Village

Crash believed to have occured in this area

Estimated time for both aircraft 10.31am

LAKE MOHAVE

Time 9.55am

DC-7 Flight Path Route

Painted Desert Line of Position

Little Colorado River

Time 9.58am

NEEDLES

PRESCOTT

WINSLOW

Grand Canyon National Park area, showing the approximate position above which the aircraft collided at the extreme eastern end of the park. The wreckage of both aircraft was found less than two kilometres apart, scattered against the canyon walls, near the junction of the Colorado and Little Colorado Rivers. The upper section of the diagram, developed from meteorological analysis during the Civil Aeronautics Bureau's investigation, shows the extent of vertical cloud development the two aircraft would have encountered as they flew eastwards. (Aero Illustrations)

comprehend. Though unusual, the transmission did not for the moment seem significant – until no Painted Desert position report came from the DC-7 as expected. Nor did the aircraft follow up its previous position report at Needles on the Flight Service frequency. The operators were concerned, not least because neither station was now able to raise the DC-7.

Equally puzzled about the same time were TWA's company radio operators in both Los Angeles and Las Vegas – the Super Constella-

tion had not reported reaching the Painted Desert line as expected at 10.31am. And it was not responding to calls.

Airliners overdue

Checks with Los Angeles Control, Salt Lake City Control and the Flight Service network revealed that no CAA controller or operator had heard from either aircraft, and none were able to make contact. Radio silence on the part of one aircraft could be explained by radio failure. But the loss of communication with the two air-

craft, apparently almost simultaneously, was deeply disturbing.

A little over half an hour later, mounting concern for the two aircraft's safety intensified. Neither had called at their next respective reporting points – Farmington in the case of the Super Constellation at about 11.06am, and Durango for the DC-7 at 11.11am.

Further checks by stations on all available frequencies proved fruitless, and by 11.50am the CAA was left with no alternative but to issue a Missing Aircraft Alert. Search and Rescue action began soon afterwards, the initial search being directed from March Air Force Base in California.

The area in which the two aircraft had vanished was a desolate expanse of barely populated wasteland on the California-Arizona state borders, comprising many thousands of square kilometres of high rugged mountains, deep barren canyons and parched desert. There were few communities, few roads, and almost no communications, its terrain ranging from the 12,000 foot San Francisco peaks to the Grand Canyon itself, the world's deepest gorge. Exploring as much of the area as possible through that Saturday afternoon, the searching aircraft found no trace of the overdue airliners.

Rising smoke

At Grand Canyon Village, a tourist settlement on the plateau adjoining the southern side of the Grand Canyon, two brothers ran a small business operating sightseeing flights.

Their light aircraft was based at the village's general aviation aerodrome a few miles to the south. Hearing only late in the afternoon that the airliners were missing, one of the brothers recalled having seen smoke in a remote, inaccessible area of the canyon during a tourist flight around midday. Rising from a point in the canyon near the junction of the Colorado and Little Colorado Rivers, it was at the extreme eastern end of the Grand Canyon National Park. Not knowing of the missing aircraft at this stage, he assumed the smoke to be from a brushfire, probably started by lightning the previous day.

The two brothers immediately returned to their airfield but, by the time they were able to take off, it was late in the day. Just on sunset they flew back over the canyon to try and identify the source of the smoke, about 40km east of Grand Canyon Village. Descending into the canyon in the fading daylight to make a low pass over the now smouldering fire, they were awed to see the unmistakable triple tail of a Super Constellation.

Perched several hundred feet above the Colorado River, it was on a rocky shelf on the canyon wall. Fragmented wreckage lay scattered nearby, and there was no sign of life. A mile or so to the north they could see smoke from another fire, but by this time it was getting too dark to investigate further. After reporting their awesome find by radio, the brothers had no option but to fly back to the airfield.

Taking off again early the following morning, the brothers returned to examine the second source of smoke. On a rocky knoll projecting from another massive outcrop high up on the side of the canyon, there was a charred area. Above it, and strewn down the near vertical canyon wall below it, were many small pieces of torn, fire blackened metal. Despite the fact there were no large pieces readily identifiable, and no visible bodies, it was undoubtedly the wreckage of the DC-7. Its point of impact was about 2500 feet above the Colorado River and at least 1500 feet higher than that of the Super Constellation. So inaccessible was the area that it was seldom visited, except by air.

As Air Force helicopters made ready to fly into the site from Hamilton Air Force Base in California and Luke Air Force Base near Phoenix in Arizona, the Director of Search and Rescue operations declared the two airliners "must have collided in the air".

The increasing risk of airline aircraft colliding in US airspace was actually under review by a Congressional committee at the time of the accident. Earlier in the year, a government advisory group had pointed out that airways were becoming so crowded and inadequately regulated that near misses were occurring far too frequently. "...there are on the average, four reported near collisions involving the airlines daily," their report declared. In a number of cases, aircraft reported passing within 35m of one another.

In a supporting statement, the Director of the CAA had been quoted as saying that deficiencies in the airways system "have been recognised as the No 1 problem in aviation. Air traffic is overloading the airways system and growing at a rate which exceeds progress in expanding the capacity of the system. The greatest single problem we face is air traffic control."

The first of the helicopters from Phoenix, carrying an Air Force medical officer, was able to make a successful if hazardous landing later in the morning at the ledge crash site of the TWA Super Constellation, establishing that no one could have survived the impact.

But the site of the DC-7 impact, although less than two kilometres away, seemed almost inaccessible. After impacting against a massive outcrop of rock on the near vertical canyon wall, its wreckage had fallen into a deep crevasse and down a sheer cliff face several hundred feet high. The prospect of landing a helicopter at the site was daunting.

At this stage, a US Army transport unit, on assignment at the time to Fort Huachuca, Arizona, offered its services and the specialised capabilities of its helicopters to the Director of Search and Rescue operations. After careful planning and trial flights, one of the Army helicopters, also with a medico on board, succeeded in landing, but the operation was difficult and highly dangerous. Again the medical officer found no one could have survived the tremendous impact against the precipitous canyon wall.

INVESTIGATION
Wreckage examination

During the days of the onsite wreckage investigations that followed, the remains of most of the occupants of both aircraft were recovered under extremely dangerous conditions. The Army helicopters shuttled to and fro, battling turbulence from vertical wind currents in the canyon, and repeatedly effecting hazardous landings on the sides of the canyon to provide transport to the otherwise inaccessible impact sites.

Recovering the human remains also entailed a good deal of personal risk to the volunteers undertaking the task. The helicopters enabled them to accomplish the grisly work successfully from the Super Constellation wreckage. But so difficult and dangerous was the near vertical disposition of the DC-7's wreckage, that experienced mountaineers had to be flown in from Switzerland to assist.

So violent had been the Super Constellation's impact in the canyon that only six of its 70 occupants could be identified. The accident was especially tragic for TWA staff, for 31 of the 70 people on board were their company colleagues. Of the 58 on board the DC-7, 29 were unable to be identified. The remains were airlifted to the Grand Canyon airfield, where they were transferred to a transport aircraft and flown to an improvised morgue at Flagstaff, Arizona.

Investigator's from the Civil Aeronautics Board's Bureau of Investigation, flown in to the impact sites by the Army helicopters, found that the Super Constellation had crashed in a shallow indentation on the northeastern slope of a prominent outcrop on the western side of the Grand Canyon, 26km northeast of Grand Canyon Village, and a little more than a kilometre south of the junction of the Colorado and Little Colorado Rivers. The aircraft struck the ground upside down, its short wreckage trail, strewn across the indentation in a southwesterly direction, showing it had done so at a steep angle.

The impact instantly disintegrated the aircraft, with an intense fire following. Even so, investigators were able to identify sufficient wreckage to determine that all the aircraft's structure was in the main wreckage area with the exception of the tail, parts of the rear fuselage, and light pieces of rear cabin interior. Significantly, several pieces of the DC-7's port outer wing were also found amongst the Lockheed's wreckage.

The main wreckage of the DC-7 lay nearly two kilometres northeast of the Super Constellation's, the aircraft having struck the south face of another major rocky outcrop, also on the western side of the canyon, but almost opposite the Little Colorado River. The investigators found that the impact occurred only about three metres below the top of the outcrop, with the DC-7 on a north-

easterly heading in a nose down and starboard wing down attitude. Again the impact resulted in severe disintegration, the DC-7's major components falling into a deep inaccessible niche in the canyon wall, as well as on to ledges in the sheer cliff face below the impact site. And again an intense fire followed. Except for a portion of its port wing, all the DC-7's major components were accounted for in, around and below the main wreckage area.

The hazardous and difficult investigation not only confirmed the two aircraft had collided in flight, but provided evidence of the relationship of the aircraft to each other at the moment of impact.

US FLIGHT PROCEDURES IN 1956

The United States Air Traffic Control (ATC) system in 1956 allowed scheduled public transport aircraft to operate either under Instrument Flight Rules (IFR), in instrument or visual weather conditions, or Visual Flight Rules (VFR) in visual weather conditions only.

Within controlled airspace ("airways"), ATC was required to separate all IFR aircraft from each other, and assigned each a specific cruising level. VFR aircraft were neither required to be in contact with ATC, nor was any separation service provided for them.

Furthermore, an IFR aircraft could request a clearance to cruise "1000 on top", requiring it to operate at least 1000 feet above the general cloud layer. When operating on such a clearance, the aircraft remained an IFR flight, but was in effect treated as a VFR aircraft, with the responsibility for its separation from all other traffic passed to the pilot in command. Aircraft operating "1000 on top" were required to obtain an amended clearance for a specific altitude before proceeding into instrument weather conditions.

Outside controlled airspace ("off airways"), all aircraft, whether IFR or VFR, were responsible for their own separation, and ATC was not required to provide any traffic information service.

The Civil Air Regulations then in force in the US required the pilot in command of an aircraft, whether IFR or VFR, on or off airways, and operating in visual weather conditions, to visually avoid all other traffic.

Some of the most telling evidence involved the port outer wing of the DC-7. Pieces of it, from its tip to a point about seven metres inboard, bore evidence of the collision. The biggest piece was found between the two impact sites about 500 metres west of the Super Constellation's wreckage. The leading edge was deformed rearwards, and dents, scratches and tears covered much of its lower surface. On the wing tip there was a deformation containing black rubber smears and red paint smudges. The smears had come from the Super Constellation's deicer boot, and the smudges from its red painted structure. Buckled pieces of the DC-7's port aileron also bore deposits of black rubber on their lower surfaces.

A section of the underside of the wing, bearing part the of DC-7's painted registration numbers, was found amongst the Super Constellation wreckage. Scrape marks on it corresponded with those found amongst the wreckage of the DC-7, while embedded in a tear in the DC-7 wing skin was a piece of headlining from the Super Constellation's rear cabin.

The Super Constellation's tail assembly had come to rest almost in one piece about 550m north of the Lockheed's main wreckage and was generally intact. Its distance from the main wreckage, with evidence of severe fuselage damage where it had separated, showed this occurred in flight after the collision. Two small pieces of the port fin's leading edge, found well away from the tail, showed unmistakable collision evidence. One piece, concaved on its leading edge, fitted precisely with damage to the DC-7's port wingtip

There was further collision evidence in the remains of the Super Constellation's rear fuselage. There were red, blue, and black scrape marks from the DC-7 along the outer surface, and on the underside were three parallel propeller slashes, less than a metre apart. Red and blue paint at the edge of one matched the paint scheme of the DC-7's propellers.

Flight operations

Both flights were planned as "high altitude operations" (above 14,500 feet) which, under procedures current at the time, permitted long range airline flights to be flown off designated airways (ie outside controlled airspace) over tracks offering the shortest distance between departure and destination. Such flights required a flightplan with numerous reporting points defining the route.

United Air Lines' policy permitted such flights on either IFR or VFR flightplans, but did not allow operations outside controlled airspace in instrument weather. TWA policy, on the other hand, permitted flights in instrument weather outside controlled airspace, but only on an IFR flightplan with an assigned altitude. When operating "1000 on top", TWA aircraft were to adhere to visual flight rules.

Captain Shirley, 48, with 17,000 hours experience, had been flying for United since 1937, and a captain for 16 years. For the past eight months he had been flying the Los Angeles/Chicago route regularly. Captain Gandy, 41, with nearly 15,000 hours, had been with TWA for 17 years and a captain for 14 years. He was also extremely familiar with the Los Angeles/Kansas City route, having flown it nearly 180 times. All members of their crews were well qualified and appropriately experienced. All were properly rested and in good physical condition. Both aircraft reported normally as the flights progressed, their company despatch offices following their progress in accordance with the airlines' current operating procedures.

When the Super Constellation asked for a change in altitude from 19,000 to 21,000 feet approaching Daggett, the TWA radio operator receiving the request called Los Angeles Control: "TWA 2 is coming up on Daggett, requesting 21,000," he advised.

The Los Angeles controller contacted Salt Lake Control at Salt Lake City. "TWA 2 is requesting 21,000 – how does it look?" he asked. "I see he is Daggett direct Trinidad, and I see you have United 718 crossing his altitude – in his way at 21,000." The Salt Lake controller replied, "Yes, their

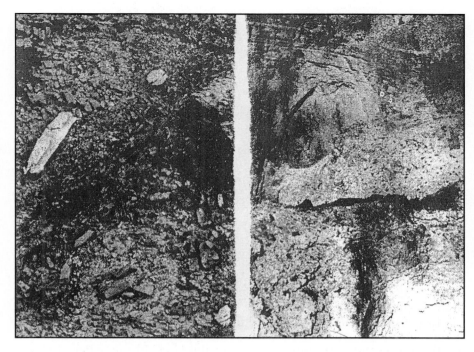

Pictures published in The New York Times *on the morning of Monday, July 2, 1956, confirming the worst fears of many throughout the United States. With the loss of 128 lives, the midair collision became the worst disaster in civil airline history.*

courses cross and they are right together." The Los Angeles controller then called the TWA operator back. "Advisory TWA 2: unable approve 21,000..."

The TWA operator interrupted. "Just a minute – I think he wants '1000 on top' – yes, '1000 on top' until he can get it." After determining from the TWA operator that the Super Constellation was by that time 1000 feet above cloud, the controller issued the amended clearance: "ATC clears TWA 2, maintain at least 1000 on top." He added, "Advise TWA 2 his traffic is United 718, direct Durango, estimating Needles at 0957."

ATC procedures

The two controllers told investigators that, because TWA 2 would soon pass from the Los Angeles ATC area to Salt Lake's, it was necessary to co-ordinate the request for the altitude change. At the time both flights were IFR traffic, operating in controlled airspace, and ATC was required to separate them. The Los Angeles controller said he offered the traffic information to the TWA radio operator merely as an explanation for ATC's denial of 21,000 feet, and not as a traffic advisory.

Enlarging on the controllers' statements, the CAA's Director of

Air Traffic Control explained that when the TWA Lockheed requested 21,000 feet, it had not reached Daggett, nor had the United DC-7 reached Needles. But in projecting their tracks eastward, although neither aircraft would be cruising continuously in controlled airspace, both would cross more corridors of controlled airspace well before they reached the Painted Desert line of position. For this reason, ATC was required to keep them separated, and so the TWA aircraft was denied 21,000 feet.

This separation was an ATC responsibility for instrument flights in controlled airspace only, and the corridors were the last such areas the aircraft would traverse for some distance to the east.

ATC maintained progress information on IFR aircraft in uncontrolled airspace only to enable their safe spacing into the next control area. Flights in uncontrolled airspace, the Director explained, whether VFR or IFR, were bound by neither by clearance nor flightplan. As the controllers' manual of procedures declared: "Clearances authorise flight within control zones and control areas only; no responsibility for separation of aircraft outside these areas is accepted."

So, when the TWA aircraft amended its flightplan to "1000 feet on top", no information concerning this was passed to the United DC-7. None was required, even though the flights were still in controlled airspace at that time. The Director of Air Traffic Control went on to explain that the clearance issued to the TWA Super Constellation required it to maintain "1000 feet on top" only while it remained within a control area. Once out of controlled airspace, the Super Constellation, although operating on an IFR flightplan, was in effect a VFR flight.

Civil Air Regulations gave no definition of "1000 on top". But the CAA's Flight Information Manual stated, "At least 1000 feet on top may be filed in an IFR flightplan, or assigned by ATC in an IFR clearance, in lieu of a cruising altitude. Even though this type of operation places the responsibility for avoidance of collision with other aircraft on the pilot, the flight is an IFR operation and must obtain an amended clearance for a specific altitude before proceeding into IFR weather conditions."

In the US at the time, aircraft separation in VFR weather depended solely on flightcrews, regardless of flightplan or clearance. Civil Air Regulations expressly placed this responsibility on the pilots – the "see and be seen" principle. Concerning IFR flights operating in VFR weather, the Flight Information Manual stipulated, "During the time an IFR flight is operating in VFR weather conditions, it is the direct responsibility of the pilot to avoid other aircraft, since VFR flights may be operating in the same area without the knowledge of ATC."

At 9.58am the DC-7 reported to the CAA's Needles Flight Service station it was over Needles at 21,000 feet, and amended its Painted Desert estimate to 10.31. The Needles flight service officer, in accordance with procedures, passed this position report to Albuquerque Control at 10.01am and at the same time tried to do so to Salt Lake Control, but there was a delay on the interphone line.

A minute later at 9.59am, the Lockheed reported to its company operator at Las Vegas that it had passed over Lake Mohave at 9.55, was 1000 on top at 21,000 feet, estimating the Painted Desert line of position at 10.31. The TWA operator at Las Vegas promptly passed this report to Salt Lake Control. The sector controller who received it was the one who had previously denied the Lockheed's request for 21,000 feet when approaching Daggett. A few minutes later at 10.13, when the landline between Needles Flight Service and Salt Lake Control was cleared, the same controller received the DC-7's 9.58am report that it too, was now estimating the Painted Desert line of position at 10.31.

Both the CAA's Director of Air Traffic Control and the Salt Lake controller were asked why traffic information was not transmitted to the two aircraft when the controller knew both were at the same altitude, both were estimating the Painted Desert line of position at the same time, and their tracks were converging.

The controller explained that when he received the reports, he had no knowledge of the track either aircraft was following. Both were by this time in uncontrolled airspace and specific tracks were not required. Because the Painted Desert line of position, stretching from Bryce Canyon to Winslow, was nearly 175nm (324km) long, the estimates from the two aircraft did not mean they would converge there, but merely both would cross the line eastbound at that time.

He was not required to pass advisory information to aircraft in uncontrolled airspace and it was only a discretionary requirement in control areas. Such an advisory service would not be possible as normal practice without some control over the flights, and without more position information. It would also need additional ATC facilities and personnel.

Supporting the controller's reasoning, the Director of Air Traffic Control said it was not the policy or concept of ATC to provide traffic information outside controlled airspace. Many aircraft could be flying in the area concerned, quite unknown to ATC. In this particular case, the controller did know about the flights, but even so, advisory information had to be viewed in its overall application. Several years before, ATC had attempted to provide this service on an evaluation basis, but the workload involved had proved too much for ATC's existing staff levels.

Weather conditions

Pilots flying in the area of the accident at the time confirmed the forecast weather conditions. The lower cloud coverage began well to the east of Las Vegas, progressively increasing eastwards, and becoming nearly overcast 20-25nm (37-46km) west of the Grand Canyon.

In the Grand Canyon area there were a number of towering cumulus clouds rising to about 25,000 feet, which appeared to be still developing. Even so, aircraft had no difficulty maintaining visual flight above the top of the general overcast, which was at about 15,000 feet.

ANALYSIS

The time of the collision was determined from the brief garbled transmission United Air Lines radio operators in Salt Lake City and San Francisco heard on the company frequency at 10.31am.

Although incomprehensible at the time, pilots who listened to a recording of the transmission during the investigation, and who knew the United crew, believed it be the voice of First Officer Harms.

The recording was subjected to spectrographic analysis, which found the transmission contained two voices, both of them under great emotional stress. The principal speaker transmitted, "Salt Lake, ah, 718...we are going in!" During the momentary pause after "718", a second voice yelled a word that could have been "look", "pull" or "come", followed by the words "up...up".

The first voice was pitched 100-200 cycles per second above that of a normal male voice. The pitch of the second voice was even higher, well above that of a female voice, although it was certainly a male voice. The transmission, obviously made immediately after the collision, began seven seconds before 10.31am.

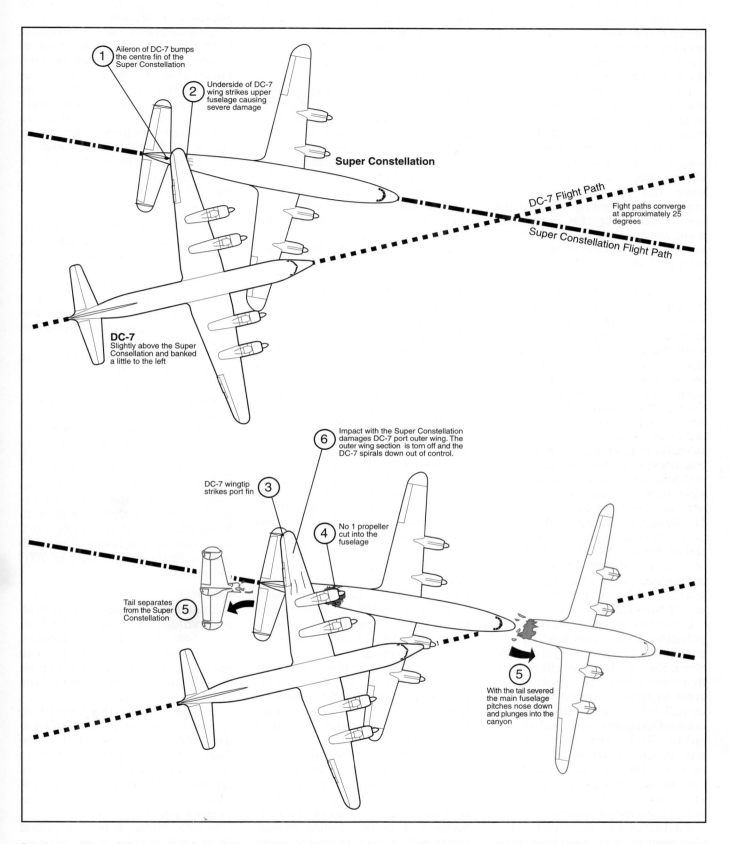

① Aileron of DC-7 bumps the centre fin of the Super Constellation

② Underside of DC-7 wing strikes upper fuselage causing severe damage

Super Constellation

DC-7 Flight Path

Fight paths converge at approximately 25 degrees

Super Constellation Flight Path

DC-7
Slightly above the Super Consellation and banked a little to the left

⑥ Impact with the Super Constellation damages DC-7 port outer wing. The outer wing section is torn off and the DC-7 spirals down out of control.

③ DC-7 wingtip strikes port fin

④ No 1 propeller cut into the fuselage

⑤ Tail separates from the Super Constellation

⑤ With the tail severed the main fuselage pitches nose down and plunges into the canyon

Relative positions of the two aircraft, as their respective tracks edged them ever closer to one other, and the collision sequence that rapidly followed. Evidence that a collision had occurred was irrefutable – the DC-7's deformed port wing tip was smeared with red paint from the Super Constellation, while propeller slashes in the wreckage of the Super Constellation's rear fuselage contained red and blue paint from the DC-7's propeller tips. (Aero Illustrations)

The collision damage found in the wreckage of the two aircraft became the basis for study of the relative attitudes of the aircraft at the instant of impact, as well as the collision sequence.

The initial impact occurred above a position just west of the Super Constellation wreckage, with the DC-7 moving from right to left relative to the Super Constellation at angle of about 25°, slowly overtaking it at the same time, the DC-7's port aileron bumping the leading edge of the Lockheed's centre fin. A moment later, the underside of the DC-7's port wing struck the upper rear fuselage of the Super Constellation with destructive impact.

As the two stricken aircraft continued to pass laterally, the port wingtip of the DC-7 hit the leading edge of the Constellation's port fin, while the DC-7's No 1 propeller cut into the Lockheed's rear fuselage, this overall sequence probably taking less than half a second.

With the Lockheed's fuselage torn open from just forward of the tail to the main cabin door, its tail assembly separated immediately, the Lockheed pitching nose-down and plunging into the canyon on a short forward trajectory. The DC-7 sustained lesser but equally critical damage. With most of its port outer wing torn off, the DC-7 spiralled down out of control, descending into the canyon on a turning path about two kilometres north of where the Lockheed struck the canyon wall.

Like nearly all other midair collisions, the accident apparently occurred in visual conditions. Yet collision studies show that effectively seeing other aircraft in time to avoid them can be difficult. Angular limits of the cockpit, angular size and shape, colour and contrast, distance and cloud obstructions, not to mention fatigue, and training – can all affect a pilot's ability to sight another aircraft on a converging collision course.

Such a "target" provides no relative motion, and searching visually needs time, and that is limited by closure speed. Attention to functions within the cockpit can also reduce the opportunity to sight another aircraft. In this acci-

dent, the aircraft could have been on either side of a cloud buildup until shortly before collision, or the buildups could have required track deviations, limiting the time available for sighting.

Assuming the limit of visual range was eight to 10km, the investigators examined possible opportunities the crews of the Super Constellation and the DC-7 could have had to sight one another's aircraft.

They found the Super Constellation would have been within the angular limits of the DC-7's window area as seen from the captain's seat during all the flightpath situations considered. Windscreen pillars would have blocked his view for only short periods of time and, with no clouds intervening, the Lockheed should have been in view for between 50 and 120 seconds. But in the most unfavourable cloud situation considered, this could have been reduced to as little as 12 seconds. From the DC-7 first officer's seat with no cloud intervening, the Lockheed would have been only distantly in view in two situations, without relative motion in one, and with relative motion in another.

In only one of the situations examined would it have been possible for the Super Constellation's captain to have seen the DC-7, and then for not more than 40 seconds. For the Super Constellation's first officer, the DC-7 should have been visible in three of the four flightpath situations considered for up to 120 seconds. But in the most unfavourable cloud situation, this could have been as little as 12 seconds.

Other factors could have kept the pilots from seeing the conflicting aircraft, especially if one of them was occupied with cockpit functions during the available sighting period.

Although the pilots obviously did not sight one another's aircraft in time to avert the accident, it is hard not to speculate on how conscious were the passengers of the developing drama, especially those seated on appropriate sides of the respective airliner cabins.

What might they have seen and felt as the aircraft came within sight of one another and the DC-7

drew progressively nearer to the Super Constellation?

Initial interest would probably have been replaced by fascination at seeing another aircraft at such close quarters, then disbelief as they loomed ever closer during those final critical seconds. Probably because the passengers would have believed the crews "knew what they were doing", a real sense of alarm might not have been experienced until the last horrific moment.

CAUSE

The Civil Aeronautics Board officially attributed the cause of the Grand Canyon accident to the obvious fact that "the pilots did not see each other in time to avoid the collision," going on to list the factors that could have brought it about, either singly or in combination:

• Intervening clouds reducing time for visual separation
• Limitations of cockpit visibility
• Preoccupation with cockpit duties
• Preoccupation with other matters, such as attempting to provide passengers with a more scenic view of the Grand Canyon
• Physiological limits to human vision, reducing the time available to see and avoid the other aircraft
• Insufficient enroute traffic advisory information because of inadequate facilities and lack of ATC personnel

Comment

Readers accustomed to Australia's traditional systems of Air Traffic Control, controlled airspace and traffic separation, might well have found their hair standing on end by the time they reached the end of this chapter!

Certainly, with the benefit of hindsight and today's fund of accident history, it is clear that the failure of the crews involved to see and avoid each other was simply the failure of an airways system – one that offered little defence against collisions.

Indeed, during a 10 year period from 1959 to 1968, there were an incredible 223 midair collisions to US registered aircraft, resulting in 528 fatalities. Moreover, the vast majority occurred in visual conditions and although most (but by no means all), involved light aircraft, their causes generally were similar to those of the Grand Canyon accident.

It has to be said that most of the failures that led to the Grand Canyon tragedy were present long before either the TWA Super Constellation or the United DC-7 took off on their fateful flights. Failure to provide the resources necessary to properly develop an air traffic management system resulted in procedures that permitted major public transport aircraft to operate in uncontrolled airspace without the safeguard of any traffic alerting service.

Furthermore, the lack of appropriate ground facilities meant that both aircraft were operating on different frequencies in the same airspace – a legacy from the early days of US airline flying when airline companies were individually responsible for communications – thus depriving the crews of the opportunity to monitor the position reports of the other aircraft.

Research and experience since that time have established the limitations of the "see and be seen" principle of air traffic separation. And in this case its application was made even more difficult by the technology of the day. While advances in aircraft design enabled higher cruising altitudes and greater speeds to be flown, the early pressurisation technology restricted them to small flightdeck windows providing only limited fields of view.

The Grand Canyon accident, with a number of subsequent midair collisions, provided the impetus for further development of the US air traffic system. Improved ground communication facilities were installed, enabling continuous communication between aircraft and ATC. The concept of narrow "airways" corridors was abandoned in favour of more flexible and all encompassing "control areas". And the widespread introduction of radar enabled the provision of a traffic information service on

The site of the DC-7's impact (circled) was about 2500 feet above the Colorado River and almost inaccessible. After impacting against a massive outcrop, the wreckage fell into a deep crevasse and down a sheer cliff face. So difficult and dangerous was the task of examining it, that mountaineers had to be flown in from Switzerland to assist. The broken line shows the route by which they reached the precipitous site. (World Wide Photos)

aircraft not otherwise participating in the ATC system.

Today, major public transport aircraft in the US cruise under IFR regardless of weather conditions, in airspace under positive control at all times, and are equipped with last defence collision avoidance systems such as TCAS. No longer is "see and be seen" relied upon as the primary means of collision avoidance.

By contrast in Australia at the time of writing, it is disquieting to note that aviation authorities are once again proposing to discontinue, on purely economic grounds, the nation's long established traffic information service in uncontrolled airspace – a service that the Grand Canyon accident, to name only one, showed to be so essential to long term air safety.

CHAPTER 10

A fatal propeller failure

In North America in the early 1950s, the advent of the sensational new Vickers Viscount turboprop, offering passengers smooth, vibration free flight for the first time, had everyone talking. But a fatal inflight blade failure early in the type's history showed its propellers were still as vulnerable to an overspeed condition as those of its piston engined predecessors.

The warm summer weather in Chicago on Monday morning, July 9 1956, was overcast with occasional light showers, but the air was clear and the day was what passengers would call a good one for flying.

At the city's O'Hare airport, amongst the rows of piston engined airliners clustered around the sprawling passenger terminal – DC-6s, DC-7s, Super Constellations and the occasional Boeing Stratocruiser – a medium sized airliner that looked and sounded different was arriving.

Carrying a Canadian registration, with the logo of Trans-Canada Air Lines on its fuselage, its four slim engine nacelles had propellers that ran at high speed even while taxiing and, in place of the familiar throb of heavy radials, emitted an ear-piercing, high frequency whine. As the unusual visitor was marshalled to its place on the apron and its engines shut down, the propellers spun freely and smoothly down to a stop.

To a knowledgeable observer,

A Trans Canada Vickers Viscount 700, about to touch down at a busy North American airport in the late 1950s. The advent of the turboprop Viscount in the mid-1950s ushered in a new era in North American short-haul airline operations.

A fine inflight study of a 700 series Viscount, operated by British European Airways in the early 1950s. This particular Viscount is named after Captain R F Scott, the Antarctic explorer. (British Airways)

the aircraft was one of the revolutionary new British turboprops, a Vickers Viscount 700, recently delivered to Trans-Canada, and now flying their regular Chicago/Toronto/Ottawa service, a distance of a little under 600nm that was ideal for the short haul Viscount.

The Canadian airline's introduction of the Viscount to North American skies was nothing less than epoch-making. The whining power of the vibration free, smooth running Rolls-Royce Dart engines was unlike anything experienced before in commercial aviation. Gone were the grunting starts of great radial engines, blowing smoke as they burst into life; gone were the lengthy, pretakeoff engine runups, when the whole aircraft would seem to stamp like some huge animal. And in cruising flight at pressurised altitudes, passengers could relax in an environment free from the continual vibration and engine noise levels of the past. Indeed, so impressed were some US domestic airlines with this new mode of air travel, that they were planning to follow Trans-Canada's lead.

The Viscount operating the service to Toronto and Ottawa on this particular afternoon was CF-TGR and, in readiness for its scheduled departure from Chicago at 1pm, its 31 passengers were ushered

aboard under the care of the two young flight attendants. They included two small boys, aged three and 21 months, and their young mother who, for her convenience, were shown to the row of seats at the front of the passenger cabin, immediately behind the forward bulkhead.

The Viscount's startup, taxi and takeoff were entirely normal, and after setting course for Toronto a few minutes after 1pm, the aircraft climbed to its nominated cruising level of FL190 (19,000 feet).

Three quarters of an hour later, the aircraft was cruising above broken middle level cloud between the Great Lakes Michigan and Erie near the town of Flat Rock, when there was a momentary drop in the rpm of No 4 engine. The engine's speed fell 200 to 300 rpm below the normal cruise figure of 13,600, returned to normal for about five minutes, then suddenly increased to about 14,000. Shortly afterwards, as the pilots attempted to feather the propeller, the overspeed condition increased appreciably and their efforts, using both the manual and automatic feathering systems, appeared to be in vain.

As the crew continued their attempts to feather the offending propeller, the Viscount's airspeed

decreased, and so did the sound of the engine's overspeed. Increasing power on the remaining three engines countered the loss in airspeed, but the increasing whine of the No 4 engine indicated its rpm was rising again.

The captain immediately declared an emergency to Detroit Control and the Viscount was cleared to descend. Reducing power on Nos 1, 2 and 3 engines, the crew began an emergency descent at close to the aircraft's maximum airspeed.

Although they had been cruising above a cloud layer, breaks in the clouds permitted the descent to be made visually and, as the Viscount descended through about 11,000 feet, the crew depressurised the cabin.

Less than a minute later, as the aircraft's altitude decreased to around 9000 feet, the No 4 propeller suddenly tore loose from its mountings, all four blades separating from the hub. Unknown to the pilots, one of the blades struck the No 3 engine nacelle, before being flung through the forward part of the fuselage, killing one passenger instantly and injuring four others, together with one of the flight attendants.

Meanwhile the pilots were continuing the descent and, on reaching 3000 feet, applied power again

Such was the passenger appeal of the recently delivered Viscounts, with their quiet, near vibration free Rolls-Royce Dart turboprop engines, that some US domestic airlines soon followed the lead of Trans Canada, even though it meant abandoning aircraft of US manufacture for the time being. Prominent among US operators of the Viscount was Capital Airlines, a company acquired by the giant United Air Lines in 1961, together with its fleet of Viscounts.

to Nos 1, 2 and 3 engines to remain at that altitude. But as they did so, the rpm of the No 3 engine failed to exceed 11,500 and its fire warning system was triggered. Although the pilots could see no fire, they immediately carried out the engine fire drill, including the feathering of the propeller.

Now flying on only its port side engines, the Viscount continued towards Windsor, Ontario, just across the Canadian border from Detroit where, 10 minutes later, with the airport fire service and ambulances standing by, the pilots carried out a successful emergency landing without brakes. Not

until the Viscount had rolled to a stop did the they learn that a propeller blade had penetrated the fuselage with fatal results. Ambulances rushed the injured to hospital.

Examination of the aircraft at Windsor disclosed that the propeller and the section of the No 4 engine forward of the propeller reduction gear mechanism had broken away in flight.

As the propeller blades separated from the hub, one blade had passed completely through the oil cooler of the No 3 engine before penetrating the forward portion of the passenger cabin and inflicting

major cabin damage in the area of the two most forward rows of seats. The woman killed was the one seated with her two small children in the front row of the cabin. Miraculously, neither child was injured, although the elder suffered a degree of shock. The other injured victims were a married couple and their three year old child, a middle aged businessman, and one of the flight attendants.

The No 4 engine, when dismantled, showed evidence of oil starvation. The engine's fuel pump, propeller control unit, and oil pump are driven by bevel gears,

(right) The flightdeck of a Vickers Viscount 700. The feathering buttons for the propellers are on the coaming panel above the instruments.

and investigation disclosed that the driven bevel gear had sustained a fatigue failure, completely disrupting the drive. The teeth of the high speed pinion of the propeller reduction gearing were also stripped, to the extent that the propeller became uncoupled from the engine. Discolouration from overheating could be seen on the pinion and thrust bearing.

All four separated propeller blades were found on the ground in the vicinity of Flat Rock. Three of the propeller blades were intact, but one blade was damaged and had a section missing from it. A small piece of propeller blade recovered from the Viscount's damaged passenger cabin was found to match the missing section of the blade

Investigators could not determine whether the No 4 engine's momentary drop of 200 to 300 rpm had any connection with events that followed. But the initial engine overspeed to around 14,000 rpm undoubtedly occurred after the bevel gear failure, and at this brief stage of the engine difficulty, the propeller could still have been feathered.

After the failure of the bevel gear drive however, the engine was being rotated by the windmilling propeller without pressure lubrication, and as a result, the high speed pinion progressively failed. The propeller oil transfer housing was damaged in the process, preventing feathering oil pressure from being directed to the propeller. No other reason for the propeller's failure to feather could be found.

The pilots told investigators that the second overspeed occurred just as they were first attempting to feather the propeller. By this time however, the damage that prevented feathering had already occurred.

Continuing to windmill at high speed without adequate lubrication, the propeller became uncou-

pled from the engine as the teeth of the high speed pinion of the propeller reduction gearing progressively stripped. By the time the Viscount was down to about 9000 feet, still flying close to its maximum permitted airspeed, the blade retaining structure of the windmilling propeller finally gave way and the propeller flew to pieces.

There was no evidence of faulty material or workmanship in the recovered components of the propeller. Rather, information from the propeller manufacturer, based on the calculated blade retention strength and tests of the propeller design, indicated that a failure of this nature could be expected in the circumstances that developed.

The problem of an uncontrolled,

decoupled propeller was not mentioned in the Viscount's training or operations manuals. At this early stage of the Viscount's operational life, the problem had not been envisaged by the aircraft manufacturers.

Even so, the investigators believed that, because the sound of the overspeed decreased with reduced airspeed and increased with a rise in airspeed, the pilots should have been conscious of the need to limit the Viscount's speed during the descent. In reciprocating engined aircraft, maintaining a low airspeed to reduce the rpm of an uncontrollable propeller had been a well known basic procedure for many years. Despite this, the captain elected to make an emergency descent at high airspeed. The investigators believed the propeller would not have failed as it did if the crew had instead maintained a moderate airspeed.

The failure of the No 3 engine to respond to the crew's power application after levelling off at the lower altitude, and the engine's subsequent fire warning, were the direct result of damage inflicted by one of the detached blades of the No 4 propeller before the blade penetrated the fuselage.

The investigators concluded that the inflight disintegration of the propeller and its fatal outcome were the result of excessive loads imposed upon it by the aircraft's descent at too high an airspeed, while the decoupled propeller was windmilling with its rpm uncontrolled.

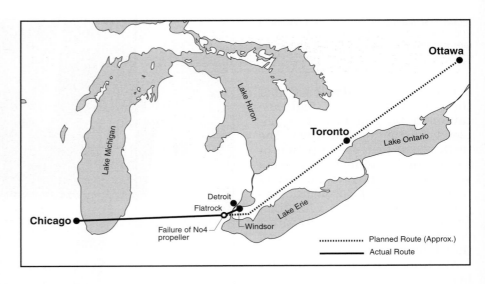

Simplified map of northeastern North America, showing the Chicago-Toronto-Ottawa air route the Trans Canada Viscount was flying at the time of the propeller failure. The town of Flat Rock, between Great Lakes Michigan and Erie, near which the separated propeller blades were later found, is indicated. Also shown is the Canadian city of Windsor, Ontario, where the Viscount made an emergency landing on only two engines. (Aero Illustrations)

Rolls-Royce Dart engines and Rotol propellers of a British Overseas Airways Corporation Viscount undergoing inspection in the airline's extensive engineering workshop in London. The No 4 propeller – that which failed on the Canadian Viscount, together with components forward of the propeller reduction gearing – is closest to the camera. A loss of lubrication, resulting from a fatigue failure in the oil pump drive, brought about the events that led to the failure of the propeller itself.

CHAPTER 11

Plagued by propeller failures

For Boeing's beautiful Stratocruiser – the "Ocean Liner of the Air" – the Brazil mystery in 1950 suggested continuing troubles related to the type's propellers. Similar problems in the years that followed did little to build crew confidence in its engine and propeller combination.

A routine trip

The day was still warm and balmy when Captain Richard Ogg and his crew reported for duty at Honolulu International Airport on Monday, October 15 1956.

On the apron in front of the international terminal, seemingly glowing in the light of the setting sun, stood their massive aircraft. Pan American's Boeing 377 Stratocruiser N90943, *Clipper Sovereign of the Skies*, having arrived from Tokyo a short time before, was being readied for the airline's nightly Pacific service to San Francisco. The trip, flown by Stratocruisers for the past seven years, would take around nine hours, disembarking the passengers in the West Coast city early in the morning.

Ogg, though still in his early 40s, was highly experienced. Having joined PanAm as a junior pilot when he was only 18, he was now one of the company's senior captains, with more than 13,000 flying hours behind him, over 700 of them in Stratocruisers. His

flightdeck crew for the trip, First Officer George Haaker, 10 years with PanAm, Navigation Officer Dick Brown, and Flight Engineer Frank Garcia, also typified the level of experience and ability expected of a major US international airline. Accompanying them as cabin staff were Purser Pat Reynolds and flight attendants Mary Daniel and Katherine Araki.

The trip to San Francisco, which the crew flew frequently, was expected to be unremarkable. They were all well rested after a break of two days in Honolulu, and the weather forecast for the 2100nm ocean (3890km) crossing was favourable. Indeed, the cabin crew were looking forward to a relaxed overnight flight, for only 24 passengers, less than half the huge aircraft's seating capacity, were ticketed to San Francisco. And only a few had taken advantage of the Stratocruiser's opulent accommodation by specifying sleeping berths.

Just after the scheduled departure time of 8.15pm local time,

with all doors shut, steps and loading vehicles rolled away, navigation and taxi lights on, and its engines idling, *Clipper Sovereign of the Skies* was ready to go. Cleared to taxi, the majestic aeroplane rolled slowly out along the lighted taxiway to the runway holding point, ran up its four great P&W R-4360 "corncob" engines in turn, lined up for takeoff, and roared off down the runway. Moments later its lights were rapidly receding specks in the already darkened Honolulu sky as it took up its north-easterly heading.

The Stratocruiser flew the first part of its trip at a comfortable 13,000 feet, cruising at a shade over 260kt (482km/h). Back in the cabin, having enjoyed the elaborate dinner that was a feature of Stratocruiser service, passengers passed the hours reading, or yarning in the lower deck lounge, a few preparing for bed as the night wore on, in the spacious dressing rooms provided for men and women at the front of the cabin. On the flightdeck Captain Ogg

A PanAm Stratocruiser departing San Francisco on one of the company's frequent scheduled 2100nm (3865km) flights to Honolulu. (Boeing)

followed his customary practice of rotating the duties from time to time, allowing each crew member to remain familiar with each other's roles. In particular, at a time when an aircraft's overwater position depended upon its crew's ability to take accurate astro navigation sights, Captain Ogg believed all on the flightdeck should remain in practice.

Mid-ocean emergency

At 1am Hawaiian time, four and a half hours after setting heading from Honolulu, First Officer Haaker called ATC on H/F to request a climb to the aircraft's new cruising level of 21,000 feet, in accordance with its flightplan.

The Stratocruiser was promptly cleared to 21,000, but just after Haaker had levelled off at the new level and ordered a resumption of cruising power, there was sudden, howling whine as Flight Engineer Garcia eased back the propeller pitch levers.

To the Stratocruiser's experienced crew, well acquainted with the aircraft type's history of highly dangerous propeller problems, the sudden, unexpected sound was chilling in the extreme. Rising in pitch and deafening in intensity, the scream could mean only one

thing: a propeller was running away – increasing uncontrollably in rpm.

The crew had good reason to be fearful. And not only because of the fate of *Clipper Good Hope* in Brazil in 1952 (see Chapter 2). Twenty months after that unexplained tragedy, *Clipper Queen of the Pacific*, N90947, enroute from San Francisco to Tokyo on December 6 1953, had lost a propeller blade two and a half hours after leaving Honolulu, the out of balance propeller immediately wrenching the massive No 4 engine from its mountings. Barely able to maintain height against the drag of the nacelle's flat face, the Stratocruiser at once altered heading for Johnson Island, fortuitously located about 700nm (1300km) southwest of the Hawaiian Islands, and made a successful emergency landing.

Not nearly so fortunate 15 months later was *Clipper United States*, N1032, which suffered a similar failure on March 26 1955, only 25 minutes after takeoff from Portland enroute for Honolulu. Although only 30nm (55km) off the coast, the crew were forced to ditch the heavily laden Stratocruiser. Two of the flightcrew and two passengers failed to escape

and went down with the aircraft. The survivors, one of whom had broken a leg, were rescued by the US Navy transport *Bayfield* after tossing for nearly three hours in inflatable dinghies.

And only four months before in April there had been Northwest Orient's Stratocruiser ditching, for reasons still unclear, only minutes after its takeoff from Seattle, which had cost another five lives. (See Chapter 8).

At his navigator's position when the propeller began to scream, Captain Ogg rushed back to his left hand seat. Haaker was pressing the feathering button for the No 1 propeller, but it was having no effect. Garcia pulled back the power to lose airspeed and Haaker lowered some flap, while Ogg tried the feathering button again. Yet still the overwhelmingly loud, high-pitched howl increased.

Even with the speed back from 260 to only 140kt (482 to 259km/h), the immense drag of the runaway propeller was too much for the Stratocruiser – it was losing height. Ogg ordered Garcia to increase the settings of the three functioning engines to climbing power, but still the altimeters unwound. There was one drastic measure left to the crew – to "freeze" the offending engine and propeller. At Ogg's instructions, Garcia closed off the lubricating oil supply to No 1 engine.

For three more anxious, howling minutes, the engine maintained its frighteningly high rpm while the Stratocruiser continued its slow but inexorable descent. Then suddenly an alarming thump shook the whole aircraft – the inertia of the great whirling propeller had sheared its driveshaft as the engine finally shook itself to a dead stop, leaving the propeller itself to continuing windmilling at high rpm, its appalling drag and mind numbing scream hardly reduced, and with the aircraft still losing height.

Somewhere out in the darkness of the mid Pacific night, not too far from the Stratocruiser's present position, the crew knew, there was a ship they had already overflown – the Coast Guard Cutter *Pontchartrain*. Heaved to, and rolling lazily in the light ocean swell, *Pontchartrain* was taking her turn, as part of the US Coast Guard's objective of "safety and security at sea," to fulfil the role of Ocean Station November, maintaining a position half way between the Hawaiian Islands and San Francisco. In the prejet era of international flying, such ocean station ships were in effect mid ocean air traffic control centres that also served as meteorological stations, and if ever needed, ocean rescue services. A World War 2 sloop type naval vessel of 80 metres, *Pontchartrain* displaced 1500 tonnes and had a crew of about 150. Her commander was Captain William Earle.

At 1.22am Hawaiian time, Ogg called *Pontchartrain* to appraise the ship of their emergency situation, reporting that it seemed likely they would be forced to ditch. He also obtained details of the wind and sea state in the ship's vicinity, and altering heading for the vessel, turned the Stratocruiser around to home on the ship's NDB.

To reduce the Stratocruiser's rate of descent as far as possible, Ogg told Garcia to maintain climbing power on the remaining three live engines. But now Garcia saw

Night departure: Engines running, PanAm Stratocruiser N1028V prepares to taxi to the runway. Lights reflecting from its spinning propellers provide an idea of their massive diameter.

from his engineer's instrument panel indications that No 4 engine was not delivering the power that it should. Juggling his engine controls, he tried all possible options his experience could suggest, but to no avail – the massive engine slowly continued to lose power

It was time to tell the passengers, already roused from their midnight sleep by the howl of the runaway propeller, the stark truth. Over the PA system, Ogg's voice was calm, as though the threatened ditching was an everyday affair. There was help near to hand, he assured them, with the ocean station vessel now only just a few miles away, and that everything would be all right. He concluded by instructing the cabin crew to begin their "preparation for ditching" procedures.

All on board now donned lifejackets, passengers were redrilled in the instructions contained in the emergency brochure issued to them when they boarded the aircraft, and the cabin crew removed inflatable dinghies from their cabin storages, ready for launching when the hatches were opened after touchdown.

A temporary reprieve

At 1.25am, with the aircraft's altitude continuing to fall, the inevitable ditching seemed imminent, and Ogg called the ship again, requesting assistance. *Pontchartrain* then transmitted the latest seastate observations, together with the most suitable ditching heading, taking into account the ocean's primary and secondary swells, and the choppiness superimposed on them by the eight knot (15km/h) wind. But as the Stratocruiser continued to descend, the crew found that, by reducing the airspeed to 135kt (250km), and retaining METO

The flightcrew of a Stratocruiser at their stations. The radio operator is at lower left, with the flight engineer at near right. The navigator's position, not visible in this picture, is further aft. Note the large area of windscreen panelling, offering the crew superb visibility.

power on Nos 2 and 3 engines, together with the limited power still being developed by the No 4 engine, they were just able to maintain height at 5000 feet.

As the Stratocruiser resumed its heading towards the ship which was still over the horizon, Ogg considered dumping fuel to lighten the Stratocruiser's load and possibly improve its chances of maintaining height. But he decided against it. If they could possibly do so without dumping fuel, this would allow more flying time to take advantage of the best pos-

sible ditching conditions. He would wait and see if Garcia's efforts to coax more power out of No 4 engine were successful.

Remembering that in previous Boeing 377 ditchings, the rear fuselage and empennage had broken off after impact with the water, Ogg called Purser Reynolds to the flightdeck and instructed her to move all the passengers as far forward in the cabin as possible, leaving the rear seats empty.

As the aircraft drew closer to *Pontchartrain's* position, one of the vessel's guns fired mortar shells to help the Stratocruiser identify it in the dark. The ship's crew also lowered a boat and laid out lighted buoys to form a flarepath not far from the ship to assist the Stratocruiser's ditching approach.

At 1.37am Hawaiian time, the Stratocruiser arrived over the ship. With a rescue crew now standing by to pluck those who survived the ditching from the water, Ogg considered his options afresh. The Stratocruiser was still holding height and despite the demands being made on them, Nos 2 and 3 engines were still delivering their power smoothly. And they had plenty of fuel.

There was no way he could consider trying to take the crippled Stratocruiser all the way to the mainland on the meagre power of two engines, even assuming they continued their trouble free operation, but the need to ditch was no longer imminent. They could stay in the air, at least for the time being, circling in the vicinity of *Pontchartrain*. And if the weather and the seastate stayed as it now was, and they could postpone the ditching until daylight, the chances of it being successful would be immeasurably improved.

The long wait for dawn began as the Stratocruiser remained in the "circuit area" of the Coast Guard cutter, the crew monitoring the operation of the engines carefully, alert for any indication of trouble that could bring on the need to go ahead with the ditching without delay. From time to time Captain Ogg conferred by radio with Captain Earle on the ship, discussing the various aspects of the proposed ditching and the measures

The flight engineer on a Stratocruiser was a busy man, playing a vital role in the management of the aircraft's systems – particularly those affecting the wellbeing of the massive P&W 28 cylinder radial engines. (Ward, Lock & Co)

for rescue that would be taken immediately afterwards. Back in the cabin, the passengers, now moved to more forward seats and thoroughly briefed as to what was to happen and what to do when the time came, did their best to relax as the hours dragged past.

Crisis averted again

At 2.45am, the flightcrew, and indeed all on board, were startled when the ailing No 4 engine suddenly backfired loudly and lost what remaining power it was delivering. The crew quickly feathered its propeller, fearing the worst as it shuddered to a stop.

But thanks to the increased fuel consumption of the Nos 2 and 3 engines running continuously at high power, the fuel load had lightened considerably and the crew found the aircraft could still maintain height at just under 1000 feet.

In fact, as more and more fuel was consumed, the Stratocruiser was even able to climb a little, giving the crew increased confidence as they planned and replanned their preditching checks. So much so that they were even able to make several practice ditching approaches.

Daylight finally dawned over Ocean Station November and still the Stratocruiser's two engined flight continued smoothly, if noisily. Below them, the now visible ocean surface appeared almost calm, save for the prevailing low swell. But Ogg knew from the sea information transmitted to him that the low chop on its surface made it a lot rougher than it looked, and the ditching would be perilous. He conferred with Garcia on their remaining fuel and the condition of the engines, and decided to further postpone the ditching to consume as much of the fuel remaining as seemed prudent. This would lighten the aircraft as much as possible.

When Ogg transmitted his plan to the ship, *Pontchartrain* requested him to give them 10 minutes warning of his intention to ditch to allow time to lay foam on the water to mark the most desirable ditching path and, as far as possible, subdue the choppiness. As the Stratocruiser continued to

The main passenger cabin of a PanAm Stratocruiser in its daytime configuration. Passenger seating, only four abreast in the wide cabin, was spacious. The well appointed galley can be seen at the rear. (Aircraft of Today and Tomorrow)

hold and the passengers waited anxiously, they could now see the Coast Guard vessel below them, rolling gently in the ocean swell from the northwest.

Survival or disaster?

At 5.40am, with little more than 30 minutes endurance remaining, Ogg called the ship to report the time had come. Getting underway, her lifeboats already swung out on their davits ready for launching, *Pontchartrain* took up a heading

of 315°, steaming into the light northwesterly wind as she sprayed fire extinguishing foam on the surface of the waves.

Aboard the Stratocruiser, the crew went through the final items on their emergency landing checklist. In the cabin, the flight attendants made a final check that the passengers had removed all sharp objects from their clothing and were ready to brace themselves for the impact. Then the cabin crew took their own seats and

The convivial lower deck lounge of the Stratocruiser allowed passengers a welcome break from the confines of their allocated seats during a long transcontinental or international flight – as well as the opportunity to stretch their legs. Flight stages of 10 or 11 hours duration were commonplace on Stratocruiser routes. (Ward, Lock & Co)

(left) The galley at the rear of the main cabin was the most comprehensive and well equipped of any airliner's when the Stratocruiser was introduced in the late 1940s. (right) Another view of the main deck. The flight attendant at right rear is standing immediately in front of the stairway to the lower deck lounge. (Air Enthusiast)

strapped themselves down firmly. All was now set. But what would be the outcome – a successful ditching or a disaster? And what were their chances of survival?

Positioning the aircraft well out to the southeast of the ship, Captain Ogg lined up with the foam path clearly visible on its eastern side. *Pontchartrain* radioed that the wind was now almost calm and the swells were four feet (1.2m) in height. Ogg announced over the PA system that there was one minute to go, and all in the cabin braced themselves. Approaching at 90kt (167km/h), with the Stratocruiser's undercarriage still retracted, Ogg waited until they neared the water, then called for full flap as he began to ease off the power on the two live engines.

The waves were coming up quickly now. Sweating with concentration, Ogg eased back the control column, raising the nose to slow the aircraft further, and the crew prepared themselves for the shock they knew was to come.

As Ogg held the aircraft off, noseup, and the airspeed decayed, there was a light impact as the Stratocruiser glanced off the top of a secondary swell. Then it hit the ocean surface as if it were something solid, the loud numbing impact throwing everyone hard against their harnesses and seat belts, and immersing the aircraft in water and spray.

Heavy deceleration and noise followed as the nose pitched down, plunging below the surface, and the whole aircraft swung wildly to the left, snapping off the rear fuselage aft of the main cabin door and taking the rearmost rows of seats with it, as Captain Ogg had feared. Then suddenly all was quiet and it was over, the Stratocruiser at rest in the water and for the moment floating level, rising and falling in the ocean swell.

Rescue

Scarcely able to believe their good fortune, the crew checked themselves, hastily undoing their harnesses. No one was hurt but the Stratocruiser was taking water fast through the stove-in nose and there was no time to be lost. Already the flightdeck was becoming submerged as the aircraft began going down nose first.

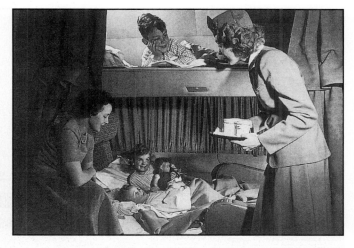

(left) Some of the cabin ceiling panels of the Stratocruiser were designed to let down to form upper sleeping berths on overnight flights. (right) The Stratocruiser cabin in its night configuration offered passengers genuinely comfortable beds, not merely reclining seats, in which to doze. (Air Enthusiast)

In the brief time it took the crew to make their way back to the cabin, passengers had undone their seat belts, got to their feet and opened the overwing escape hatches. Some had already thrown one liferaft clear of the aircraft and were inflating it. For a short time the broken away tail section, still floating, trapped this liferaft beside the main door, but it quickly sank, and leaving the

rear of the cabin open to the elements. There was another fracture of the fuselage just above the front of the cabin, but it had opened up only slightly.

The broken rear fuselage actually assisted the crew in the evacuation of the aircraft and all on board were quickly transferred to inflated liferafts. As they paddled away from the sinking Stratocruiser, motor lifeboats

from *Pontchartrain* bore down on them. One lifeboat came alongside the Stratocruiser while a crewman boarded it through the broken fuselage to check that no one had been left behind, then the lifeboat crews took the survivors aboard. In a few minutes they were rejoicing in the security of the ship, their ordeal finally over. Five passengers had sustained minor abrasions, but none required medical attention.

Minutes later *Clipper Sovereign of the Skies* raised her broken tail to the sky for the last time and slipped nose first below the waves, on her last journey to the ocean floor.

As news of the successful ditching and rescue was transmitted to the world, four US Navy ships racing towards the scene, including the destroyer USS *Johnson* with a navy surgeon on board, were recalled, and San Francisco Coast Guard headquarters directed Captain Earle to bring the survivors to port. *Pontchartrain* would be replaced at Ocean Station November by the cutter *Klamath*. *Pontchartrain* reached San Francisco with them all two days later.

The Civil Aeronautics Board investigation that followed could not fault the airline's operational procedures, nor those of the crew. In fact, the story of Captain Ogg's

(left) A classical view of a Pan American Stratocruiser. Sistership Clipper America *in the heyday of the type's airline operations in the early 1950s.*

Twenty months after the loss of PanAm's Clipper Good Hope *in Brazil in 1952 (see Chapter 2),* Clipper Queen of the Pacific, *N90947, enroute from San Francisco to Tokyo on December 6 1953, lost a propeller blade two and a half hours after leaving Honolulu, wrenching the No 4 engine from its mountings. Barely able to maintain height, this Stratocruiser was fortuitously able to make an emergency landing on Johnson Island, 700nm (1295km) southwest of the Hawaiian Group. (Peter R Keating/Propliner)*

successful ditching, saving all on board with only a few minor injuries, was to become an epic – a highly professional textbook example – in the annals of transocean aviation.

As to what brought about the drama that led to the loss of the aircraft, the investigators were unable to do other than speculate – their evidence lay halfway between America and the Hawaiian Islands in four kilometres of water.

CAB finding

But from the Stratocruiser's accident and incident history, the likely scenario seemed all too obvious. The CAB apparently thought so too, for as a result of a recommendation arising from the aircraft's loss and two subsequent Boeing 377 incidents, the oil transfer mechanism in the propellers was modified with redesigned components.

The CAB officially ascribed the cause of the Stratocruiser's loss to "an initial mechanical failure, which precluded feathering of the No 1 propeller and a subsequent mechanical failure, which resulted in a complete loss of power from the No 4 engine, the effects of which necessitated a ditching."

Yet troubles for Pan American's Stratocruiser operations in the Pacific were by no means over. A year later, in almost the same place, a far more disastrous episode was to overtake yet another

Newspaper photograph of the US Navy transport Bayfield *picking up survivors from* Clipper United States, *N1032, which suffered a similar failure on March 26, 1955, only 25 minutes after leaving Portland for Honolulu. Unable to maintain height, the crew was forced to ditch the heavily laden Stratocruiser 30nm off the coast. Two of the crew and two passengers failed to escape. (Associated Press Wirephoto)*

An armed patrol vessel operated by the US Coast Guard service. These substantial Coast Guard ships, of which *Pontchartrain, Minnetonka* and *Klamath* were typical, have always been designated "Coast Guard cutters". (US Coast Guard)

company Stratocruiser flying the same route, but in the opposite direction.

History repeats

On November 9 1957, *Clipper Romance of the Skies*, another sistership to *Clipper Sovereign of the Skies* and the next on the US register, N90944, took off from San Francisco in fine weather at 11.40am Pacific Standard Time.

Under the command of Captain Gordon Brown, it was bound for Honolulu, Wake Island, Tokyo, Hong Kong and Rangoon. On board, in addition to the crew of eight, were 36 passengers. Carrying fuel for 13 hours flying, the Stratocruiser was loaded to its maximum permissible weight of 66,680kg, limiting its initial cruising level to 10,000 feet.

The aircraft transmitted normal hourly position reports, and five and a half hours after its departure, the radar operator aboard the Coast Guard cutter *Minnetonka* (a sistership to *Pontchartrain* and *Klamath*),

maintaining Ocean Station November at the time, fixed the Stratocruiser's position passing 10nm (19km) east of the vessel. The regular position reports from the Stratocruiser continued, and at 5.04pm Pacific Standard Time it gave its position as 890nm (1650km) from Honolulu. The aircraft was encountering headwinds stronger than forecast, but there were no problems and operations were normal.

This proved to be the Stratocruiser's last transmission. When no report was received from it at 6pm as scheduled, there was no

immediate concern, for H/F communication over such distances was unreliable at times, particularly near sunrise and sunset.

But there was concern an hour later when nothing further was heard from the aircraft, and when it again failed to report at 8pm Pacific Standard Time, the commander of the US Coast Guard District in Honolulu ordered out a search aircraft and alerted the crews of two Coast Guard cutters to be ready to join the search. Meanwhile, two Navy submarines, USS *Cusk* and *Carbonaro*, exercising to the northwest of the

Flightplanned route of Stratocruiser N90943, Clipper Sovereign of the Skies *and its approximate position when the No 1 propeller ran away uncontrollably. After turning back, the aircraft ditched several hours later close to the US Coastguard cutter maintaining position at "Ocean Station November". (Aero Illustrations)*

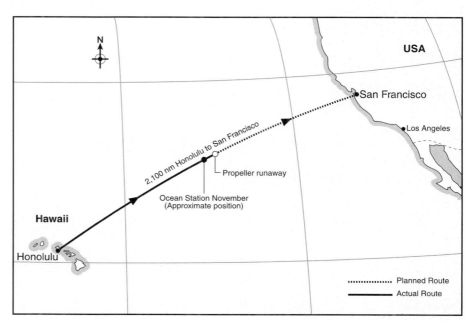

(above) Lined up with the foam path laid on the ocean surface by Pontchartrain's crew, Clipper Sovereign of the Skies makes its literally final approach. (below) Ditching! Green water and spray almost cover the Stratocruiser as Captain Ogg skilfully puts the aircraft down in difficult conditions on the choppy sea. (Air Classics)

(below) Success: The Stratocruiser comes to rest largely intact and floating. As Captain Ogg feared, the aircraft's wild swing during the ditching snapped off the rear fuselage, taking the rearmost rows of seats with it. Foreseeing this possibility, Captain Ogg had the passengers moved forward before touchdown. (Air Classics)

Hawaiian Islands, were diverted to the area of the Stratocruiser's last report. Merchant ships in the area were also alerted

Hopes that the Stratocruiser's failure to report was only because of radio failure were dashed after the aircraft failed to reach Honolulu as scheduled, and the search effort was intensified, US Navy and Air Force aircraft joining those of the Coast Guard to scour a 90nm (167km) wide path from 950 to 300nm (1760 to 555km) east of the Hawaiian Group. As well, the aircraft carrier, USS *Philippine Sea*, sailed from the naval base at Long Beach to join the search with its complement of long range anti-submarine aircraft.

Eventually, on November 14, five days after the Stratocruiser disappeared, aircraft from *Philippine Sea* found floating debris from the aircraft, together with a few bodies, 820nm (1520km) east of Honolulu.

The subsequent Civil Aeronautics Board investigation into the loss of the aircraft calculated that, taking into account the effects of ocean currents and wind over those five days, the aircraft had come down about 90nm (167km) west of its last reported position and about 30° off course to the north.

But what befell the Stratocruiser and its occupants during the last 20 minutes of its flight could only remain a matter of speculation. Whatever overtook the aircraft had probably happened suddenly and unexpectedly, for there had not been the slightest hint of difficulty during the crew's last radio report, and no emergency call at any time afterwards.

It could only be surmised that the fate of *Clipper Romance of the Skies* over the Pacific Ocean was similar to that of *Clipper Good Hope* over the Brazilian jungle, five and a half years earlier – a fate that might easily have also been that of a military version of the aircraft type, flying the same route only three months before the Pacific mystery. The story of that Boeing C-97's remarkable escape is told in the next chapter.

(right) Map published in The New York Times *for November 10 1957, reporting the disappearance of PanAm's* Clipper Romance of the Skies, *N90944, en route for Honolulu the previous day. Five days later, searching aircraft from the US aircraft carrier* Philippine Sea, *located floating debris and bodies 820nm (1520km) east of Honolulu.*

(above) Clipper Sovereign of the Skies *overflies the Coast Guard cutter* Pontchartrain *at Ocean Station November prior to ditching. Note the stationary No 4 propeller. (Air Classics)*

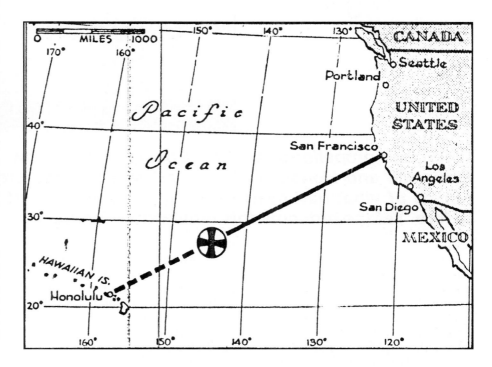

Passengers and crew board inflatable dinghies as motor lifeboats from Pontchartrain *speed to their rescue. All on board the Stratocruiser were rescued, only five sustaining minor injuries. (Air Classics)*

CHAPTER 12

The captain who refused to give up

When one propeller of a USAF Boeing C-97 ran away, midway between San Francisco and Honolulu, the situation facing the crew was an almost exact replica of what had overtaken Clipper Sovereign of the Skies, *nearly a year before. Yet the outcome this time was different.*

Pan American, Northwest Airlines, and United Air Lines were not the only major operators of Stratocruisers to suffer the problems inherent in the type's engine-propeller combination. During the 1950s, the USAF's extensive Military Air Transport Service was also a prolific operator of the type – at least of the military transport from which the Stratocruiser was derived, the Boeing 367.

Boeing delivered no less than 888 Boeing 367s to the US armed forces before production ceased in 1956. Most were completed as KC-97 tankers, equipped with boom inflight refuelling equipment, but a substantial number of the transport version, designated the C-97 by the USAF, were assigned to the Military Air Transport Service. Some were configured as passenger aircraft for the many daily scheduled trips which MATS operated for the movement of military personnel and their families between the nation's far flung and often worldwide military bases.

On August 8 1957, one such C-97, attached to MATS' Pacific Division, was flying the regular daily 10 hour, 1990nm (3690km) MATS trip from Travis Air Force Base northeast of San Francisco, to Hickam Field, Honolulu. This military airfield, established before World War 2, now adjoined what had become Honolulu International Airport, developed immediately to its east, and shared its longer runways.

Under the command of Major Samuel Tyson, USAF, a pilot of 6000 hours experience, no less than 2000 of them in C-97s, the massive aircraft with its crew of 10 was carrying 57 passengers, including four army wives and 10 children. After an evening departure from Travis to fly through the night, the aircraft was scheduled to reach Hickam in the morning, Hawaiian time.

In a repetition of events aboard *Clipper Sovereign of the Skies* (except that the C-97 was flying in the reciprocal direction), trouble for the then massive aircraft and its occupants began half an hour after passing the calculated Point of No Return. At the controls in the right hand seat, one of Tyson's two copilots had just climbed the aircraft to its new enroute altitude of 16,000 feet, and was in the process of levelling off to re-establish cruising flight.

All seemed as it should be, and in the commander's left hand seat Major Tyson was leaning back, relaxing. He was waiting until the flight engineer on duty had reset cruising power before he walked back into the cabin again to see how his passengers were faring on the long trip. Cabin visits by the commander were a part of MATS' policy on its long distance flights. But it was also policy that the commander be present on the flightdeck whenever the configuration of the aircraft was being changed.

In any case, having full responsibility for the flight and everyone on board, it was his practice to keep an eye on things while power adjustments were made and the

A USAF Military Air Transport Service Boeing 367 of MATS' Pacific Division, identical with the aircraft flying from California to Honolulu under the command of Major Samuel Tyson. Designated the C-97 by the USAF, a substantial number of these "military Stratocruisers" were assigned to MATS as transport aircraft. The situation that faced Major Tyson was almost a replica of what developed aboard Clipper Sovereign of the Skies *a year earlier. (Boeing)*

aircraft was settled again in its cruise configuration. It was a habit he had developed from the time he became an aircraft captain.

Suddenly, rising above the relatively quiet, smooth throbbing of the four massive engines that was normal on the flightdeck of a Stratocruiser or C-97, there was suddenly the growing, spine chilling whine of a runaway propeller.

The flight engineer on duty, his attention suddenly riveted to his instrument panel by the unexpected sound, saw the No 1 engine rpm needle rise rapidly to hover around a frightening 3800rpm. Major Tyson, instantly alert, reached forward over the centre pedestal, retarded No 1 throttle and mixture control, pushed its feathering button, then pulled the aircraft's nose up to lose airspeed, at the same time calling for 55% flap. But though the abnormally high rpm of No 1 engine decreased to a degree as the airspeed fell off, the propeller refused to feather.

Drag created by the violently windmilling propeller in its ex-treme fine pitch position was yawing the aircraft hard to the left, and with the airspeed now back to an indicated 130kt (240km/h), the crew pulled off the power on all engines and again attempted to feather the No 1 propeller. But again there was no result.

To maintain height for the time being, cruising power was restored on Nos 2, 3 and 4 engines. The crew on this flight, in addition to the usual flight engineer, included a student flight engineer and his instructor for training purposes. All three were now on the flightdeck, but even their combined expertise was insufficient to persuade the No 1 propeller to feather.

Tyson considered his options. Still a daunting 1050nm (1945km) from their destination, they were of course even further from the west coast of the United States. Should he try to ditch the C-97 successfully near a ship, as had Captain Ogg his PanAm Stratocruiser so skilfully 10 months before?

But there were no ships in the C-97's immediate vicinity, and even the Coastguard cutter maintaining position at Ocean Station November now lay at least 200nm (370km) behind them. Tyson determined they would continue – for as long as it remained possible to stay in the air.

The oil quantity gauge for the No 1 propeller was now indicating zero, so there was no longer any possibility that it would feather. The crew's only alternative was to shut off the oil supply to the engine itself in order to "freeze" it – and hopefully stop the propeller that way. As a drag reduction measure, the drastic step would not be as effective as a successful feathering, but it could improve the desperate situation they were in. He instructed the engineers to do it.

Aware that the speed of a windmilling propeller was a function of true airspeed, and that the lower the aircraft's altitude, the lower would be the actual windmilling rpm, Tyson decided as well to descend to a lower altitude. There was also the important consideration that the aircraft would

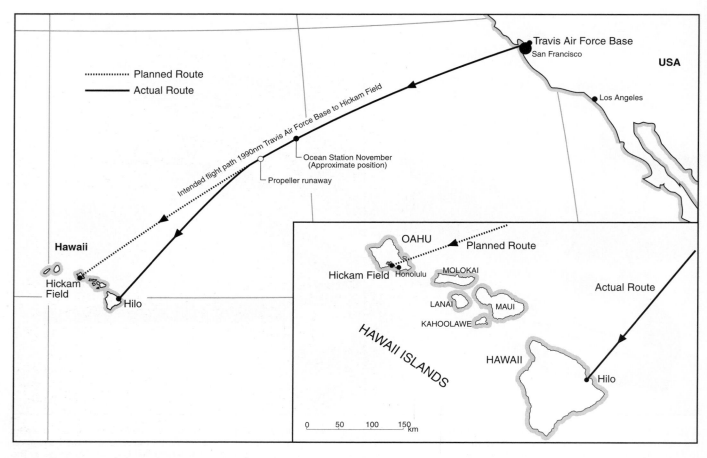

The flightplanned route of the USAF C-97, and the diversionary route the crew succeeded in flying after the propeller runaway, to reach Hilo on the island of Hawaii. (Aero Illustrations)

perform better in its abnormal configuration at a lower altitude.

So as not to exacerbate the windmilling problem, the crew eased the C-97 into a slow descent. With the manifold pressure gauge for the No 1 engine now meaningless, its rpm was varying between 2100 and 2200. Both Tyson and his copilot were now at the controls, holding on full rudder as well as having wound on full rudder trim to keep the aircraft straight against the enormous drag of the outboard runaway propeller.

Meanwhile the whole crew were going about their emergency procedures. The copilot not flying had transmitted a Mayday call on H/F, detailing the nature of their emergency and requesting an Air Rescue Intercept from any aircraft or ships in the area. The three engineers were monitoring their instrument indications. Overheating of the three live engines – now operating at high power at low airspeed – could become a problem, and the correct setting of the en-

gine cowl cooling gills was critical. They were also frequently checking the condition of the overspeeding engine and propeller installation visually.

The two navigators were fixing the aircraft's exact position, seeking to maintain an up-to-the-minute plot of its progress and working out new ETAs and "fuel remaining" figures. Calculating true airspeeds and winds as accurately as possible and cross checking with expected fuel flows determined by the engineers, they informed Tyson that in the aircraft's reduced speed configuration, continuing the flight to Hickam would take six hours, 30 minutes. But with the present high power settings on the three functioning engines, the fuel remaining was sufficient for only six hours, four minutes flying.

Back in the cabin, the flight attendants were getting passengers into lifejackets and briefing them on the preparations necessary for ditching. Over the aircraft's PA system, Major Tyson explained

the situation, assuring the passengers that though these precautions had become necessary, there was no immediate danger.

As the C-97 descended through 11,000 feet, the No 1 engine, starved of lubricating oil, finally seized with a violent thump, and its rpm dropped to zero. But as was the case with *Clipper Sovereign of the Skies*, the inertia of the enormous spinning propeller sheared its drive shaft and it continued to windmill with its rpm and overpowering scream unabated. A few minutes later, as the C-97 sank through 7500 feet, the flightcrew saw to their consternation that the hub of the No 1 propeller, deprived of its lubricant, was developing a red discolouration – it was obviously becoming red hot.

This could mean only one thing – the propeller assembly was near to final, probably catastrophic, failure or disintegration. And when that happened, the great propeller blades could be hurled with the force of an artillery shell into the fuselage, or into

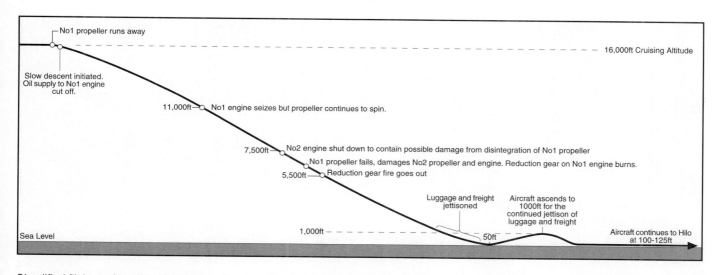

Simplified flight profile of the C-97's operation from the time its No 1 propeller ran away uncontrollably in mid-ocean. The crew's achievement in reaching Hilo safely displayed outstanding airmanship. (Aero Illustrations)

the spinning No 2 engine and propeller alongside it. If the latter occurred and a section of a blade on the No 2 propeller was broken off, the resulting violent out of balance condition would immediately tear the whole engine from its mountings, as had happened in other accidents to this type of aircraft.

Mindful of these possible appalling consequences, Tyson took further drastic precautions to minimise the possibility of damage, even though he knew this might jeopardise their chances of being able to remain in the air. Firstly, shutting down the No 2 engine, he feathered its propeller. If it was struck now by the disintegrating No 1 propeller, the fact that No 2 was stationary would prevent further structural damage to the aircraft.

Next, when it had shuddered to a stop in the feathered position, he banked the aircraft 40° to the right and held it in that attitude, hoping that when the No 1 propeller did finally fail, it would be flung harmlessly over the top of the fuselage.

His precautions paid off – not long afterwards No 1 propeller finally separated from its engine. In doing so it struck one of the four blades of the feathered No 2 propeller, slicing one metre off it, as well as damaging the No 2 nacelle and engine mounting. Although it also dented the top of the fuselage and the tail section, the still spinning propeller fortunately just missed inflicting serious damage

to the fuselage before falling into the ocean.

At least the unnerving propeller scream had gone. But another hazard was now evident – a small magnesium fire, friction ignited by the overheated hub of the flailing propeller, was burning in the reduction gear casing on the nose of the No 1 engine. The crew watched it intently. To everyone's relief, in another eight minutes, it burnt itself out.

The C-97's altitude was now down to 5500 feet. Unbelievably, only 20 minutes had passed since the propeller had run away. Day was now breaking, revealing a limitless ocean stretching to the horizon in every direction. For the pilots, directional control, though slightly improved, was still extremely difficult. And in one way the emergency had become more serious – two engines were now out, both of them on the one side.

But the crew were not accepting defeat yet. Word of the emergency had been received at MATS Headquarters in Washington, DC, and a communications patch set up to provide the fastest possible information on the C-97's situation. Navy ships on the aircraft's track to Hawaii were alerted by radio to stand by, and Air Rescue aircraft and crews at Hawaiian bases were readied. Another MATS C-97 that had departed from Travis Air Force Base for Hawaii an hour before Major Tyson's, turned back to intercept and escort the stricken aircraft.

At 2500 feet, with the aircraft still descending slowly, the navigators, continuing to calculate furiously, reported to Tyson that if there were no further complications, there was a slight possibility of being able to reach Hilo, the nearest airfield to their position, on the northeastern coast of the island of Hawaii itself, nearly 100nm (185km) closer than their original destination on Oahu.

Back in the cabin, the flight attendants, working with calm determination, now had all the passengers as ready as they could be for any likely eventuality. Shoes removed and in stockinged feet in case of ditching, they were to remain seated and strapped into snugly adjusted lifejackets for what was probably the longest ordeal many of them would ever face.

Major Tyson, setting the flaps between five and 10% to minimise the buffeting being produced by the partially open engine cooling gills, and to increase the aircraft's lateral stability, ordered the crew members who could be spared from the flightdeck to assist the flight attendants to jettison all possible luggage and freight, as well as the mail bags on board. It now appeared as though the C-97 might be capable of continuing on its two remaining engines, even though they were both on the starboard side. But there was a discouragingly long way yet to go.

One of the flight attendants opened the port side rear emergency hatch and the crew began

The spacious flightdeck of the massive transport aircraft, normally accommodated captain, co-pilot, flight engineer, navigator and radio operator. The MATS flight to Honolulu in this case was carrying additional USAF crew members for training purposes. (BOAC)

jettisoning. Watching their belongings being hurled into the sea, the passengers made not a single complaint. Through the cabin windows they could see the ocean swell and the waves apparently growing in size as the C-97 continued to lose height – opening the hatch had only increased the aircraft's drag and with it, its rate of descent.

When the C-97 was down to only 50 feet above the waves, Tyson ordered the hatch to be closed and called for METO power on the two live engines. The huge aircraft laboured back to 1000 feet to allow the crew to reopen the rear hatch and continue the jettisoning. After they had thrown out everything on board that could be spared, they closed the hatch again and the aircraft, its high power settings reduced but slightly, flew on at low altitude.

On the flightdeck, the three pilots were taking turns at the controls, two of them at a time

holding on rudder and aileron against the drag of the dead engines on the port wing. The No 1 propeller assembly was missing entirely of course. The No 2 propeller, feathered and useless, with one of its four huge blades cropped by the No 1 propeller as it flew off, was hanging from an engine that was drooping slightly on its mountings.

In its exaggerated asymmetrical condition, the aircraft's tendency to yaw was still extreme. To maintain heading, despite the use of full right trim, the pilots had to brace themselves against their seats and use both feet to hold the right rudder pedal forward. After the first change of copilots, their shift times had to be reduced.

When the copilot working the first shift climbed out of the seat, his legs crumpled under him. And when Major Tyson tried to relax his grip on the controls for the first time, he found he had to pry the fingers of his left hand free

from the wheel. The taut wrist muscles and sinews had broken his watch band.

The flight engineers were nursing the two starboard engines with all the care they could muster, alert for the slightest sign of hesitation at their high power settings. Even a partial loss of power on either one, they knew only too well, would mean an imminent ditching.

A little later, after Tyson had conferred again with the navigators, the crew were able to transmit: "Estimate Hilo in five hours, at 2120Z (21.20 GMT). Fuel remaining 5:04 hours. Airspeed 134 knots." The situation was still far from encouraging. But the crew had coped with the emergency so far, and they were still flying. Now the engineers were able to reduce power a fraction more – and with every revolution of the engines, fuel was being consumed and the aircraft was becoming lighter.

As a professional pilot, Major

The flight engineer's station, immediately behind the pilots' control seats, to which they gained access from their outboard sides. The flight engineer could either face forward to adjust the engine controls on the centre pedestal between the pilots or, as in the preceding picture, face his instrument panel on the right to monitor the aircraft's systems. (Smith's Industries)

Tyson knew about ground effect. He knew that, in theory, as an aircraft descends to within its wingspan of the surface of ground or water, its induced drag is decreased. Deciding he would never have a more opportune time to put the theory to the test, he descended the C-97 further, holding it close above the two and a half metre swell that was sweeping under the nose in the early morning sunlight.

As before, his decision paid off handsomely. The airspeed improved. Engine power could be cut back slightly more, reducing the fuel flows and helping to lighten the load on the two engines being called upon to do the work of four.

Back in the cabin, the flight attendants continued to do what they could for the passengers. But little could be done to ease their tension. Movement in the cabin had to be restricted to a minimum, for there

would be little time to scramble back into a seat and fasten a safety belt should the feared ditching suddenly become necessary.

As if the pressure of the emergency was not enough in itself, the temperature inside the aircraft, its cabin air conditioning system shut down to help conserve precious fuel, increased steadily as the sun rose higher out of the sea, exposing the fuselage to the brightening, sub-tropical morning heat of its rays. It increased until it reached more than 43°C, soaking crew members and passengers alike in perspiration, and adding to the discomfort of their closely fitting lifejackets.

But though little could be done to alleviate their condition, to the passengers the distress imposed by the heat seemed insignificant compared to the slow passage of time. For all on board, the world now comprised only the C-97 itself, the hostile heaving ocean,

stretching in all directions just beneath them, and an invisible line, hopefully leading in time to a landing ground on a distant island. Their best therapy was the continuing, reassuring roar of the two starboard engines and the steadily advancing hands of the aircraft's clocks and passengers' watches.

The passengers were now heartened by an announcement from Major Tyson over the PA system, conveying encouraging news from the navigators. The aircraft's latest position, determined from astro navigation observations of the sun, showed that, in addition to the slight gain in airspeed at their wavetop level, they had actually picked up a tailwind of about 20kt (37km).

As the flight continued, Major Tyson made further encouraging progress reports, strengthening the bond that now existed between passengers and crew – they were all in this together. One of these was the reassuring information that Navy ships were now standing by off the coast of Hawaii, ready to render any assistance that became necessary.

Each announcement from the flightdeck showed the aircraft's chances to be progressively improving, so time seemed to become even more vital. No one in the cabin could resist glancing frequently at their watch – there was no other diversion. They were still flying – and would keep flying for just as long as those two engines could sustain what was being asked of them.

The hours ground slowly on, the yawing C-97 now encountering a little light chop in the slightly turbulent air near the ocean surface. Experimenting with small changes in altitude had shown the crew that 100 to 125 feet was the optimum altitude at which to fly.

As time passed and the C-97 became lighter, the load was easing further on the two starboard engines, still operating at high power settings, despite the small reductions the flight engineers had been able to make from time to time.

With just under 200nm (370km) to run to Hilo, USAF air-sea rescue aircraft from Hawaiian bases intercepted the C-97, cheering its crew and passengers alike by taking up station to either side. If a ditching now became inevitable, additional inflatable rafts and other emergency equipment could be dropped to them at once.

Just after 11am Hawaiian Time, Major Tyson announced the glad news to the passengers that only 15 minutes remained to ETA Hilo, and he eased the C-97 up to 500 feet in preparation for landing. There below them now they could see the aircraft carriers USS *Bon Homme Richard* and *Thetis Bay*, with their destroyer escort, USS *Taylor*, waiting for them. The passengers occupying the window seats pressed their faces to the glass, straining to see ahead. Land was in sight! The atmosphere in the cabin became electric — after the heart-in-mouth tension and worry of the past hours, the reality was almost beyond belief.

The duty runway at Hilo's Lyman Field, only slightly less than 2000 metres long, was almost into wind and suitable for a near straight-in approach. Nearing the circuit area with the landing checklist completed and approach flap lowered, Tyson called for the undercarriage to be lowered, and the copilot moved the selector to the down position. There was the usual noise and thump of the undercarriage extending.

"The left gear is not down!" one of the engineers warned as only two of the three green lamps illuminated on the instrument panel. He added quickly: "But you have enough fuel for a go-round."

Without hesitation Major Tyson pushed Nos 3 and 4 throttles forward to METO power, calling at the same time for the undercarriage to be retracted again and the flaps reset to the climb setting.

Climbing the C-97 back to 500 feet, he flew a circuit, extending the downwind leg sufficiently to allow the engineers to crank the undercarriage down manually. But after a few turns of the crank, the mechanism became unyielding. Looking out at the No 2 engine nacelle, the engineers surmised the reason – the nacelle was drooping enough as a result of its earlier damage to jam the undercarriage doors shut.

Pushing and pulling desperately on the crank with all their strength, two of them at a time, the engineers finally succeeded in forcing the undercarriage assembly through the closed doors, distorting the structure and bursting rivets, but in time for Major Tyson to continue his approach to a smooth and uneventful landing – a fitting anticlimax to the anxiety of the past hours.

The C-97 slowed towards the end of the runway, turned off, and began to taxi in. Thanks to their careful and skilful fuel flow management, the engineers had the satisfaction of knowing that fuel for another 30 minutes flying still remained in the tanks.

So involved were Tyson and his crew with the handling of the emergency landing that the crowd of several thousand people gathered at Hilo Airport had made little impression. In fact, when the crew first sighted them as they overflew the field to go around for the second approach, Tyson commented they would apparently be disrupting whatever occasion was underway at the airport. Not for a moment did they realise the crowd was but a tiny fraction of the American population who, following broadcasts of the crippled C-97's progress, were anxiously anticipating the outcome of the drama.

The plight of the disabled C-97 and the 67 people on board had been flashed across the nation. Progress reports were transmitted as they came in, and the aircraft's struggle to stay in the air was followed with mounting fascination throughout the US. Few listeners when they heard the news of its peril had given the C-97 much of a chance, but as the hours wore on, more and more began to feel there might be some hope.

They were not disappointed. The aircraft's two remaining engines had laboured at high power settings for more than six hours to bring the saga to a successful conclusion. And thanks to the efforts of the flight attendants, as well as to Major Tyson's reassuring words of explanation over the PA system every now and then, there were no histrionics from the 57 people whom he later described as "the best passengers in the world".

Major Tyson had won a Distinguished Flying Cross flying B-24 Liberator bombers on operations in the closing stages of World War 2. He won a bar to his DFC during the Korean War for returning a Douglas C-124 Globemaster to a safe landing in Japan after an engine had caught fire, disintegrated and fallen from the aircraft.

Now, as a result of his determination and superb airmanship in beating overwhelming odds to bring the C-97 to a safe landing at Hilo, when a watery grave seemed its certain fate, he was awarded a second bar to his DFC. His accomplishment also elicited a rare tribute from the Military Air Transport Service's most senior officer, Lt General J Smith. He declared it to be the "most splendid example of flying to come to his attention in his six years as commanding officer".

Like Pan Am's Captain Richard

Ogg 10 months before, Major Tyson saved the lives of all for whom he was responsible by dint of skilful, knowledgeable and resourceful flying under extremely demanding conditions. But unlike Ogg, he was able to save his aircraft as well.

Their Boeings were almost identical, were operating in similar conditions, and their propeller failures both occurred in almost the same position in midocean. So what made the difference?

The answer undoubtedly lay in the drag created by the windmilling, overspeeding propellers, the aerodynamic effect of which in these conditions is similar to a flat disk of the same diameter in front of the engine concerned.

In Ogg's case, the offending propeller continued to windmill throughout the time his Stratocruiser remained in the air, demanding near maximum power and fuel flows from all three remaining engines up to the time of the ditching, thus precluding any possibility of being able to reach the nearest land.

Tyson's aircraft, on the other hand, lost its windmilling propeller within half an hour of the development of the problem. And even though it effectively took with it a second engine-propeller combination, the great reduction in aerodynamic drag that resulted was sufficient to allow the remaining two engines and fuel to keep the C-97 in the air through the long hours needed to reach safety at Hilo.

Mission accomplished: the MATS C-97 overflies the airport at Hilo, Hawaii, after achieving the near impossible flight from mid-ocean on only two engines. The No 1 engine is without its propeller, while the No 2 engine and propeller, with portion of one of its blades sheared off, is feathered and stationary. (MATS Flyer)

CHAPTER 13

The Lockheed Electra saga

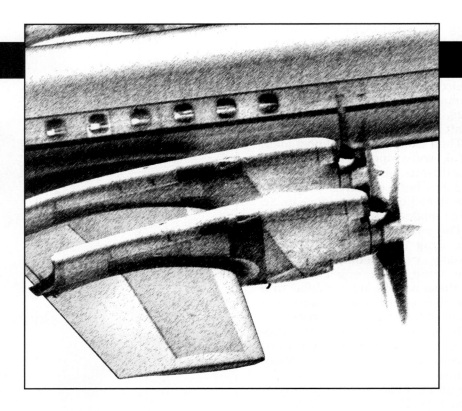

The advent of Lockheed's turboprop Electra in 1959 quickly won aclaim from US airline executives, aircrews and passengers alike. But the euphoria for the new type in the country of its origin was unfortunately to be short lived.

Vickers' revolutionary turboprop Viscount airliner that took Europe by storm in the early 1950s initially had little impression on the conservative US domestic airline industry, with its vast fleet of heavy four engined aircraft, all powered by great, snorting, supercharged reciprocating radial engines.

It was not until Air Canada introduced Viscount services to North America, that US airline executives suddenly realised that the era of smooth, near vibration free, turbine power for airline operations had dawned.

The Lockheed Aircraft Corporation, working on a US government contract for the development of a military transport, was about to fly its prototype YC-130A Hercules, powered by Allison T56 turboprop engines. Inspired by Lockheed's innovative design work, and greatly impressed by the British Viscount's performance, economics and passenger appeal, the forward thinking Capital Airlines approached Lockheed in early 1954 to see if it would also

be interested in developing a turboprop airliner for the US domestic market.

Lockheed was indeed willing. But no other US airlines appeared to be impressed by the proposal, so it seemed that such a development could prove uneconomic. For this reason Lockheed decided not to go ahead. Left with no alternative if it were to steal a march on its US competitors by becoming the first US turboprop airline operator, Capital Airlines in 1954 ordered no less than 60 Viscount 700s.

But a year later, American Airlines, after showing interest in a proposal for a twin engined turboprop that also failed to eventuate, called for a four engined, longer range turboprop design from Lockheed. Eastern Air Lines then joined in the negotiations, which finally resulted in specifications for what was to become the Lockheed 188. A fast, low wing aircraft seating around 90 passengers with a range of up to 3000nm (5557km), it would be powered by four Allison 50l-D gas turbine engines.

Named the Electra after the elegant little twin engined, twin tailed 10 passenger Lockheed 10 Electra that had established the company's reputation as a major airliner manufacturer in 1934, the first L-188 was completed late in 1957. By that time Lockheed had orders for 129 of the aircraft, with options for at least another 48.

Eastern Air Lines introduced the new Electra to its passengers on January 12, 1959, when the type flew the company's New York-Miami service. Eleven days later on January 23, American Airlines followed suit on its New York-Chicago service.

From the start the Electra's smooth, high speed flight made a great impression on passengers and crews alike. At the same time its unusual economy of operation appealed to the companies' accountants. The future for Lockheed and the airlines introducing the Electra seemed assured. But as seems to happen all too often with a promising new type of aircraft, soul-searching disappointment lay just around the corner.

The original Lockheed 10 Electra, developed at the Burbank factory in 1934, after which the Lockheed 188 Electra was named. With Boeing's Model 247 and Douglas's DC-2, the L-10 Electra was among the first of the new generation of all-metal monoplane airliner designs that took the aviation world by storm in the mid 1930s. The success of the L-10 Electra established the Lockheed Aircraft Corporation as one of the world's major transport aircraft manufacturers. In Australia prewar, Macrobertson-Miller Aviation, Guinea Airways and Ansett Airways operated a number of these 10 passenger aircraft on regional services. One the former Ansett aircraft, VH-UZO, is still airworthy today.

Lockheed's new 188 Electra quickly won acclaim from US airline executives, aircrews and passengers for its smooth, near vibration free, turbine power, its high performance, and operating economics. The first L-188 prototype was completed in December 1957 and the type entered airline service just over two years later. This picture was taken during the Electra's extensive flight evaluation program. (Lockheed)

A few minutes before midnight on February 3, 1959, only 12 days after American Airlines had inaugurated its Electra services, Lockheed Electra N6101A was inbound to New York's La Guardia Airport at the conclusion of the company's Flight 320 from Chicago. On board were 68 passengers and a crew of five, under the command of veteran Captain Albert DeWitt, 59, a pilot whose total flying experience was nearing 30,000 hours.

The winter weather was poor, so much so that although the aircraft had left Chicago at 9pm and was due to land at La Guardia at 11.05pm, it was forced to hold nearing the New York area and was not able to be cleared for an instrument approach to La Guardia's Runway 22 until 11.54pm. The cloudbase at the time was 600 feet, with visibility below it varying in fog and rain.

La Guardia Airport lies on the Manhattan side of Long Island, towards its southwestern end, and aircraft making an approach to Runway 22 cross the broad East River to the northwest of the airport before reaching the runway threshold.

Nothing more was heard from the Electra after it acknowledged La Guardia's clearance for an instrument approach, but 16 minutes later at 12.12am, the Coast Guard service telephoned the Tower to report an aircraft was down in the river. It had crashed into the water near Rickers Island, to the west of the approach path to Runway 22. Several small vessels, including a harbour tug, were endeavouring to rescue survivors from the water. Despite the poor visibility and darkness, a Coast Guard helicopter was preparing to fly to the accident site.

The first vessel to reach survivors from the Electra was the tug. Owned by a dredging company, it was towing two barges down the river in foggy conditions when its captain heard "a terrific crash" less than 300 metres away. Switching on his vessel's searchlight, he quickly picked out the wreckage of an aircraft that was sinking as he watched. Only a seven metre section of the fuselage appeared to be still intact. Immediately he cut the barges loose, heading the tug at full speed towards where the wreckage was going down. "There were people and bodies all over," the tug captain said later.

Survivors struggling in the water were crying out for help, and as the tug reached them, the captain and other crew members of the tug leaped into the icy water to assist. Other members of the crew reached out with boathooks to bring survivors alongside the vessel and haul them aboard.

Meanwhile, a police boat, several small craft, and a fire float had joined the rescue effort, but the fast running outgoing tide in the river was carrying bodies away in the darkness and poor visibility. Although the vessels succeeded in recovering 22 more bodies, all had succumbed by that time to hypothermia. Only eight of the 73 persons on board the Electra were finally found to have survived the accident. They included the first officer, the flight engineer, and one of the two flight attendants.

Investigators from the Civil Aeronautics Board in Washington DC found that the aircraft had flown into the river more than a kilometre short of the runway threshold. At the time the Electra began its approach to Runway 22, ground visibility on the airport was about three kilometres, but fog lay over the river itself.

It seemed inconceivable to the CAB that Captain DeWitt, one of American Airlines' most senior and experienced captains, and his highly experienced first officer, should have made such a fatal error of judgement. Yet no evidence of any failure or malfunction could be found in the wreckage of the near new Electra or its systems.

The official investigation dragged on for more than a year before the CAB was able to issue its final report. When it did so, it sheeted home the ultimate cause of the accident to the crew's premature descent below landing minimums as a result of preoccupation with the aircraft and its environment, to the "neglect of essential flight instrument references". But the report qualified this finding by referring to a number of contributing factors.

"There is no one factor so outstanding as to be considered the probable cause," the report declared. "On the contrary...the accident was an accumulation of several factors which together compromised the safety of the flight."

These included the crew's limited experience on the Electra which, in the captain's case, amounted to less than 50 hours, possible misinterpretation of the new type of altimeter fitted to the Electra, a faulty approach technique in which the autopilot was used in the heading mode, the lack of adequate approach lighting to Runway 22, marginal weather in the approach area, and the possibility of a sensory illusion that the aircraft was higher than it actually was, resulting from visual reference to the few lights in the approach area – a not uncommon phenomenon when making an approach over water at night in restricted visibility.

On the new type of drum pointer altimeter fitted to the Electra, hundreds of feet were indicated by a single radial pointer, with thousands of feet shown on a rotating drum viewed through a "window' in the face of the dial. Readings of less than 1000 feet were emphasised by a crosshatching on the drum adjacent to the figures.

Interpreting this type of altimeter requires first noting the number below the index on the drum for the thousand foot level, then the radial pointer for the hundreds of feet. In level flight or at low rates of climb or descent where the drum is almost station-

The Electra was very much a "pilot's aeroplane". One of the reasons for its great responsiveness is evident in these two pictures – the massive 3.8m four-bladed propellers, driven by Allison 501D turbine engines, swept a powerful slipstream over an unusually high proportion of the total wing area, while the generous flap area made for highly flexible approach characteristics. (Lockheed & John Vogel)

ary, care has to be taken to associate the correct "thousands" reading with the "hundreds" reading. A dangerous misinterpretation could occur at low level if a pilot mistakenly associated the pointer indication with the "1" slightly above the drum index, rather than the "0" below it. The result, for example, could be an erroneous reading of 1800 feet, rather than 800 feet as actually indicated.

American Airlines had used conventional three-pointer altimeters in the training of their initial Electra crews, and the investigators believed that, unfamiliar as they were with the new type of altimeter, a misinterpretation could have occurred under the conditions of the restricted visibility approach on this occasion. As a result of the East River accident,

the FAA temporarily raised Electra landing minimums pending the re-installation of conventional three-pointer altimeters

The CAB recommended that the Civil Aeronautics Administration (today the Federal Aviation Administration or FAA) establish autopilot approach criteria and limitations applicable to all air carriers, taking into account the type of autopilot used, the aircraft involved, and the approach facilities available. The CAB also recommended that all air carriers develop simulator training programs before introducing new types of aircraft that required substantially different operating techniques. Finally the CAB suggested that all large air transport turbine aircraft be equipped with flight recorders.

Another of Lockheed's pre-production Electras during a proving flight off the coast of California. The type's evaluation program included an around-the-world test flight. (Lockheed)

Although there was some public uneasiness about the fact that an Electra had been involved in a fatal accident only a matter of days after its introduction to airline service, the investigation completely exonerated the airworthiness of the radically new turboprop, and its glowing reputation remained largely unaffected.

For the following eight months, Electras, now being operated by airlines in the US and overseas, continued to build on their reputation for fast, smooth and economical operation. Passenger reaction was extremely favourable, crews enjoyed the aircraft's performance and responsive handling characteristics, and airlines operating the Electra rejoiced in the fact that its operating economics even exceeded the manufacturer's specification.

The Electra's wide flightdeck offered the pilots comfortable working space, with power levers provided for both captain and first officer positions. The crew included a flight engineer, who occupied a centre seat, giving him access to all engine and system controls. (Lockheed)

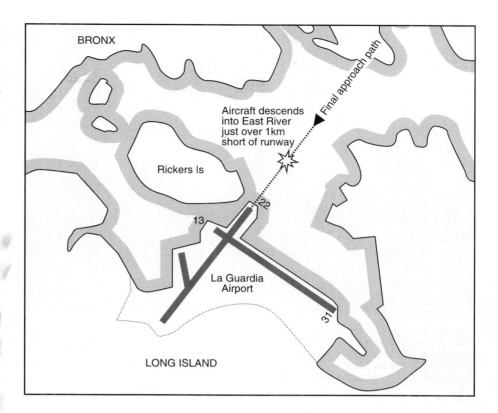

Diagram illustrating the approach of American Airlines' Electra N6101A to La Guardia Airport at the conclusion of a scheduled flight from Chicago in poor weather on the night of February 3, 1959. Finally cleared for an instrument approach to Runway 22 after being held for nearly an hour because of fluctuating visibility, the aircraft descended into the East River more than a kilometre short of the runway threshold. The major US airline had inaugurated its Electra services only 12 days previously. (Aero Illustrations)

Few technical difficulties came to light as operational experience accumulated on the type. The most serious was the finding that the outboard propellers became more highly stressed than the inboard as the airspeed increased because of a change in inflow angle resulting from slight torsional downward bending of the wing. Aboard the aircraft, this was felt chiefly as excessive vibration in the passenger seats situated in the plane of the propellers. After a thorough investigation of the problem, Lockheed overcame it with a modification that altered the incidence of the engine nacelles on the wing three degrees upwards. The inboard nacelles were similarly modified to reduce vibration in the cabin. The manufacturer bore the cost of the modification program which amounted to $7 million for the near 100 Electras now in service.

One other modification required was the reinforcement of the wing upper skin inboard and outboard of the inboard engine nacelles carrying the main undercarriage legs, to better withstand landing impact loads. And a problem was also encountered as a result of faulty procedures during pressurised refuelling operations on one Electra. Because the fuel inlet valve was left open after a tank was filled, the pressurised fuel line caused some deformation of the integral wing tank structure.

But on the night of September 29, 1959, all the public and airline industry approbation that held the Electra in such high regard was to change forever.

At Houston, Texas, Braniff Airways' Electra N9705C, was being prepared for the company's Flight 542 to New York via Dallas and Washington, DC. The aircraft, delivered by Lockheed only 10 days before, was brand new, the fifth Electra of the nine on order from Braniff, and was under the command of Captain Wilson Stone, another veteran airline pilot with more than 20,000 hours flying experience.

After a 20 minute delay occasioned by a faulty generator, 28 passengers boarded the aircraft, and with a crew of six, it took off for Dallas at 10.44pm into the warm, almost clear Texas night.

At 11.05pm the Electra reported to San Antonio ATC that it was over the Leona VOR, cruising at 15,000 feet, and in accordance with ATC procedures, it was instructed to call Fort Worth on 120.8 mHz for ongoing clearance to Dallas. Immediately afterwards, the crew called Braniff Airways at Dallas on the company frequency, reporting the generator problem was solved but there were two other minor electrical problems requiring attention when the aircraft landed. This transmission, concluding at 11.07pm, was the last to come from the Electra.

A minute later, on a small property near the township of Buffalo, Texas, a farmer, in bed for the night and dozing off to sleep, was startled by a deafening, extremely high pitched screaming, something like the sound of a jet fighter. The screaming sound was superimposed over heavy metallic grinding noises.

Dashing outside, he was just in time to see a blinding yellow light that filled the sky quickly fading. Then came shrill, whistling sounds that gradually increased in intensity to a great roar, before a vast explosion and a flash of fire not far away shook the ground under his feet.

Moments later massive metallic objects came crashing to the ground behind his farmhouse. Finally there came what seemed to be a brief light shower, despite the fact that the stars were shining. But the droplets were plainly not rain – they smelt like kerosene!

Grabbing a torch, the farmer shone it towards where some of the debris had fallen. Strewn over the ground were pieces of fragmented aluminium and torn yellow plastic foam that looked like acoustic insulation. And caught in the branches of a big tree beyond them was the battered and broken off tail assembly of a huge aircraft. "Fly Braniff" the lettering on the fin and rudder read.

The team of CAB investigators that descended on the little Texas

The rear fuselage and tail section of the Electra being raised from the icy waters of the East River during the investigation of the near-inexplicable accident. Of the 68 passengers and five crew members on board, only eight were rescued, most of them by a tug that happened to be passing at the time of the crash. Others who survived the impact succumbed to hypothermia before they could be pulled from the water. (UPI/Bettman)

farm at first light, found the main impact crater only 70 metres from where the farmer saw the Electra's broken tailcone in the tree. Buried within it was the fragmented nose section, including the remains of the flightdeck, some forward fuselage structure, and that of a few passenger seats. Back in the direction from which the Electra had come, close to the suspended tailcone, were the fragmented remains of the centre fuselage.

Other major items of wreckage were found further back along the flightpath – a portion of the starboard wing more than 500m away, the port and starboard elevators 1250m and 620m away respectively, the port wing 2600m away, and the No 1 engine and gearbox more than 3000m away.

To the investigators, it was clear from the entire wreckage distribution pattern that there had been an inflight failure of the port wing, followed by a disintegration of the aircraft under the effect of aerodynamic forces. But what had brought about the initial failure?

Numerous witnesses on the ground that night had heard a sound like that of jet fighter, or a propeller running at supersonic speed, then seen an apparent explosion in the air which they described as an electric arc, or a huge exploding flashbulb, followed by a flash of fire.

Did the wing fail because of this supposed explosion? Or was the flash of fire the result of fuel spilling from an already ruptured wing?

There was no indication in the wreckage of structural failure having resulted from metal fatigue. Nor was there any suggestion of an inherent structural weakness in the design. And the weather throughout the night remained fine; partly cloudy, but with no turbulence, no thunderstorms or lightning, and no rain.

Could an uncontrollable fire have broken out in the No 2 engine, weakening the wing structure to the extent that it failed?

One possible source of inflight fire was thought to be the magnesium cased port side starter compressor, mounted in the rear section of the No 2 engine nacelle. Other fire sources considered were an overheated wheel brake, or a landing wheel tyre blowout that could have ignited hydraulic fluid spilling from severed hydraulic lines.

But if such a fire had developed from any of these causes, why had the crew not transmitted a MAYDAY call? Could the structural failure be put down to sabotage?

Following established air accident investigation techniques, a "reconstruction" of pertinent sections of the aircraft structure from the fragmented wreckage was undertaken in a Dallas warehouse. This established quite positively that the inflight fire had occurred *after* the structural failure, and not as a result of it, thus ruling out all the possible explanations so far put forward. It also established that the wing failure had occurred close to the fuselage as a result of powerful torsional forces.

Other possible explanations considered were earlier damage to the wing structure as a result of tank over-filling during pressure refuelling, a runaway engine or

Braniff Airways took delivery of a total of nine Electras. Its fourth aircraft, N9704C (pictured), entered service only shortly before the ill-fated N9705C. Braniff's fifth Electra broke up in flight enroute from Houston to Dallas, Texas, on the night of September 29, 1959, only 10 days after being delivered, and eight months after the type had begun airline operations.

propeller, or some type of control problem that resulted in the Electra entering a high speed dive.

But the wreckage examination could support none of these theories, and from a plot of the probable wreckage trajectories, it was evident that the structural failure had begun when the Electra was still at its cruising altitude of 15,000 feet. There was also evidence that the No 1 propeller, which had separated from its engine, had been precessing or "wobbling" as much as 35° from its normal plane of rotation before it did so.

After six months of intensive, painstaking work, CAB investigators were ready to admit they had nowhere else to turn. An Electra wing had failed in cruising flight, yet all the assembled evidence could offer no explanation for it. Indeed, that same evidence showed it was almost impossible for an Electra wing to fail in the circumstances it did. The CAB could find not the slightest reason to believe there was anything amiss with the Electra design, and the investigation had certainly not revealed any basis for curtailing the type's operations in any way.

By the beginning of March 1960, the investigation of the mysterious loss of Braniff's N9705C was about to be concluded as unsolved. But by the middle of that same month another Electra air tragedy would reopen the whole wound, at the same time posing a major question mark over the entire future of Lockheed 188 Electra operations.

A flight to Florida

On the cold autumn afternoon of March 17, 1960, Northwest Airlines' Lockheed Electra, N121US, was scheduled to operate the company's Flight 710 from snowy Minneapolis, Minnesota, to Miami, Florida, via Chicago.

Captain Edgar LaParle, 57, a veteran airline pilot who had been flying for Northwest since 1937 and had more than 27,500 flying hours, was in command. With him on the flightdeck was First Officer Joseph Mills, 27, with nearly 3000 flying hours, and Flight Engineer Arnold Kowal, 40, with over 5000 flying hours. Flight Attendants Mitchell Foster, Constance Nutter

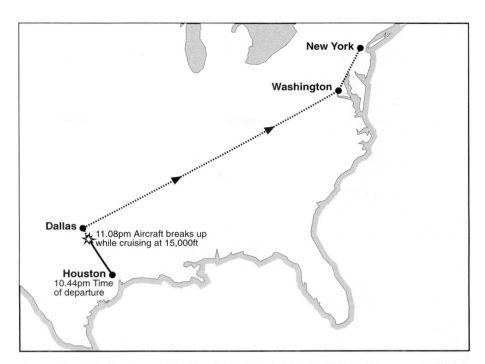

Proposed route of Braniff's Flight 542 to New York via Dallas and Washington, DC, on the night of September 29, 1959. The last transmission to come from the Electra was at 11.07pm, only a minute before the aircraft broke up, apparently in cruising flight. The aircraft transmitted no distress call, nor was there any other indication that it was in difficulties. (Aero Illustrations)

and Barbara Schreiber comprised the cabin crew.

Before departing from Minneapolis, the company's meteorologist briefed the crew on the weather they could expect along the route. There were thunderstorms in Florida, and the jet stream over the southeastern states appeared to be growing in intensity.

The wrecked tail section of Braniff's Electra N9705C, after being recovered from the branches of a tree on a farm near Buffalo, Texas. The tail section was the biggest remaining piece of the disintegrated aircraft. (United Press International)

The Electra took off at 12.50pm. Cruising at 15,000 feet at 340kt (630km/h), the flight to Chicago proceeded normally, the aircraft landing at Midway Airport at 1.55pm. Some of the passengers leaving the Electra at Chicago remarked the landing was hard; others felt it was quite normal.

The aircraft was on the ground at Chicago for 30 minutes. While it was being refuelled, Captain LaParle went to the company operations office to review the latest weather information on the flight on to Miami.

A low pressure area was centred over the northern portion of the lower peninsula of Michigan, while a troughline at all altitudes extended southwards from this low along the Illinois-Indiana border. The wind change across the troughline varied between 30° and 60°, generally increasing with altitude. A ridge of high pressure extended from the southern plains northeastwards across Arkansas, western Tennessee, central Kentucky, and into southern Ohio. There was a broken to overcast cloud deck extending south from the Chicago area into Indiana, with an average base of 1500 feet. Above this was a second broken to overcast layer with a base of

FLIGHT ENGINEERS LOG

The fire-damaged Flight Engineer's Log, recovered from the scattered wreckage of the Electra at Buffalo. The last entry was made at 11pm, only eight minutes before the inflight disintegration. The aircraft was cruising at 15,000ft at the time and all engine indications appeared normal. (Civil Aeronautics Board)

about 4000 feet, with its tops around 7500 feet near Chicago but reducing to 5000 and 6000 feet further south. Generally clear conditions prevailed above these clouds, with unrestricted visibility. The available weather forecasts made no mention of the possibility of clear air turbulence.

The crew's flightplan for the trip from Midway Airport to Miami specified a cruising altitude of 18,000 feet, a true airspeed of 337kt (624km/h), and an estimated time interval of 3 hours, 37 minutes.

With 57 passengers on board, including one child, the Electra left Chicago at 2.38pm. Its gross weight was calculated as 107,661 pounds (48,878kg), well within the maximum takeoff weight of 110,590 pounds (50,208kg), and its centre of gravity was within prescribed limits.

At 2.45pm, it reported to Indianapolis Control that it was over Milford, Illinois, at 18,000 feet, estimating Scotland, Indiana, at 3.12pm. Almost on time at 3.13pm, the Electra reported over Scotland. It was maintaining 18,000 feet, and estimating Bowling Green, Kentucky, at 3.35pm. Acknowledging the position report, Indianapolis Control instructed the Electra to contact Memphis Control on 124.6 mHz at 3.30pm.

It did not do so, and then failed to reply to a number of calls from both Indianapolis and Memphis Control. The aircraft had transmitted no distress calls, nor was there any other indication that it could have been experiencing difficulties.

At about 3.15pm that afternoon, numbers of people on the ground in the vicinity of the neighbouring towns of Tell City and Cannelton, Indiana, on the Ohio River about 100km southwest of the city of Louisville, noticed a Lockheed Electra passing overhead at high altitude on a southerly heading. The day was cold, with about 30cm of snow lying on the ground, but the weather remained clear except for scattered cumulus clouds at about 4000 feet. Visibility was good.

Suddenly, two puffs of white smoke were seen to come from the aircraft, followed seconds later by a big cloud of dark smoke. Then came the sound of two loud explosions, and a large object dropped out of the smoke, trailing smoke and flame, and fell almost vertically to the ground. Smaller objects were then seen falling.

The aircraft appeared to continue in level flight for a few seconds, before descending in an increasingly steep trajectory. It finally plunged into soft ground and exploded on a farm about 10km east of Cannelton and just over a kilometre north of the Ohio River. So great was the impact that debris and mud were thrown nearly 250 feet into the air.

At 4.40pm, Northwest Airlines' headquarters at Minneapolis received telephoned reports that its Flight 710 had crashed near Cannelton. The wreckage appeared to be widely scattered and there was no possibility that any of the aircraft's occupants could have survived.

★   ★   ★

Wreckage Distribution

The fuselage and tail, with the port wing and the No 2 engine and propeller still attached, had plunged into the ground almost vertically, in a soft, half acre field of soya beans in a small valley. The enormous impact and explosion hurled small pieces of wreckage in all directions for up to 500m and dug a crater four metres deep and more than 10 metres in diameter.

Only a few fragments of wreckage were visible in the bottom of the crater, most of the aircraft structure having disintegrated and been buried. A shallow depression extended southwards from the crater for five metres. Fragments of the port wing lay in it, while

With American Airlines and Eastern Air Lines, Minneapolis based Northwest Airlines was one of the three principal operators of Electras in the US. The picture shows Northwest's N123US, one of the 18 the company purchased, and delivered only a short time after N121US entered service. At the time of its inflight breakup at 18,000ft over Indiana, N121US was less than eight months old and had flown only 1786 hours. A troughline lay along the Illinois-Indiana border on the autumn afternoon of the accident, with unforecast clear air turbulence.

portions of the fin and tailplane were embedded in the rim of the crater. A smouldering fire burnt in the bottom of the crater for several days after the accident until extinguished during the excavation of wreckage.

A survey of the accident area from a helicopter disclosed that the main portion of the starboard wing, both outboard engines and propellers (Nos 1 and 4), and many small pieces of wreckage lay widely scattered to the north and northeast of the impact site. The starboard wing was nearly three and a half kilometres northeast, while the Nos 1 and 4 engines and their respective propellers, with their reduction gears, were found in four separate pieces within 600m of the wing. Scattered parts of both wings and the outboard nacelles were distributed along a path 11km long.

Airborne witnesses

At the time of the accident, six USAF aircraft – three KC-l35 tank-ers and three B-52 bombers – were conducting a refuelling exercise in the area at between 31,000 and 32,000 feet.

Visibility was good and the crews first sighted the smoke left by the disintegrating Electra at 3.32pm. At an altitude estimated to be about 25,000 feet, there was a cloud of smoke the shape of a child's spinning top, dark in colour as if produced by burning fuel, with a corkscrew shaped base partly obscured by scattered cumulostratus clouds. A horizontal streamer of dark smoke extended a considerable distance north from it.

The USAF crews were 26nm (48km) to the north-northwest when they first sighted the smoke. Their own aircrafts' heading of 170°M was nearly parallel to the Electra's track, and they passed abeam the smoke cloud at 3.39pm, by which time they were about 12nm (22km) to its west. During the seven minutes that elapsed from their first sighting of the smoke, the cloud and streamer retained their original form, with little indication of breaking up.

During the afternoon of the accident, from after 1pm until around 6pm, crews of a number of other aircraft, both airline and military, flying in the general area of the forecast troughline along the Illinois-Indiana border and up to 80nm to its east, reported unforecast moderate to severe clear air turbulence between 15,000 and 25,000 feet. Some of these aircraft were forced to reduce speed and descend because of the severe airspeed fluctuations and turbulence they were encountering.

Wreckage examination

The wreckage and its distribution showed that the complete starboard wing, the Nos 3 and 4 engines, propellers and engine support structures, the outer section of the port wing, the No 1 engine nacelle, and the outboard section of the port elevator, had

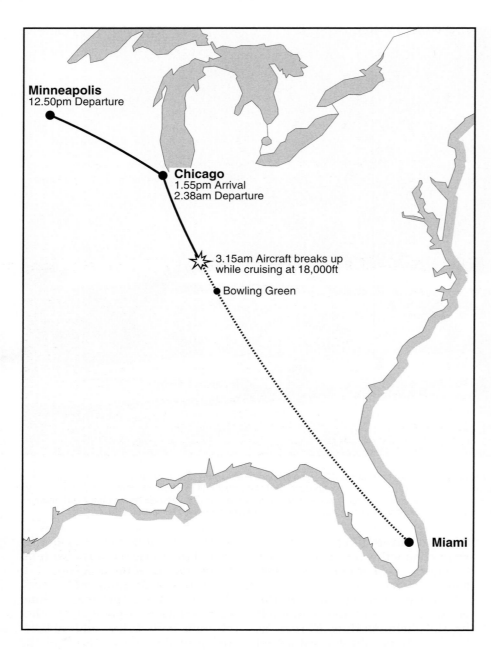

Minneapolis
12.50pm Departure

Chicago
1.55pm Arrival
2.38am Departure

3.15am Aircraft breaks up
while cruising at 18,000ft

Bowling Green

Miami

amination disclosed no evidence of fatigue cracking, substandard material, overtorquing of nuts, or missing attachments. But they did yield evidence as to the direction of the loads that produced the failures.

Where the starboard wing separated from the aircraft between the fuselage and the inboard nacelle, there was a shattering of the upper and lower wing planks, with many pieces falling to the ground separately. The long upper and lower aluminium planks in the Electra's wing structure form spanwise stiffeners integral with the wing skin. In the lower plank, irregular sawtoothed fracture lines indicated repeated loading reversals during the breakup, with laboratory examination revealing evidence of both tension and compression, resulting from alternate upward and downward loadings of the wing.

The first component of the wing's No 4 engine support to fail was the upper port attachment to the firewall, which did so in tension. The front of the engine support then moved downwards and to the right, rotating with the propeller until it broke away. The mountings supporting the propeller reduction gearbox were found to have been damaged by abnormal loadings in various directions.

A "reconstruction" of the port wing disclosed that from an irregular fracture line outboard of the engine nacelles, the outer wing and a section of the aileron fragmented and separated from the aircraft in flight. But the bulk of the port wing and flap remained attached to the fuselage until the aircraft plunged into the ground. The fracture of the outer wing had resulted from the fuel in the partly filled outboard tank being violently rammed into its outer end by high gyrational forces as the aircraft broke up. Similar but lesser damage was found at the outer end of the starboard wing.

separated very rapidly from the aircraft in flight. So severely damaged was the wreckage that detailed study was necessary to identify the nature of the failures.

This Electra, like Braniff Airways' N9705C that crashed in Texas during the night flight to Dallas less than six months before, was a near new aircraft. Less than eight months old, it had flown a total of only 1786 hours. Having undergone a major inspection a mere eight days before the accident, it had spent only 74 hours in the air since that time.

In the 14 months since the type was introduced to airline service, no less than three new Electras had now been lost. Public confidence in the type was rapidly evaporating, and both the US press generally and certain members of Congress were now calling for the Electra's grounding pending further investigation of the type's airworthiness.

In this unfavourable climate, all the pieces of aircraft structure recovered from the vicinities of Tell City and Cannelton were taken to the Lockheed Aircraft Corporation at Burbank for detailed examination and testing. Meanwhile, what was left of the engine and propeller assemblies were taken to the Allison works at Indianapolis.

The numerous pieces of wreckage subjected to metallurgical ex-

The 10m diameter crater, formed in the soft earth of an Indiana farm when the fuselage and port wing of the Electra plunged into the ground 10km east of the town of Cannelton. The impact hurled wreckage in all directions for up to 500m. Fire smouldered in the crater for several days after the accident. (United Press International)

Damage to the No 1 engine support showed that the lower starboard fitting aft of the firewall failed in tension first, allowing the front of the engine support to move upwards and to the left until it separated from the nacelle. Again laboratory examination of the mountings supporting the propeller reduction gearbox disclosed evidence of abnormal loadings in various directions, with numerous curved scratches indicating large cyclic motions of the engine relative to the wing before the engine support structure broke away.

There was no fire damage to any of the engine assemblies. All the propeller blades were found in the vicinity of their respective hubs, with the exception of the No 2 propeller, dug from the main crater together with the remains of the No 2 engine assembly.

Re-evaluation of the Electra design

As a precautionary measure three days after the accident, the FAA issued an emergency airworthiness regulation reducing the Electra's normal operations speed (V_{no}) from 324kt (600km/h) to 275kt (510km/h). But a week later, because the investigation indicated both this and the previous Electra accident in Texas had occurred in cruising flight near a speed of 275kt (510km/h), a second FAA emergency regulation further limited the V_{no} to 225kt (420km/h) and established a new never exceed speed (V_{ne}) of 245kt (454km/h). A comprehensive structural inspection of all Electras in service, including an internal examination of the entire wing, was also to be carried out.

At the same time, the FAA requested Lockheed to conduct an engineering re-evaluation of the Electra with the objective of detecting any design or operational characteristics that could possibly produce structural effects more critical than those originally pro-

vided for. The comprehensive program encompassed flight tests, structural investigations, aerodynamic investigations, wind tunnel experiments and design studies. In carrying out this re-evaluation, Lockheed had assistance from NASA, Boeing, Douglas, and other organisations. A similar program was also carried out on the engine and propeller designs.

The engineering re-evaluation revealed two discrepancies in the design of the Electra:
• Loads imposed on the wing ribs between the fuselage and outboard nacelles by wing skin distortion had not been included in the design loads.
• The response of the outboard nacelles to turbulence was different from that provided for in the original design, with the result

that torsional loading of the wing inboard section was increased.

In addition, it was found that if the stiffness of an engine assembly installation became reduced, for example through damage, normal propeller oscillations could become destructive at the cruising speed of the Electra at the time of the accident.

ANALYSIS

Meteorological evidence showed that severe clear air turbulence was highly probable at the time of the accident, and the Civil Aeronautics Board believed that both the US Weather Bureau and Northwest Airlines should have mentioned the likelihood of clear air turbulence in their forecasts.

Trajectory studies of the wreckage indicated that the Electra was

in level flight at 18,000 feet, on a track of 170°T at an IAS of about 260kt (480km/h) when the disintegration began. The first parts to separate were pieces of the starboard wing upper surface just outboard of the fuselage. The engine assembly and wing disintegrations then followed within six to 10 seconds, taking place almost simultaneously.

Although the engine assemblies themselves showed no evidence of any malfunction which could have contributed to the accident, the similar structural failures within Nos 1 and 4 engines had been brought about by abnormal loads. Aluminium deposits on the thermocouples and turbine inlet guide vanes of these engines had resulted from air inlet and compressor case distortion after disruption of the engine supporting structure, so that loads normally taken by the structure were imposed on the engine itself.

Overall, the examination of the wreckage narrowed the significant inflight structural failures to the outboard engine support structures and the inboard portion of the starboard wing. *These were the components which appeared to have been involved in the catastrophic disintegration of the aircraft.*

Damage progression

The outboard engine support structures showed additional evidence of cycling damage indicative of the propellers having oscillated violently for a short time, causing a rapid progression of damage to the supporting structure before its gross displacement and disintegration.

Damage to the starboard wing structure between the fuselage and the inboard nacelle disclosed numerous indications of damage progression during rapid reversals of loading. The irregularly saw-toothed diagonal fracture lines in the wing's lower plank offered further evidence of reversing loads, both bending and torsional, and this type of damage progression was consistent only with catastrophic flutter.

All the flutter tests and analyses made by Lockheed during the original certification process and the re-evaluation showed the Electra to be flutter-free at and above normal operating speeds. It further disclosed that the Electra wing had a high degree of inherent damping and that an oscillating motion of the structure would die out rapidly when the exciting force was removed. The most significant damping effect was the result of opposing aerodynamic forces, absorbing energy from the oscillation. But if a major change occurred in the wing assembly that allowed the aerodynamic forces to become additive to the exciting force, the oscillation would grow and the result would be flutter.

Tests conducted during the engineering re-evaluation also produced the significant finding that on the Electra, the propeller oscillation known as "whirl mode" could, under certain conditions, induce such wing oscillations. In other words, the re-evaluation showed that a "wobbling" outboard propeller, resulting from a weakened nacelle structure, could lead to flutter and structural disintegration

"Whirl mode"

Because a propeller has gyroscopic characteristics, it will tend to stay in its plane of rotation until displaced by some external force such as turbulence or an abrupt manoeuvre. And when such a force is applied, the propeller reacts in the same way as a gyroscope, its plane of rotation tending to precess or "wobble". This effect on a propeller is called "whirl mode" and its direction of "wobble" is opposite to that of the propeller's rotation.

Normally, whirl mode effect is

The starboard wing and engine nacelles of the Electra were found nearly three and a half kilometres northeast of the main impact site. Smaller pieces of wreckage lay widely scattered further to the north and northeast. (United Press International)

limited by the stiffness of the propeller's supporting structure, and is quickly dampened, especially on piston engined aircraft where the propeller is bolted to the front of the crankshaft. If, however, the stiffness of the propeller's supporting structure (which on turbo-prop aircraft is usually separate from that of the engine) has been weakened in some way, the damping effect will be correspondingly reduced.

Weakness in the propeller's mounting structure does not alter the conditions under which whirl mode can be triggered, but makes it a greater potential danger in three ways:

• The greater flexibility of a weakened support structure increases the possibility for whirl mode to develop, and allows it more freedom, so it can become more violent.

• In an already weakened installation, the increasing violence of whirl mode can further damage the supporting structure, leading progressively to more violence and further damage.

• As the structural damage increases, the amplitude of whirl mode increases.

The natural frequency of whirl mode in an Electra's propeller with an undamaged engine nacelle installation is about five cycles per second. The Electra's wing torsional frequency is about 3.5, and its wing bending frequency is about two cycles per second.

As whirl mode progresses in a damaged Electra engine-propeller installation, its frequency can reduce from five to three cycles per second, at which point it will begin to resonate with the wing in torsional and bending oscillations. These oscillations reinforce and perpetuate the whirl mode, so inducing a form of flutter. Wind tunnel tests conducted during the Electra engineering re-evaluation showed this could occur at airspeeds far below that at which classical aerodynamic flutter can develop.

On an undamaged Electra engine-propeller installation, whirl mode cannot induce wing oscillations at any speed below 120% of the design dive speed. If, however, the strength of the engine-propeller mounting structure is reduced, induced oscillations become possible at lower airspeeds. The tests showed that under these conditions, whirl mode of catastrophic proportions could develop to resonate with the wing and induce flutter in as little as 20 to 40 seconds.

The investigators now believed that whirl mode provided the driving force that destroyed the Electra's starboard wing. Yet the sequence of events that led to whirl mode becoming destructive at the Electra's normal cruising airspeed remained elusive.

Prior damage?

One possibility was that there was sufficient prior damage to the mountings in one of the outboard engine nacelles to reduce its strength to the range where, once triggered by turbulence, whirl mode became self sustaining and rapidly increased in amplitude. This possibility assumed that the damage to one of the engine-propeller mountings was severe. Yet this condition was unlikely to have escaped detection during the detailed examination of the wreckage.

Another possibility was previous damage to the wing; for example, partially disrupted ribs. Severe clear air turbulence in such a condition could conceivably result in

Newspaper photograph of the Electra's severed starboard wing lying on the snow covered Indiana ground. A broken off main undercarriage leg, with the landing wheels still attached, lies in the foreground. (Associated Press Wirephoto)

rapid progression of wing damage. This could also change the already more critical than expected response of the outboard nacelles to turbulence, as found during the engineering re-evaluation, damaging the outboard engine-propeller support structures sufficiently to allow whirl mode to become self-sustaining.

The landing of the Electra at Chicago earlier on the day of the accident might well have caused damage to the wing structure, even though some of the passengers considered it a normal touchdown. In different parts of the cabin of large aircraft, passengers can experience different forces during a landing because of the flexibility of the aircraft structure Furthermore, side impacts on the undercarriage sufficient to cause structural damage are smaller than damaging vertical loads, and can occur without alarming passengers.

The investigators' conclusion

Two months after the accident in Indiana, the Civil Aeronautic Bureau's investigation finally concluded that although severe clear air turbulence contributed to the initiation of whirl mode and the resulting flutter that destroyed the starboard wing, it appeared to be insufficient to produce the nacelle damage necessary to render whirl mode self-sustaining. It seemed probable therefore, that undetected damage existed in the wing or outboard nacelles, making the effects of the turbulence more critical than on an undamaged aircraft.

This at last provided an acceptable explanation of the Cannelton accident. But what about the earlier, outwardly similar Electra accident in Texas? Was the destruction of that aircraft initiated in a similar way? Yet that breakup occurred on

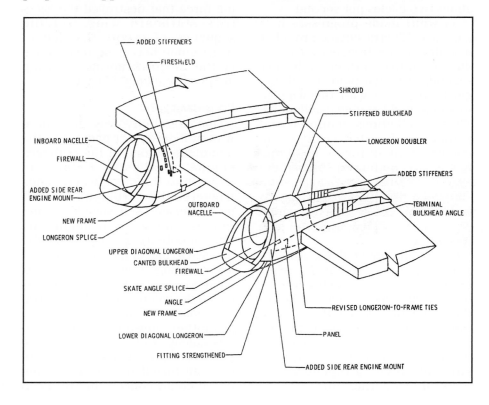

ADDED STIFFENERS
FIRESHIELD
SHROUD
STIFFENED BULKHEAD
LONGERON DOUBLER
INBOARD NACELLE
FIREWALL
ADDED STIFFENERS
ADDED SIDE REAR ENGINE MOUNT
OUTBOARD NACELLE
TERMINAL BULKHEAD ANGLE
NEW FRAME
LONGERON SPLICE
UPPER DIAGONAL LONGERON
CANTED BULKHEAD
FIREWALL
SKATE ANGLE SPLICE
ANGLE
NEW FRAME
REVISED LONGERON-TO-FRAME TIES
LOWER DIAGONAL LONGERON
PANEL
FITTING STRENGTHENED
ADDED SIDE REAR ENGINE MOUNT

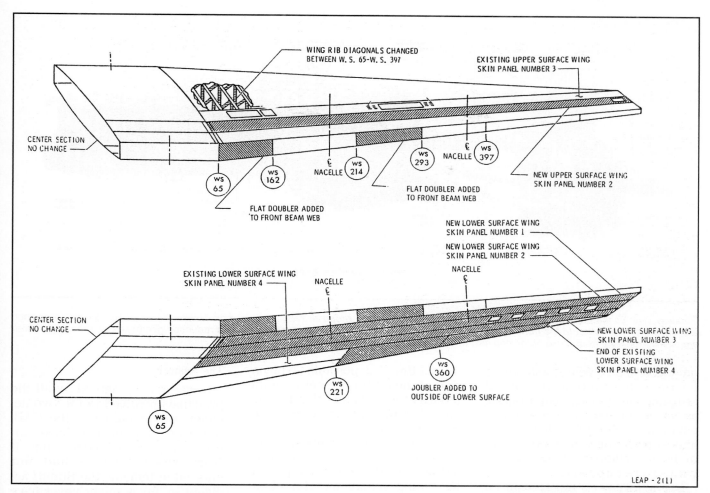

WING RIB DIAGONALS CHANGED
BETWEEN W.S. 65-W.S. 397

EXISTING UPPER SURFACE WING
SKIN PANEL NUMBER 3

CENTER SECTION
NO CHANGE

WS 65

WS 162

NACELLE

WS 214

WS 293

NACELLE

WS 397

NEW UPPER SURFACE WING
SKIN PANEL NUMBER 2

FLAT DOUBLER ADDED
TO FRONT BEAM WEB

FLAT DOUBLER ADDED
TO FRONT BEAM WEB

NEW LOWER SURFACE WING
SKIN PANEL NUMBER 1

NEW LOWER SURFACE WING
SKIN PANEL NUMBER 2

EXISTING LOWER SURFACE WING
SKIN PANEL NUMBER 4

NACELLE

NACELLE

CENTER SECTION
NO CHANGE

WS 65

WS 221

WS 360

DOUBLER ADDED TO
OUTSIDE OF LOWER SURFACE

NEW LOWER SURFACE WING
SKIN PANEL NUMBER 3

END OF EXISTING
LOWER SURFACE WING
SKIN PANEL NUMBER 4

LEAP - 2(1)

(Opposite and this page) Structural modifications made to the Electra's engine and propeller gearbox mountings, engine nacelles, and wing structure during the Lockheed Electra Achievement Program (LEAP) which the company developed with the approval of the FAA and the CAB. The modifications, taking 20 working days per aircraft, added more than 600kg to the Electra's empty weight. Lockheed underwrote the cost of the entire the modification program. (Lockheed)

a fine and almost clear night, with no suggestion of the aircraft having encountered atmospheric turbulence

Another puzzling difference in the mode of breakup was the way in which the wings had failed. Although in both accidents, the wing failures had occurred close to the fuselage, in the earlier Braniff case, the wing had initially folded upwards, the failure having resulted from a high positive loading, in other words, apparently from a sharp pull-up. By contrast, the Northwest Electra's wing failure followed severe flutter, with the wing folding to the rear.

The finding that an Electra's engine nacelle structure had to be

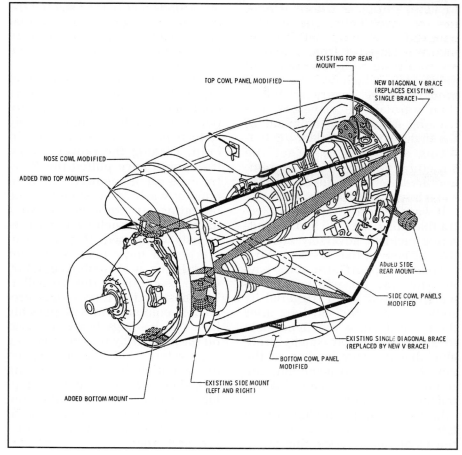

TOP COWL PANEL MODIFIED

EXISTING TOP REAR
MOUNT

NEW DIAGONAL V BRACE
(REPLACES EXISTING
SINGLE BRACE)

NOSE COWL MODIFIED

ADDED TWO TOP MOUNTS

ADDED SIDE
REAR MOUNT

SIDE COWL PANELS
MODIFIED

EXISTING SINGLE DIAGONAL BRACE
(REPLACED BY NEW V BRACE)

BOTTOM COWL PANEL
MODIFIED

EXISTING SIDE MOUNT
(LEFT AND RIGHT)

ADDED BOTTOM MOUNT

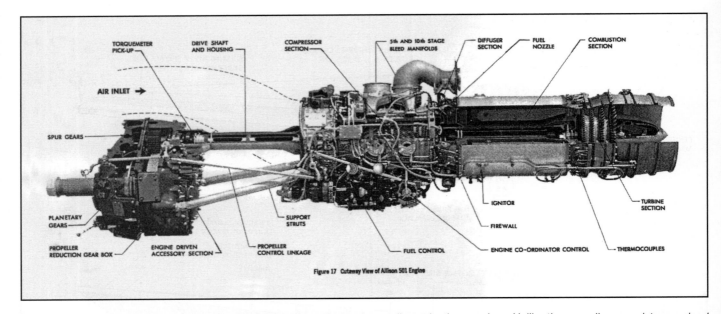

Cutaway view of the Electra's Allison 501-D13 turboprop engine and propeller reduction gearbox. Unlike the propellers on piston engined aircraft, which are bolted to the front of the engine, the supporting structure for the propellers and reduction gearboxes of turboprop aircraft are usually separate from those of the engines. (Lockheed)

damaged before whirl mode could become destructive at normal cruising speeds was also a puzzle as far as the earlier accident was concerned. Braniff's Electra was almost brand new, with no history of heavy landings or encounters with severe turbulence.

But it had been involved in an incident during a training flight just one week before the disaster over Buffalo. During that flight, an incorrect recovery from a deliberate stall resulted in a second stall developing, which was accompanied by more severe buffeting than normal. Nevertheless, the training captain in command of the flight did not consider the buffeting sufficient to affect the structural integrity of the aircraft, and he did not ask for the Electra to be inspected after the flight.

It was the port wing of this Electra that failed first. So had the buffeting incident adversely affected the stiffness of that Electra's No 1 propeller support structure, paving the way for whirl mode to manifest itself when triggered by some other factor? So long after the event itself, it was impossible to know. It seemed equally probable that a heavy landing in the new Electra could have gone unreported, as could a damaging turbulence encounter.

In the light of the findings of the later Northwest Electra accident, the Civil Aeronautics Bureau finally offered a possible explanation of the difference between the modes of wing failure that had occurred in the two otherwise similar accidents.

Witnesses to the Braniff accident in Texas had heard what seemed like the sound of a propeller "going supersonic" for about 30 seconds before they sighted the ball of fire high in the sky that clear night. So had that Electra initially been afflicted by a runaway propeller?

The investigators reasoned that the first reaction of a flightcrew, confronted with a runaway propeller, would be to immediately reduce power and slow the aircraft. Closing the power levers, they could have pulled the Electra into an immediate climb to quickly wash off airspeed. If the mounting structure in the No 1 nacelle had somehow been previously weakened, this manoeuvre would have been sufficient to trigger a destructive whirl mode reaction in the propeller. The destructive forces thus created, in combination with possibly high "G" loadings being imposed on the aircraft by the crew as they desperately tried to reduce speed and dampen both the alarming propeller overspeed and the rapidly escalating airframe vibration, could ultimately have been sufficient to fail the port wing structure at its root.

The answer

It was readily agreed by all the principals involved in the two accident investigations – the CAB, the FAA, and the Lockheed Aircraft Corporation itself – that if Northwest's Electra had not crashed in Indiana, the Braniff accident in Texas might never have been fully explained. But as a result of both investigations, with the enormous amount of testing, analysis and engineering re-evaluation that followed them, there could no longer be any doubt that the destructive effect of undampened propeller whirl mode was the culprit in both cases.

Lockheed, conscious of its reputation and mindful that its otherwise superb Electra had an inherent structural weakness, announced to the world that it would bear the financial responsibility of modifying every Electra that it had sold or was in production, to eliminate this Achilles' Heel. All that operators of the Electra were required to do was to meet the cost of ferrying their aircraft to and from Lockheed's plant at Burbank, California.

The modification process, called the Lockheed Electra Achievement Program (LEAP) involved a comprehensive strengthening of the engine nacelle structures, the engine and gearbox support structures, and the engine mounts themselves, while the nacelle cowlings were also modified to reduce vibration. The wings themselves were strengthened too, with heavier gauge planking on the upper and lower surfaces, heavier gauge wing ribs in critical places, and some additional internal bracing. In total, the modifications added more than 600kg to the Electra's empty weight

An exhaustive program of flight testing followed, during which several test aircraft were repeatedly pushed to their limits in a schedule lasting six months. The flight test program included deliberately inducing whirl mode, but on each occasion the increased stiffness of the wings and the nacelle mounting structure damped out the phenomenon well before it could develop to dangerous proportions.

Lockheed's extensive modification program, which cost the company $US25 million, proved entirely successful and in February 1961 the FAA lifted its speed restrictions on the Electra.

Identifying the reason for the two whirl mode accidents, finding a solution and modifying the world's entire fleet of Electra's at its own expense, justifiably enhanced Lockheed's reputation for integrity. It also finally vindicated the aircraft itself within the aviation industry.

Unfortunately, all this action would not spell the end of the Electra's accident history in the US, as the following two chapters relate. But the integrity of the Electra design would never again be in question.

Yet sadly, as far as the travelling public was concerned, the damage had been done. Its confidence in the Electra dented, the public was by now looking hopefully to the new generation airline jets. Despite a major advertising effort for the economical, high performance Electra, Lockheed was to receive no further new orders for the type.

CHAPTER 14

A flock of starlings downs an Electra

Seven months after Tell City, yet another Electra disaster sullied the reputation of the high performance turboprop that was now the butt of criticism throughout the USA. This time the operator was Eastern Air Lines, another old established domestic operator, and an Electra launch customer.

Lockheed Electra N5533 touched down at Logan International Airport, Boston, on the afternoon of October 4 1960 after a flight from New York. Refuelled and serviced, it was to leave Boston at 5.30pm for Atlanta via Philadelphia, Charlotte, and Greenville.

In command was 59 year old Captain Curtis Fitts, a pilot for Eastern since 1934, with more than 23,000 hours. Fitts' crew also represented the level of experience expected on a large aircraft of major US airline: First Officer Martin Calloway, with Eastern for seven years, had nearly 6000 hours, while Flight Engineer Malcolm had nearly 8000. He was also an experienced ground engineer. Two stewardesses, Patricia Davies and Joan Berry, completed the crew.

In preparation for the flight, the crew lodged an IFR flightplan, cruising at 10,000 feet. Sixty seven passengers boarded the aircraft and at 5.35pm it taxied from the terminal. The weather was fine, with layers of scattered cloud at 6000 feet, a visibility of 15 miles,

and wind from the southeast at 11 knots.

Taxiing to the threshold of Runway 09 for an easterly takeoff that would take the Electra over the waters of Winthrop Bay, the crew were passed their airways clearance, and at 5.39pm the tower cleared them for takeoff.

The takeoff was uneventful at first, with a normal rotation, initial climb and undercarriage retraction. But suddenly a puff of grey smoke came from the port engines and the Electra momentarily veered left before resuming the runway heading. Seconds later, at a height of less than 200 feet, the aircraft swung hard to the left and, still nose-high, sank to about half the height it had gained. Steeply nose-up, it then rolled to the left, the nose dropped, and it plunged into the bay, striking the water between moored yachts about 200 metres from shore.

The rear fuselage broke off, spilling passengers and their seats into the cold water and floating for a short time. But the major section of the aircraft disappeared

immediately, taking most of those on board to the bottom with it. Small craft that swarmed to the scene plucked 10 survivors from amongst the floating wreckage. Among them were the Electra's two flight attendants. Nine of the survivors were seriously injured.

Investigation

As darkness fell, a large number of dead birds were found to the left of Runway 09 where the Electra had begun its initial climb. Scattered over an area 130 metres long and 65 metres wide, were the remains of about 80 starlings, killed only a short time before.

Meanwhile, at the scene of the accident, a US Coast Guard vessel took over from the volunteer rescuers, guarding the impact area throughout the hours of darkness and making what efforts it could to recover wreckage. Full scale salvage operations by the Navy began the following morning.

A number of witnesses told how the Electra lifted off after a run of about 800 metres along the 2140 metre runway, flying level at 30 to

40 feet for a hundred metres or so before establishing a climb. After the undercarriage retracted, several witnesses saw a puff of grey smoke come from No 1 engine while others saw fire from No 2 engine.

Describing the aircraft's speed as 'very slow', they saw it veer to the left, then return to its original heading during its brief climb. Two took photographs of it, the first picture showing the Electra heading 030°M at a height of 120 feet. It was about 2000 metres down the runway, but displaced about 400 metres to the north. With a body angle of about 9°, it was banked 8.5° to the left. The second photograph, taken a second later, showed the aircraft at the same height and on the same heading, but both the body angle and bank had increased to 14°.

Witnesses said the Electra then did what looked like a 'wingover', the nose attitude increasing as the port wing dropped nearly vertical. The nose then fell rapidly, and the aircraft dived into the water, still rolling to the left. Only 48 seconds had elapsed from the beginning of takeoff.

Three pilots in an Aero Commander on final approach for Runway 15 had an unobstructed view of the Electra's takeoff. They were watching it closely because the Electra had to be clear of the Runway 09-15 intersection before they touched down. They first saw it as it passed the intersection when their Aero Commander was at about 400 feet. Already airborne, the Electra was beginning a left turn well before crossing the end of the runway. It was also excessively noseup. Either a puff of smoke or flame came from the Electra's No 2 nacelle shortly after it passed Runway 15.

Nine of the Electra's 10 survivors corroborated the observations of all these witnesses. Both flight attendants, seated on the left of the lounge for the takeoff, felt vibration shortly after becoming airborne, and both recalled a sudden burst of power as they realised the aircraft was in trouble. Both felt a sharp left turn and one heard the engines become unsynchronised.

Eastern Air Lines Lockheed Electra N5533 immediately after taking off from Logan International Airport's Runway 09 at Boston on the afternoon of October 4 1960. Already the aircraft is in serious trouble. After a normal rotation and undercarriage retraction, grey smoke came from the port engines and the Electra veered left before resuming the runway heading. Seconds later, the aircraft swung hard left and, still nose-high, sank to about half the height it had gained. Seconds after this picture was taken, it rolled left and plunged into Boston Harbour. (Associated Press)

Four surviving passengers spoke of a sharp, flat turn to the left shortly after becoming airborne. One, seated amidships on the starboard side, said one of the engines on the port side shot out flames. Another, in the rear of the cabin, recalled a slight bump, unlike that of undercarriage retraction, shortly after takeoff. Looking out his starboard window he saw a 'dark smudge' pass through the propeller arc and over the engine nacelle.

A former military pilot, seated in the lounge opposite the flight attendants, told investigators "something happened" to the en-

Seeking survivors of the accident, police and other rescuers drag a portion of the wreckage of the Electra ashore in Boston Harbour's Winthrop Bay. (United Press International)

Firemen and volunteers search though the rearmost section of the Electra cabin. The rear fuselage broke off when the aircraft crashed, spilling passengers into the water. The majority of the 10 survivors were seated in this part of the aircraft. (Associated Press)

gines on the port side shortly after takeoff. He was conscious of the difference between the sound of the port and starboard engines, and estimated the skidding turn occurred five to seven seconds after lifting off.

Investigators determined the Electra struck the water almost vertically, but slightly port wing first while rolling to the left, tearing off all four engines. The undercarriage was retracted and the flaps symmetrical at their takeoff setting. There was no evidence of any control, hydraulic or electrical failure, and all damage to the airframe was the result of the Electra's plunge into the bay. The aircraft's gross weight was well below its maximum, and its load properly distributed. The Electra was just under 16 months old and had flown only 3500 hours.

All four engines and propellers were recovered. The No 1 propeller was fully feathered and the engine shut down, but the other engines were all under power at the time of impact.

Foreign matter was found in different sections of all four engines. That removed from Nos 1, 2, and 4 engines contained bird tissue and

starling feathers. There was substantially more in No 1 engine than in Nos 2 and 4, and several feathers were found in the nacelle airscoops supplying cooling air to the engines' generators and oil coolers. No bird remains were found in No 3 engine.

The No 1 emergency shutoff handle had been pulled. This handle feathers the propeller, closes the oil tank shutoff valve, and shuts off the engine's fuel flow.

Tests by the engine manufacturer demonstrated that substantial power interruptions and emissions of flame from the tailpipe could occur when birds were ingested.

Another test program, being conducted under the auspices of the FAA in Lockheed's wind tunnel at Burbank, was examining the problem of turbine engine bird ingestion generally when the accident occurred. This program now sought data pertinent to the Boston accident, and an Electra engine was fitted with a modified inlet duct to permit a controlled introduction of birds. Various numbers of starlings were then ingested

into the engine at different power settings and wind tunnel speeds.

It was found that a single bird ingestion at takeoff and cruise power settings produced a negligible effect. A two bird ingestion decreased the engine's output by 10% at takeoff power, and by 15% at cruise power after recovery.

Ingesting four starlings at takeoff power resulted in the engine's output falling below 50% for one to three seconds, and a 15% power loss after recovery. An autofeathering signal was also generated in one of the three tests. Six birds decreased the shaft horsepower by 23% after recovery, and in one instance the engine failed to recover. In another test, less than 50% power was available for four seconds. In the last four bird test, the engine flamed out, relighted, then produced 50% power after seven seconds. Autofeathering could occur in all cases.

Eight starlings ingested at takeoff power produced an autofeathering signal in all three tests conducted. In two of the tests the engine failed to recover and one test had to be terminated because of surging and overtemperature.

Analysis

The bird remains in the engines and the carcasses on the runway showed that the Electra's Nos 1, 2, and 4 engines ingested starlings when the aircraft encountered a large flock during its takeoff. Apart from possible structural damage, the bird ingestion blocked airflow, decreased compressor efficiency, and distorted the gaspath. The tests showed that an engine's efficiency could deteriorate to the point where it became unable to deliver propulsive power or became incapable of surge-free operation. Ingestion of more than three starlings could trigger the propeller's autofeathering system, cause engine flameout, or reduce the power output substantially for several seconds. Engine recovery after simultaneously ingesting eight or more starlings was unlikely.

The Electra's No 1 propeller probably autofeathered. But because autofeathering of any one propeller disarms the system, none of the others moved into the feathered position. The autofeathering of the No 1 propeller also suggested this engine was the first affected by the birds, and that it ingested at least four.

The investigators believed No 2 engine ingested about six birds, with the result that its power output was the most adversely affected. The Electra's loss of performance, together with its yaw to the left, indicated a substantial power interruption on the port side. Furthermore, witnesses saw flames coming from an engine on the port wing, several saying they were from the tailpipe of No 2 engine. Flames from the tailpipe indicated a torching relight, and it was evident that No 2 engine flamed out after ingesting the birds, but relighted and recovered power. But for as long as six to seven seconds, less than 50% power would have been available from it.

It was evident that the No 4 engine ingested fewer birds than engines 1 and 2, and its power loss was the least severe. The encounter with the starlings was taken more on the port side of the aircraft and the flightpath suggested considerable power asymmetry

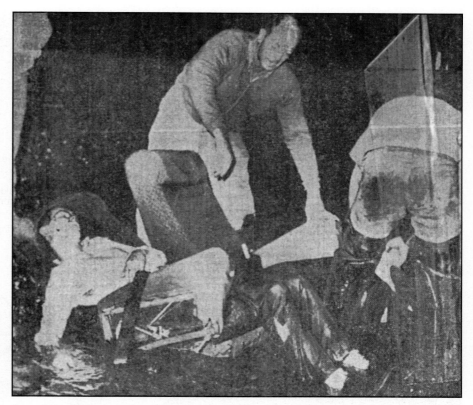

One of the Electra's passengers, still strapped into his seat, is brought ashore by rescuers. (United Press International)

with most power on the starboard side. There was no evidence that No 3 engine ingested any birds.

To study the controllability of the Electra under conditions of multiple engine failure more critical than those required for certification, the Lockheed Aircraft Corporation undertook a series of flight tests. They sought to determine V_{mc} in various angles of bank with one or two engines inoperative, and to define the maximum asymmetric power at which a heading could be maintained at a constant low airspeed.

With the No 1 propeller feathered and the other three engines developing 3800shp, V_{mc} ranged from 110 knots with 5° of right bank to 136 knots with 5° of left bank. With No 1 propeller feathered, No 2 propeller windmilling, and engines 3 and 4 each developing 3800shp, V_{mc} was found to be 125 knots with 5° of right bank and up to 154 knots with 5° of left bank.

Other tests demonstrated that, to maintain directional control with two engines inoperative on the port side, the total power output of both starboard engines

could not exceed the maximum power of a single engine.

Further study determined that the excessive yaw associated with a flat turn of small radius produces drag requiring abnormally high power to prevent the airspeed rapidly deteriorating. At 110 knots, 10° of bank, and a turning radius of 2000 feet, the power required would be more than available. The radius of the Electra's flat turn from its takeoff direction on to a north-easterly heading was less than 2000 feet.

Calculations based on the two photographs taken by witnesses produced an airspeed of 118 knots at the time of the first photograph and 103 knots in the second. During the one second interval between the two photographs, the aircraft was approaching the stall at the rate of about 15 knots per second, and at the time of the second photograph, was already below its stall speed of 108 knots at the aircraft's weight, flap extension, and attitude.

Extreme yaw angles also result in the fuselage shielding one wing from the airflow, while a skidding turn reduces the lift generated by the shielded wing. Together with

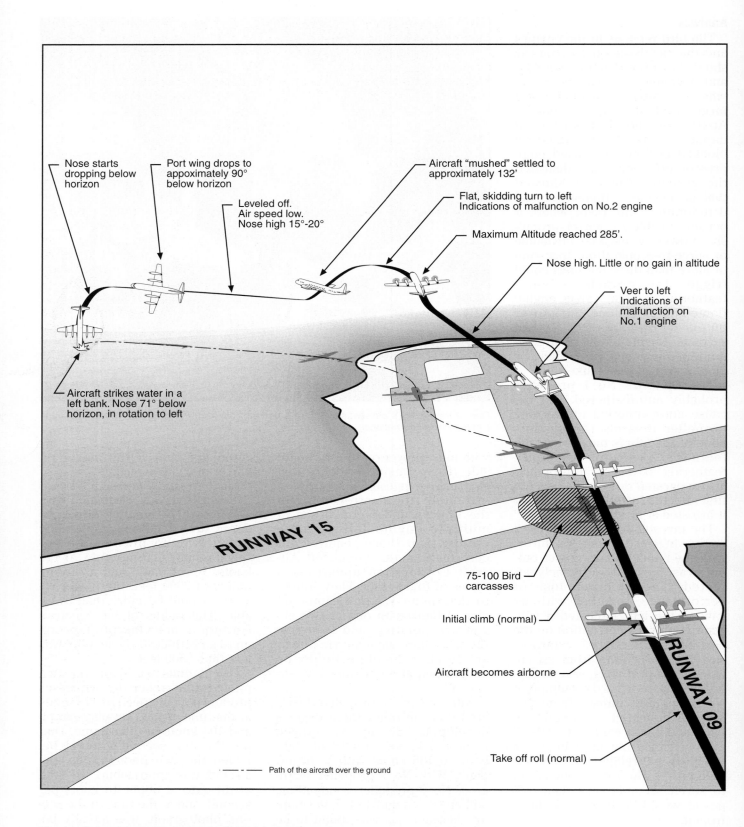

Nose starts dropping below horizon

Port wing drops to appoximately 90° below horizon

Leveled off. Air speed low. Nose high 15°-20°

Aircraft "mushed" settled to approximately 132'

Flat, skidding turn to left Indications of malfunction on No.2 engine

Maximum Altitude reached 285'.

Nose high. Little or no gain in altitude

Veer to left Indications of malfunction on No.1 engine

Aircraft strikes water in a left bank. Nose 71° below horizon, in rotation to left

RUNWAY 15

75-100 Bird carcasses

Initial climb (normal)

Aircraft becomes airborne

RUNWAY 09

Take off roll (normal)

——— - ——— Path of the aircraft over the ground

Diagram illustrating the Electra's takeoff, flightpath and plunge into the waters of Boston Harbour, as described by eye witnesses. The aircraft struck the flock of starlings just before it reached the Runway 15 intersection. (Aero Illustrations)

the additional lift resulting from the increased slipstream over the unshielded wing, this produces a rolling tendency. The condition could normally be countered by opposite aileron and rudder, but at low airspeeds, a point could be reached where the tendency to roll becomes greater than the countering effect of the control surfaces.

To explore the difficulties faced by the Electra crew, the investigators devised a series of simulator tests. "Flown" by qualified Electra pilots, they demonstrated that the control problems which suddenly confronted the crew could well have been insurmountable.

The total time from the beginning of takeoff to impact was only 47.5 seconds, and the Electra was in the air for approximately 27.5 seconds. It was evident that the aircraft struck the birds about six seconds after lift-off, so allowing one second for the ingestions, the engines would have taken another six seconds to recover power. This left only 14.5 seconds before impact and, as three seconds of this would have been occupied by the aircraft's uncontrollable plunge into the bay, the interval available to the crew for corrective action was extremely brief indeed.

From all the evidence, the investigators concluded that about seven seconds after lift-off, engines Nos 1, 2, and 4 ingested sufficient numbers of birds to cause a loss of power, and that Nos 2 and 4 recovered six seconds later. But they believed the key to the disaster lay in the critical sequence of events that rapidly followed.

The fact that No 1 propeller autofeathered rather than an inboard propeller was unfortunate in that it increased the power asymmetry that was to follow. The flameout of the No 2 engine, coupled with only a partial loss of power on No 4, then placed the

aircraft in the condition of having no power on the port side but substantial power on the starboard side. The severe yaw to the left was aggravated by No 4 engine recovering full power before the relight of No 2 engine.

The high yaw angle produced so much drag that the recovery of No 2 engine was unable to prevent a rapid loss of airspeed. And though No 2 engine's recovery reduced the power asymmetry, it could not compensate for the high power being delivered by the two starboard engines. With this asymmetric condition continuing to produce yaw and roll to the left, coupled with the effects of roll resulting from the yaw, and with the aircraft rapidly approaching a stall, control effectiveness quickly deteriorated. As a result the aircraft rolled further to the left, stalled, and entered a spin.

The birds probably also struck the windscreen and blocked the pitot heads. The noise of the bird

strikes, the reduction in visibility, with the possible loss of airspeed indication, would have been highly distracting to pilots in an already critical situation.

The investigators concluded that an emergency of great complexity was suddenly thrust upon the crew, with insufficient time and height in which to take action to recover control.

For the Lockheed Corporation, Electra operators worldwide, and the travelling public generally, there was at least the satisfaction that the investigation found no sign of any structural failure or mechanical malfunction in the aircraft type that could have contributed to the accident.

Prominent among the investigation's findings was the recommendation that the FAA initiate a research program to improve the tolerance of turbine engines to bird ingestion, and that a study be made of ways of preventing birds entering turbine engines.

The rear fuselage and tail section of the Electra being raised from Boston Harbour. Most of the survivors were seated in this part of the aircraft. (Associated Press)

CHAPTER 15

A needless tragedy waiting to happen

Lockheed Electras had experienced their share of problems since Eastern Air Lines first introduced the type to airline service in 1959. But modifications to the wing and engine mountings had been thought to overcome early structural shortcomings. Even so, another horrific accident, just after takeoff at Chicago, once more appeared to call the integrity of the design into question.

A recently delivered Lockheed Electra, N137US, was operating Northwest Airlines' scheduled service from Milwaukee to Miami, with intermediate stops at Chicago, Tampa and Fort Lauderdale, on the morning of September 17 1961.

The crew flying the first leg of the service that morning, designated Flight 706, were the same ones who had brought the Electra to Milwaukee the previous afternoon. They were going off duty when they landed at Chicago's O'Hare Airport shortly after 9am.

Arriving at O'Hare Airport, the aircraft was given normal turnaround servicing and a preflight inspection. A new crew, under the command of Captain Ralph Hagstrom, came aboard and, at 9.50am, with 32 passengers under the care of two young flight attendants, the Electra was despatched for its next leg to Tampa. The weather was fine and mild, but hazy, with a visibility of 10km and a southerly wind of eight

knots (15km/h). The Electra was cleared for takeoff while taxiing, and after turning on to the threshold of Runway 14R took off into the southeast.

The takeoff appeared normal until the aircraft attained a height of about 100 feet, some 2500 metres down the runway, when there was a slight change in the sound of its engines. Still climbing, the Electra then began a gentle turn to the right with its bank angle slowly increasing. When this angle reached about 35°, with the aircraft at a height of between 200 and 300 feet, there was a brief, garbled radio transmission from the aircraft, and it began to lose height.

Within moments, now banked more than 50° to the right in a tightening turn, its starboard wing struck 38,000 volt high tension powerlines carried on 20 metre high towers adjacent to the railway embankment bordering the southwestern boundary of the airport, severing them with a huge

blue flash that lit up the whole aircraft. About 100 metres further on, by now banked about 85°, and 10° nosedown on a westerly heading, the Electra's wing struck the 10 metre high embankment itself, cartwheeling the aircraft on to its nose more than 100 metres further on. Falling upright, the aircraft slid tailfirst among scattered trees for another 250 metres, disintegrating as it went and strewing burning wreckage over an area 100 metres wide. It finally exploded into a mushroom cloud of orange-red flame, and heavy black smoke. All on board died instantly.

The accident occurred in front of relatives and friends at the airport to see passengers off. One young couple had travelled to O'Hare Airport to see elderly parents leave for a holiday trip to Florida. They had won the holiday in a national contest. A former Marine had just farewelled his wife and four young children who were going to Tampa to visit her

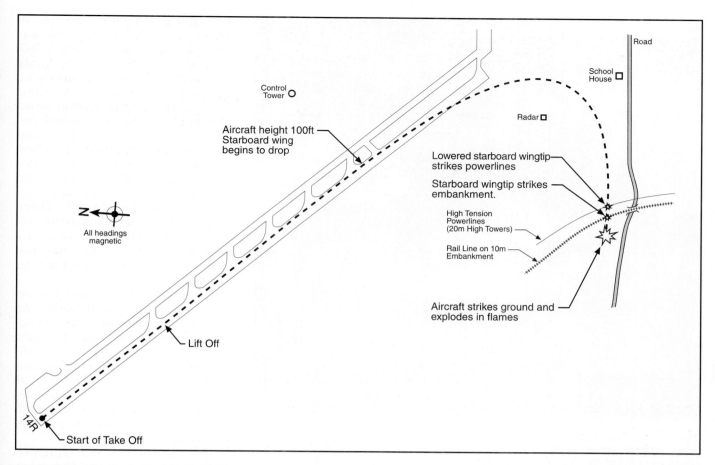

Diagram of the Electra's takeoff from Chicago's Runway 14R, steadily steepening turn to the right, impact with the high tension powerline and railway embankment, and the crash site. The entire crash sequence took less than two minutes from the commencement of takeoff. All on board died instantly. (Aero Illustrations)

parents. The youngest child was only four months old, "This is the end of my world," the father cried when told there were no survivors.

A young woman who lived directly south of where the Electra finally struck the ground said: "I ran over after the impact, but I couldn't get close – they were burning too badly. I just went into hysteria for a minute. Then I turned and ran and called the police and fire department."

Eye witnesses and some of the media reported that the Electra "had suffered a double engine failure". And one daily newspaper went on to point out that "Electra airliners have been in six fatal crashes in the United States in the last 31 months."

But a Civil Aeronautics Board supervisor countered: "This is not of the same nature as the earlier ones at Buffalo and Tell City. In those you had a breakup of the airframe at high altitude. This one barely got into flight when diffi-

culties began." The chairman of the CAB added: "We have no reason to question the structural integrity of Electra aircraft."

Investigation

Most of the aircraft's structure was destroyed by fire where it came to rest, and there was evidence of fire amongst the trees at various points along the wreckage trail. At the time of impact the flaps were still at the takeoff setting and the undercarriage was retracted. All four engines and propellers had separated from the aircraft as it broke up and were scattered along the wreckage trail.

Propeller slashes along the ground, as well as detailed examination of the engines themselves, showed they were all rotating at impact, and none exhibited any evidence of operational distress. The blade angles of all four propellers indicated they were in the flight idle position when the aircraft struck the ground, probably

because the crew had closed the power levers when they saw that impact was imminent.

Examination of airframe wreckage suggested that a malfunction might have occurred in the aileron control system. Marks made on the starboard aileron inboard indicated that it was deflected upwards 3° at impact, corresponding to a flight control position of starboard-wing-down. The rudder and elevator boost units were in their engaged positions, but the aileron boost unit was disengaged.

The boost units showed no evidence of any malfunction, but the aileron boost unit had seized as a result of fire damage in a position consistent with starboard-wing-down control movement. The lateral position of the first officer's control wheel at impact could not be determined, but the captain's wheel had been turned almost fully port-wing-down. Other than the possible aileron control malfunction, the wreckage examination indicated that the aircraft, its

Heavy black smoke billows from the fiercely burning wreckage of the Electra after it struck the railway embankment bordering O'Hare Airport and cartwheeled into a field. The accident occurred in front of horrified relatives and friends who were seeing the aircraft off. (Associated Press Wirephoto)

engines and its systems, were operating normally.

The Lockheed L-188C Electra, N137US, was almost new, having been delivered to Northwest Airlines on 22 June 1961, less than three months before the accident. Although actually built a year before this, the aircraft, before being sold, had undergone the modifications introduced by the manufacturer under the Lockheed Electra Action Program resulting from the Whirl Mode wing structural problem experienced by some of the first L-188 Electras built. (See Chapter 13). This work was completed early in 1961 and the aircraft was then subjected to a second final acceptance flight. The aircraft, equipped with four Allison 501-D13 engines, had a total flying time of only 614 hours.

The pilot in command, Captain Ralph Hagstrom, 50, had been flying for Northwest Airlines since 1942, and had nearly 16,000 hours experience, more than 300 of which were in Electra aircraft. First Officer Richard Anderson, 33, with the company for 10 years,

had over 6500 hours, including 90 in Electra aircraft, while Flight Engineer Wayne Fuller, 34, had been with Northwest for almost as long and had almost 3500 hours, 55 of them in Electras. The two Flight Attendants were Rosemary Bilski, 28, and Jeanette McKenzie, 22.

O'Hare's Runway 14R, from which the aircraft took off, has an elevation of less than 700 feet, and at the time of the accident, was 11,600 feet (3536 metres) long. Although no witnesses saw the Electra actually lifting off, eyewitness evidence indicated it assumed a normal climbing attitude and reached a height of between 50 and 75 feet when 3000 to 4000 feet down the runway. By the time it passed the 8000 foot marker, it had climbed about 100 feet, slightly lower than normal at this stage of its takeoff. The flaps were extended to some degree for takeoff and the undercarriage had retracted after liftoff.

When the Electra was nearing the 9000 foot runway marker, now at a height of around 250 feet,

eyewitnesses heard a change in engine note and the aircraft was seen to begin an apparently coordinated turn to the right, during which the rate of bank slowly increased. The crew made their brief, garbled transmission when the angle of bank reached between 30° and 45°, and from that point on the aircraft began to lose height. There was no sign of fire or smoke before it struck the powerline, and nothing was seen to fall from the aircraft. There were no birds in its flightpath and the aircraft made no abrupt or violent manoeuvre, other than the progressively increasing bank to the right.

The crew who had flown the aircraft to Chicago told investigators that the Electra was operating entirely normally during the flight from Milwaukee. No abnormalities were detected during its routine maintenance checks at Chicago before the aircraft's departure for Tampa, and the company's despatch procedures were correctly complied with.

The Electra was not equipped with a Cockpit Voice Recorder, but a four parameter Flight Data Recorder was installed in the nose wheel compartment of the fuselage. High impact forces had unfortunately cracked and sheared its stainless steel magazine and fragmented the metallic recording foil it contained. Parts of the recorder and foil were found strewn along the wreckage trail, but the section bearing the record of the aircraft's final takeoff could not be found.

However, the investigators found it possible to reconstruct the flightpath with reasonable accuracy from observations of other Electra aircraft taking off on the same runway, and by use of the aircraft type's performance data. From this it was determined that the aircraft lifted off 3200 feet (975 metres) down the runway, and reached a height of approximately 300 feet. It was descending at an angle of 5° when it struck the powerlines.

After their acknowledgement of the takeoff clearance, there were no further transmissions from the crew until the aircraft had reached the bank angle of between 30° and 45°. The garbled transmission made at this time lasted seven seconds and, delivered in a tense, high pitched voice, was poor in signal quality. As closely as could be determined by acoustic laboratory examination of the ATC recording, the transmission was: "We're in trouble (break)... and all units holding this is Northwest 706, alert. I still don't have release...right turn...no control (intake of breath). A more garbled phrase, higher in pitch and more rapid than the preceding utterances, then followed what could have been "can you" or "have you".

A portion of the Electra's primary aileron control system consists of two cables which run from the pilots' control wheels through a series of pulleys to form a closed loop at the aileron boost unit's input quadrant. The cables carry a signal input from the control wheels to the aileron boost unit when boost is engaged, as well as providing for manual operation of the ailerons when the boost is disengaged. The cable connected to the captain's control wheel is in tension for a starboard-wing-down movement, while that to the first officer's control wheel is in tension for a port-wing-down movement

All the aileron cable connections recovered from the wreckage between the captain's control column and the aileron boost unit were intact, except for a threaded cable connector to a slack takeup spring in the final flexible cable run to the boost unit. This connection to the end fitting of the slack absorber, as it is called, was found to be partly unscrewed, only a third of its normal thread being engaged in the end fitting. In addition, sooting of the assembly indicated that locking wire, required to ensue the connector remains tightened, had not been installed. Laboratory examina-

The wreckage trail of the Electra, photographed from a helicopter, looking back towards the railway embankment. The burnt-out main wreckage is in the foreground. (Associated Press Wirephoto)

tion confirmed there was no locking wire on the connector at the time of the accident.

Even more significantly, the corresponding slack absorber assembly in the flexible cable on the other side of the aileron boost unit, leading back to the first officer's control wheel, was not in place and could not be found in the wreckage at all.

The captain's and first officer's cables run parallel to each other from the aileron boost unit, passing through their respective guide holes in a pulley bracket, each guide hole being 0.6 inches (15mm) in diameter. But indentations around the guide hole for the first officer's cable indicated that some larger object had been forced through the hole. The missing slack absorber assembly was too big to have been pulled through the hole, but the cable connector to the slack absorber, if completely unscrewed, would

have been capable of making the indentations round the guide hole if forced through it.

Flexible cables, as widely used in most aircraft flying control systems, have a natural tendency to unscrew from their connectors under tension. Tests conducted by the Lockheed Aircraft Corporation during the investigation of the accident, using identical parts to those installed in the crashed Electra's aileron control system, proved that without locking wire installed, a cable would inevitably unscrew from its fitting over a period of time.

All this evidence indicated that the flexible cable connectors to the end fitting of the slack absorbers on the cable runs to both the captain's and the first officer's control wheels, because they had not been lockwired, were gradually unscrewing in service, and that the first officer's cable finally parted completely as the aircraft took off. The connector was then pulled through the cable guide hole as the aircraft broke up after hitting the railway embankment.

Using another Electra aircraft, the Lockheed Corporation also tested the effects resulting from a failure of this aileron cable. With hydraulic pressure applied, boost engaged and the ailerons held in a neutral position, the cable was severed. Although the pilot holding the control wheel at the time felt only a slight pulse when the cable was cut, and did not realise what had happened, a starboard-wing-down signal was immediately imparted to the aileron boost input quadrant because of the tension on the slack absorber on the cable run to the captain's control wheel.

With the port-wing-down cable thus disconnected at its slack absorber, it would not be possible for the pilots to apply opposite aileron to bring the starboard wing up.

Police, firemen and emergency crews examine the main wreckage soon after the fire was extinguished. The underside of the rear fuselage and tailplane is the only recognisable part of the Electra remaining. (Associated Press Wirephoto)

The tests also showed that the control system would tend to return the ailerons to neutral in about seven seconds, provided no part of the linkage binds. However, if the severed cable became caught up in the structure, preventing the ailerons returning to neutral, control of the aircraft would quickly become unmanageable.

Because witnesses saw the aircraft's angle of bank increasing steadily, and the starboard aileron was found after the accident in a position consistent with starboard-wing-down, the investigators believed it reasonable to conclude that the cable became disconnected, then became caught up in the aircraft structure somewhere within the aileron control system. In this situation, recovery techniques such as the use of opposite rudder, asymmetric power on the engines, and adjustment of the aileron trim tabs might have been effective in overcoming the increasing bank, but only if sufficient time and altitude had been available.

Tests were also conducted to eliminate the possibility of the control restriction having resulted from interference between the wing flap and the aileron. But it was found that, even in the unlikely event of this interference having occurred, the pilots would have been quite capable of overcoming it with the aileron controls, with or without aileron boost engaged.

The aircraft's logbooks disclosed that, during the period from June 27 to July 11 1961, during which the aircraft made 29 flights, eight "snags" in the aileron system were recorded. These referred to a sluggish feel in boost, delayed reactions of boost, sticking or binding of aileron boost, boost pulses at all speeds, and ailerons erratic at all speeds. Most of the corrective action recorded consisted of ground checks, one entry showing that the boost valve and hydraulic filter had been replaced. Another merely carried the entry "noted'.

On July 11, more than two months before the accident, the Electra became due for an extensive maintenance check. As aileron boost problems were still occurring, it was decided to replace the aileron boost unit during the maintenance. It so happened that this was the first time North-west Airlines's line maintenance personnel were required to replace a Lockheed Electra's aileron boost assembly. The company's maintenance instructions stipulated that, in doing so, maintenance engineers were to follow the steps prescribed in the Electra maintenance manual supplied by Lockheed.

Three shifts were operating in the Northwest Airlines maintenance hangar in which the work was carried out, and the aileron boost unit was removed by ground engineers employed on Shift 2. Following the steps described in the Lockheed Electra manual, these engineers removed the locking wire from the cable connectors at the forward end of the slack absorber units, then unscrewed the connectors to relieve the cable tension, thus facilitating removal of the boost unit.

The replacement boost unit was installed by Shift 3. But neither of the two maintenance engineers actually engaged on the work had been given any training in flight control systems. Indeed, one of them had no formal engineering training. Although the airline workshop had an on-the-job training scheme, with instructors available for guidance on unfamiliar work, the engineers concerned did not take advantage of this during the aileron boost replacement. This was despite the fact that it was the first time this workshop had performed the task. Even more surprisingly, neither man followed the Lockheed manual step by step, referring to it only when he encountered difficulty.

Although both maintenance engineers later claimed that they checked each other's work on completing the boost unit installation, neither could recall reading the instructions on re-rigging the aileron control cables, or actually checking to ensure that the previously loosened cables were properly re-tensioned and lock wired again. Neither had read the removal instructions to determine the components that had been disconnected or rendered inoperative.

The shift foreman, who also had not read the instructions in the Lockheed manual, made a cursory examination of the installation

The aileron cable slack takeup spring, with its threaded cable connectors, as recovered from the burntout wreckage of the Electra. The slack absorber assembly formed part of the aileron control circuit between the captain's control wheel and the aileron boost unit. The cable connector on the left of the spring was correctly tightened and lockwired, but that on the right was partly unscrewed. No locking wire had been installed on this connector. The corresponding slack absorber in the aileron cable leading back to the first officer's control wheel was missing. Indentations around one of the cable's guide holes indicated that, having become completely unscrewed at one end as the aircraft took off, the missing slack absorber assembly had been pulled through the guide hole as the aircraft broke up. Tests showed that, without locking wire, an aileron cable connector would inevitably unscrew over a period of time. (Civil Aeronautics Board)

when the engineers had finished their work, and functionally checked the controls. He then signed out the work as completed. But he did not ensure that the work was inspected by a company inspector, as required by a maintenance directive. The following morning the aircraft was flown on a satisfactory test flight.

Northwest Airlines' maintenance manual prescribed a comprehensive system to ensure that details of work commenced by one shift but not completed, were made known to the following shift. In addition it required red Unit Inoperative tags to be attached to cockpit controls when locking wire was removed from cable connectors for any reason, so as to prevent the release of an aircraft in an unsafe condition when work had been performed in an inconspicuous place. This particular directive specified that a Unit Inoperative tag could only be removed by an inspector, who was himself responsible for signing the tag after being satisfied that the affected cables had been re-tensioned and lock wired.

Evidence from the engineers and inspectors concerned with the work, showed that these procedures had not been followed, and that there was a lack of co-ordination between maintenance supervisors and the inspection department. Although the inspectors knew that the aileron boost unit was being changed in Electra N137US, they failed to inspect the completed installation.

Despite the existence of several managerial directives which should have ensured the aileron boost unit change was properly completed, the evidence clearly indicated to the investigators that little attention was paid to the prescribed methods of assuring job continuity between shifts, as well as to overall compliance with other company instructions. Indeed, the line maintenance and inspection personnel concerned with the work on the Electra displayed both ignorance and disregard of published directives and instructions.

Analysis and conclusions

Reviewing all the evidence that

had a direct bearing on the accident, the investigators believed that:

• The change in engine sound heard by several witnesses before the accident was attributable to a normal power reduction after the aircraft lifted off. All four engines were capable of normal operation up to the time of impact.

• Shortly after the Electra took off on the fatal flight, it developed a rolling movement to the right. But because of a failure in the aileron primary control system between the pilots' control wheels and the boost input quadrant, the roll could not be corrected by the crew. This made it impossible for the crew to decrease the steepening bank. At such a low altitude, the crew had no hope of affecting a recovery by any other means before the collision with the powerline.

• The control failure was caused by a separation of the port-wing-down aileron cable, running from the first officer's control wheel to the aileron boost unit, at its slack absorber.

• Although marks made on the

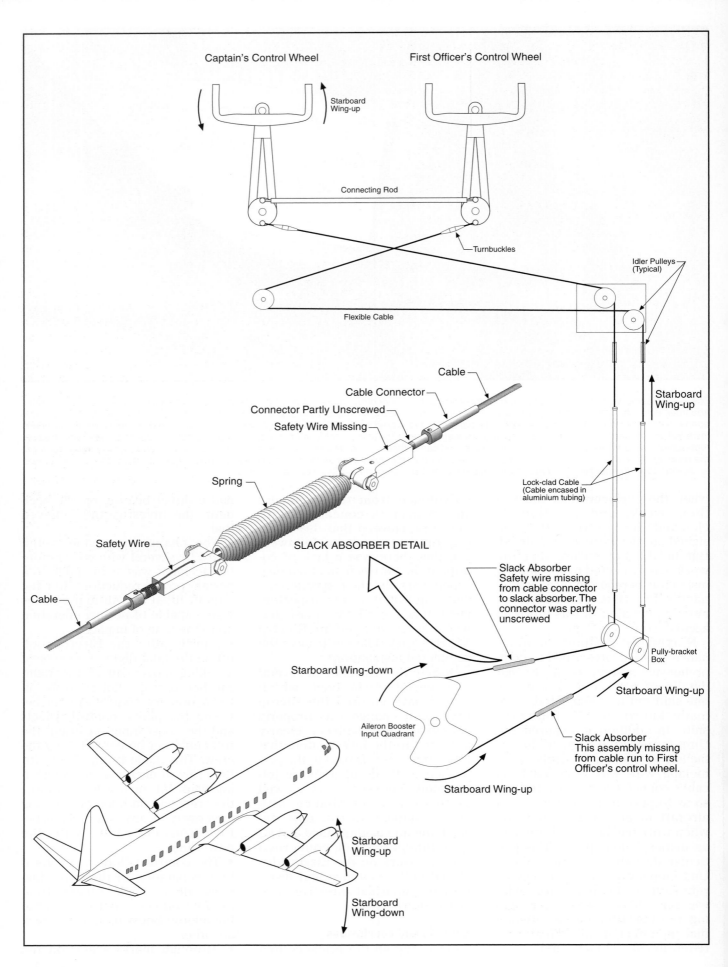

Captain's Control Wheel

First Officer's Control Wheel

Starboard Wing-up

Connecting Rod

Turnbuckles

Idler Pulleys (Typical)

Flexible Cable

Starboard Wing-up

Cable

Cable Connector

Connector Partly Unscrewed

Safety Wire Missing

Spring

Lock-clad Cable (Cable encased in aluminium tubing)

Safety Wire

SLACK ABSORBER DETAIL

Cable

Slack Absorber Safety wire missing from cable connector to slack absorber. The connector was partly unscrewed

Pully-bracket Box

Starboard Wing-down

Starboard Wing-up

Aileron Booster Input Quadrant

Slack Absorber This assembly missing from cable run to First Officer's control wheel.

Starboard Wing-up

Starboard Wing-up

Starboard Wing-down

starboard aileron indicated a starboard-wing-down aileron displacement, the captain's control wheel was positioned for a full port-wing-down aileron movement. This showed the pilots were attempting to recover from the starboard bank, but the ailerons were not responding.

• The rudder, elevator, and aileron boost units were each capable of normal operation. The rudder and elevator boost units were recovered in the engaged position, but the aileron boost unit was found disengaged. It was probably disengaged by the crew in a vain attempt to solve the difficulty with the aileron controls.

• The crew's last transmission, "I still don't have release...right turn...no control," was uttered almost without a break. The first part, "I still don't have release" probably referred to the unsuccessful attempt to control the roll by disconnecting the aileron boost, and the second part, "...right turn...no control," indicated the lack of control response.

• Two months before the accident, the cable connections to both slack absorbers were unlocked and loosened while the aileron boost unit was being changed. The engineers who fitted the replacement unit did so without knowledge of the work done during the previous shift, and completely overlooked the cable rigging instructions prescribed in the Lockheed manual.

As a result, these cables were not re-tensioned and the connectors again lock wired before the aircraft was released for flight. In the course of subsequent flying, both the cable connectors gradually unscrewed, one of them finally separating from the slack absorber immediately after the aircraft took off on its last flight.

Commenting on the eight aileron control defects recorded between June 27 and July 11, 1961, the investigators considered that the entries showed that little effort had been made to analyse the cause of the problems or to correct them. The manner in which the work was carried out reflected a casual attitude on the part of company's maintenance personnel towards a potentially hazardous condition. This same attitude was evident in the replacement of the aileron boost assembly.

The training of Northwest Airlines line maintenance personnel on the Lockheed Electra appeared to have been sporadic and inadequate, particularly with regard to flight control systems. Although the changing of the aileron boost unit provided an excellent opportunity to make use of the company's on-the-job training scheme, this opportunity was missed.

Cause

The Civil Aeronautics Board determined that the probable cause of the accident was a mechanical failure in the aileron primary control system resulting from incorrect replacement of the aileron boost assembly. This caused a loss of lateral control of the aircraft at an altitude too low to effect recovery.

Further vindication – but too late

With one exception, this needless accident at Chicago was the last Electra disaster involving a major US airline company. That exception occurred on the afternoon of May 3 1968, when Braniff's N9707C's, operating a Texas intrastate service from Houston to Dallas at Flight Level 200 (20,000ft), attempted to turn back after inadvisedly penetrating a line of severe thunderstorms that lay across the route.

Upset by severe turbulence during the turn, the Electra entered a high speed, steeply banked spiral dive. As the crew attempted to level the wings and recover, the high aerodynamic loads imposed on the airframe exceeded its ultimate design strength, and the starboard wing failed. All 85 occupants were killed when the wreckage struck the ground.

A thorough investigation, involving readouts of the Electra's FDR and CVR, and a detailed "reconstruction" of the failed wing, once again entirely vindicated the Electra design. The cause of the disaster was formally prescribed by the National Transportation Safety Board as "the stressing of the aircraft structure beyond its ultimate strength during an attempted recovery from an unusual attitude induced by turbulence associated with a thunderstorm."

Yet even this further affirmation of the soundness of the Electra did little to save its future as a frontline domestic airliner.

With a history of several major accidents early in its US operational life, its concept was by this time being overtaken by the introduction of new domestic jetliners, notably the Boeing 727 and the DC-9. As a result, Electra production never realised the type's full potential. Even so, its performance and economics, particularly over short routes, was outstanding. Block times close to those of the jets were consistently achieved on far lower fuel consumptions.

During the late 1970s, Lockheed considered putting an updated version of the Electra back into production, its design to be based on a longer fuselage version of the Orion maritime surveillance aircraft. But to the disappointment of airline financial managements, Lockheed finally decided it would not be a commercial proposition."

(Opposite) Schematic diagram of the Electra's aileron control circuit between the pilots' control wheels and the aileron boost unit. Detail of the aileron cable slack absorber units is shown in the enlarged drawing. (Aero Illustrations)

CHAPTER 16

The Dag Hammarskjold Mystery

Every reasonble precaution was taken for the safety of the UN Secretary-General's African flight. But all were to be undone by a simple and classic approach error.

Rebellion in the Congo

When the former Belgian Congo was granted its independence in June 1960, the new republic's provisional constitution, agreed upon at a conference in Brussels, provided for a democratically elected national government, whose upper house members would be designated by the six Congolese provinces.

Congolese leaders fell into two groups: those favouring a strong central government, and those wanting a looser federal system, When the centralist Congo National Movement led by Patrice Lumumba emerged as the dominant party and he was appointed President, confusion developed almost at once. Tribal violence broke out, Belgian forces had to protect Belgian residents, and the new government broke off official relations with Brussels.

President Lumumba asked the United Nations to intervene, a UN force was sent to the Congo, and Belgian forces withdrew. Meanwhile, the leader of the Katanga provincial government in the Congo's south, Moise Tshombe, refus-

ing to accept the new centralist authority, proclaimed Katanga as an independent state.

Soon afterwards, a new Congolese army chief, Colonel Joseph Mobutu, dismissed President Lumumba and his prime minister and established a committee to administer the government. Lumumba was arrested and transferred to Katanga for "safe custody". But five months later he was killed, allegedly by villagers "while attempting to escape". He was in fact assassinated.

The UN Security Council now agreed to use its forces in the Congo to prevent civil war. But in July 1961 the Congolese national parliament reconvened without representatives from Katanga, and two months later decided to send troops into Katanga for "the restoration of law and order". Fighting broke out in the province almost immediately.

Within two weeks, the military situation in Katanga had deteriorated and the fighting was intensifying. With much of the 20,000 strong UN military contingent under serious threat, the Secretary-

General of the United Nations, Mr Dag Hammarskjold, sought to intervene personally to pave the way for a peaceful settlement.

After flying to the Congolese capital of Leopoldville (today Kinshasa), Mr Hammarskjold arranged to meet with Katanga's President Tshombe, on neutral ground at Ndola, a town in Northern Rhodesia. Ndola was chosen for the meeting because, while it was readily accessible to Mr Tshombe, it lay in the British colonial Federation of Rhodesia and Nyasaland. To hold the meeting, arranged with the assistance of the British Government, covert arrangements were made for Mr Hammarskjold to fly to Ndola from Leopoldville in a chartered DC-6B aircraft.

Preparation for the flight

The United Nations's base at Leopoldville had the DC-6B on permanent charter, primarily for the use of the UN military commander in the Congo, General McKeon. Carrying the Swedish registration SE-BDY, the DC-6B was owned and operated by

An Australian National Airways Douglas DC-6, similar to the UN operated, Swedish registered DC-6B SE-BDY, engaged to transport the UN Secretary-General, Mr Dag Hammarskjold and his party, from Leopoldville to Ndola on the night of September 17 1961. (Ansett)

Transair Sweden, and flown by a Swedish civilian crew.

The best transport aircraft available, the DC-6B was immediately placed at the disposal of the Secretary-General and his party for the long flight to Ndola. Planned for the night of Sunday, September 17, it was hoped the trip would enable Mr Hammarskjold and President Tshombe to reach agreement, as a first step to peace, on a permanent ceasefire between Congolese and UN forces on the one hand, and forces of the self-declared independent Katanga on the other.

Ndola lies on the main north-south African railway, 970nm (1797km) southeast of Leopoldville and 333nm (617km) north of Salisbury (today Harare), the then capital of the Federation of Rhodesia and Nyasaland. Set in thickly forested, generally flat country more than 4000 feet above sea level, Ndola's popula-

tion at the time was around 44,000, more than 5000 of whom were Europeans. A town of substantial development, it was connected by bitumen road with a major copper mine at Mufulira, 61km to the northwest.

Ndola's airport, on the town's southeastern outskirts, was equipped with control tower facilities, runway lights, and high intensity approach lighting. Its main east-west runway, 4160 feet AMSL and more than 1600m long, was capable of handling all heavy propeller driven aircraft. An NDB located 4km to west of the runway provided for non precision instrument approaches into Ndola.

Covert arrangements –

The Swedish crew allocated to Mr Hammarskjold's flight was under the command of Captain P B Hallonquist, 35, a pilot of 8000 hours experience, including some 1350 hours on the DC-6 and DC-6B. He was also an experienced navigator. On board the DC-6B as well, because of the expected duration of the outward and return flights, was reserve Captain N Ahreus, 32, with similar experience to Captain Hallonquist. The rest of the crew included a well qualified first officer, a flight engineer, and a radio operator. The radio operator was carried because it was possible that Mr

The decoy aircraft type: A DC-4 identical to the Belgian owned OO-RIC that flew the British Parliamentary Secretary for Foreign Affairs and his party to Salisbury via Ndola, earlier the same night. The DC-4 and DC-6B are generally similar in appearance, and the flight of OO-RIC was intended to divert attention away from the UN Secretary-General's covert journey. (Rob Finlayson)

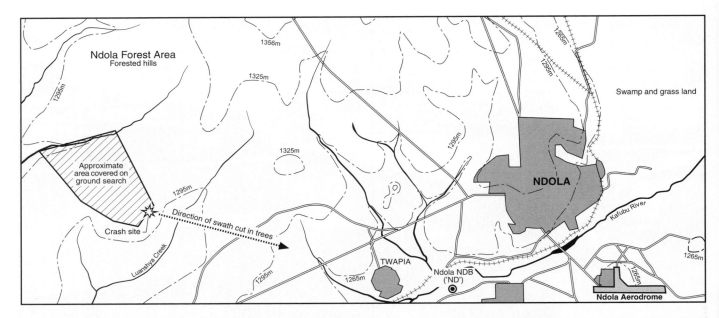

Comparison of the route flown by DC-4 OO-RIC with that probably flown by DC-6B SE-BDY. While the DC-4's flight was conducted normally on full reporting basis, SE-BDY maintained radio silence after clearing Leopold Tower until it called Salisbury FIC more than four hours later, seeking information on OO-RIC. By this time the DC-6B was evidently clear of Congolese territory. It resumed position reporting soon afterwards. (Aero Illustrations)

Hammarskjold might require long-range communication in the course of his trip.

Mr Hammarskjold's party consisted of 10 other passengers. They included his staff of UN officials, a secretary, and three armed UN military personnel – two sergeants and a private – acting as bodyguards.

– and a decoy

Because of the highly volatile political situation in the Congo, arrangements for Mr Hammarskjold's flight from Leopoldville were, as far as possible, kept secret. To confuse any possible interference, plans were made for another four engined aircraft, a DC-4, to act as a decoy for the Secretary-General's movements.

The Belgian owned and registered DC-4, OO-RIC, while being readied for flight at Leopoldville, would be made to appear to be embarking the Secretary-General and his entourage. But it would in fact be carrying the British Parliamentary Secretary for Foreign Affairs, Lord Lansdowne, and his party to Salisbury via Ndola.

After OO-RIC's crew lodged a normal flightplan at Leopoldville, the DC-4 would take off well ahead of the DC-6B, SE-BDY. It would then fly an almost direct track to Ndola via Villa Henrique de Carvalho in Angola, in full ra-

dio contact, with navigation lights on throughout the flight. By the time the DC-4 reached Ndola, it was expected that the DC-6B carrying the Secretary-General and his party would be well on its way by an undisclosed route. The DC-4 would continue its flight to Salisbury shortly before the DC-6B reached Ndola.

Apart from the crew of the DC-6B, few people knew of the plans for Mr Hammarskjold to travel in this aircraft. Captain Hallonquist told Leopoldville Air Traffic Control that, for security reasons, he would not lodge a flightplan and that his aircraft would maintain radio silence. No preflight briefing was carried out, and no one except the crew of SE-BDY had any knowledge of the proposed route or the flight levels it would maintain. But at the suggestion of Leopoldville ATC, Captain Hallonquist agreed to lodge a false flightplan nominating Luluabourg, a Congolese town 435nm (806km) southeast of Leopoldville in the general direction of Ndola, as the aircraft's destination. According to this plan, the aircraft would cruise at 13,500 feet.

The weather was fine with a slight haze, but no cloud. Although the night would be dark and moonless, visibility was expected to be at least five miles.

There was only a light southeasterly wind of 10 knots, and no operational problems were expected for either flight.

The DC-4, OO-RIC, carrying Lord Lansdowne and his party, took off from Leopoldville for Ndola at 5.04pm. The DC-4's trip to Ndola was expected to take five and a half hours. The flight of the DC-4 continued normally without incident, with OO-RIC making all routine position reports.

Radio silence

SE-BDY followed nearly an hour later at 5.51pm. But after taking off and clearing Leopoldville Tower on VHF, nothing further was heard from the Secretary-General's aircraft for more than four hours, the DC-6B evidently maintaining radio silence as Captain Hallonquist had indicated. SE-BDY finally broke its radio silence just after 10pm, when it called Salisbury Flight Information Centre on H/F, seeking information on OO-RIC's position and that aircraft's ETA for Ndola. This was Salisbury FIC's first indication that SE-BDY was flying in its airspace, and in reply to the Salisbury operator's request for information, SE-BDY advised that it was a DC-6, also enroute from Leopoldville, and that it was estimating Ndola at 00.35am.

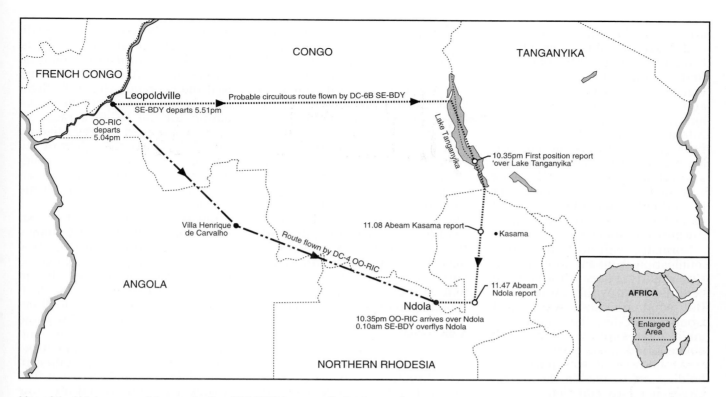

Map of the Ndola area and the crash site of SE-BDY, in generally flat forested country, more than 4000ft AMSL. Flying a westerly heading, the lights of the DC-6B were seen passing to the north of the airport in the direction of the Ndola NDB at about the normal height for an initial approach. Radio contact with the aircraft was then lost. Evidently attempting a visual night approach, rather than following the prescribed NDB procedure, the aircraft descended into the trees while turning at low level on to an easterly heading to line up with the runway lights. (Aero Illustrations)

At 10.35pm the DC-6B again reported to Salisbury. It advised it was now "over Lake Tanganyika", flying an unspecified route at 17,500 feet that would avoid Congolese territory. While this communication exchange between SE-BDY and Salisbury FIC was actually taking place, OO-RIC arrived over Ndola after a trouble free flight, joined the circuit, and landed. Its safe arrival was reported to SE-BDY a few minutes later.

At 11.08pm the DC-6B reported to Salisbury that it was "abeam Kasama", a town 87nm (151km) south of the southern tip of Lake Tanganyika and 235nm (435km) northeast of Ndola. It advised that its ETA "abeam Ndola" was 11.47pm, and requested a clearance to descend to 16,000 feet. Approving the clearance, Salisbury then asked SE-BDY its intentions after arriving at Ndola. But apart from saying it was to take off again almost immediately, the DC-6B gave Salisbury no other information.

Contact with Ndola

Salisbury FIC at 11.32pm instructed SE-BDY to contact Ndola Tower on VHF on 119.1 MHz. The

aircraft did so, advising its ETA Ndola was 00.20am. Ndola Tower then gave the aircraft the current Ndola weather as: "Surface wind 120°, seven knots, QNH 1021, QFE 877, visibility 5-10 miles in slight smoke haze." Ndola Tower asked the aircraft when it would require a further descent clearance, and SE-BDY requested descent at 11.57pm. The Tower cleared the aircraft to 6000 feet on QNH at that time, and instructed it to report when commencing descent.

On time at 11.47pm, the aircraft reported it was now "abeam Ndola" and a radio bearing on its transmission, taken from Ndola Tower, indicated SE-BDY was then due east of Ndola. Twenty-three minutes later at 0.10am, 10 minutes before its previously reported ETA, the DC-6B reported, "Lights in sight, overhead Ndola, descending, confirm QNH." Responding, Ndola Tower confirmed the QNH as 1021 and instructed the aircraft to report when it had descended to 6000 feet. The airport's runway lights and high intensity approach lighting were on at the time, set to maximum intensity.

The elevation of Ndola Airport, in flat to slightly undulating bush country, is 4160 feet, and about this time a number of people at or near the airport heard or saw the DC-6B overhead, flying in the direction of the Ndola NDB, four kilometres to the west of the airport, at about the normal height for an aircraft making an initial approach (6000 feet on QNH – 1840 feet above aerodrome level),

Contact lost – for security reasons?

Although requested to report reaching 6000 feet on descent, no such report came from the aircraft and the Tower received no further transmissions from it. The Tower controller expected the DC-6B to land by about 00.20am and when it failed to do so and there was no response to the Tower's further transmissions, the controller notified Salisbury FIC that all contact with the aircraft had been lost.

Despite the fact that SE-BDY had lodged no flightplan, the Ndola controller knew a good deal about the importance and movements of the flight. He had been told the Secretary-General of the United Nations was expected to arrive at Ndola in a second aircraft leaving from Leopoldville, he had participated in controlling the first aircraft's arrival, with Lord Lansdowne and party on board, and Salisbury FIC had advised him that SE-BDY was enroute for Ndola with an ETA of 00.35am. From 11.35 onwards the controller was in VHF contact with the aircraft and knew its ETA was amended to an earlier time. And he certainly knew the DC-6B had passed over the airport, heading towards the Ndola NDB.

Normally, with no further communication from the aircraft, the Uncertainty Phase should have been declared within 30 minutes. But when no more was heard from the DC-6B, the controller's initial impression was that it had not reported at the base of its descent because it was purposely holding off to enable the Secretary-General to complete a communication with a distant station.

The Ndola airport manager, to whom the controller was responsible, was of a similar view, believing the lack of communication from the DC-6B was for security reasons. The airport manager had returned to Ndola from leave only the day before, a Saturday, intending to resume duty on the Monday. But on Sunday 17 he was called to attend a meeting at the airport to discuss security and accommodation arrangements for the proposed meeting later that day between President Tshombe and Mr Hammarskjold.

From 2.30pm, strict security, with strong detachments of police, was imposed at both the airport and the residence of the Senior Provincial Commissioner, where Mr Hammarskjold and his party were to stay.

At the airport, Royal Rhodesian Air Force personnel took over the crew briefing room, and the airport manager's office was set aside for the projected meeting between the two political leaders. From 4pm that afternoon, President Tshombe and the British High Commissioner for the Federation of Rhodesia and Nyasaland, Lord Alport, made use of the office.

From the conversation there be-

tween President Tshombe and Lord Alport, the airport manager gained the impression some doubt still existed about the arrival of the Secretary-General. But after Lord Lansdowne arrived in the DC-4, OO-RIC, he confirmed to them that the Secretary-General was in fact on his way. He was not expected to arrive until after OO-RIC had left for Salisbury.

SE-BDY actually overflew Ndola Airport while Lord Landsdowne and his party were boarding OO-RIC to depart for Salisbury. But when the airport manager returned to the terminal after seeing Lord Lansdowne off, he learned that SE-BDY was no longer responding to the Tower's calls.

A diversion?

Because the DC-6B had passed over the airport in a northwesterly direction, appearing to be on a heading back towards Leopoldville, the airport manager thought the Secretary-General's aircraft might have diverted for some reason to another destination, and was again maintaining radio silence.

The British High Commissioner, Lord Alport, waiting to meet Mr Hammarskjold, agreed. Knowing that any meeting between the Secretary-General and President Tshombe was contingent upon a temporary cease-fire in Katanga, he feared some breach of the arranged armistice had forced the Secretary-General to change his plans.

The airport manager instructed the tower controller to report the situation to Salisbury FIC, and to continue calling SE-BDY. He also requested Salisbury FIC to check with Leopoldville for any available information on the DC-6B's movements. But an hour and a half later, when nothing more had been heard from the DC-6B, the controller, after conferring with the airport manager, declared the Uncertainty Phase of Search and Rescue action at 1.42am.

By 3.15am, when there was still no word of SE-BDY, the airport manager decided to return to his hotel, giving instructions to the airport switchboard operator that

he was to be contacted immediately if any information came to hand. Still convinced the unusual arrangements that had characterised the Secretary-General's flight from Leopoldville, were the explanation for the DC-6B's radio silence, the airport manager had no real concern for the safety of the aircraft at this stage. He considered the overdue measures already taken were adequate in the circumstances.

Earlier however, at the residence of the Provincial Commissioner in Ndola only a few minutes after SE-BDY had passed over the town, one of the police in attendance had noticed a flash and a glow in the sky in the direction of what he supposed was the aircraft's track. Bush fires and lightning flashes are common occurrences during September in the Ndola area, and no one at first associated the flash and the glow with the aircraft. But when the police party learnt the aircraft had not landed, the information was passed to Ndola police station, and an Assistant Inspector thought it justified reporting to the airport.

When the airport switchboard operator on duty was informed at about 3.30am, he directed the police to the airport manager's hotel. Two Assistant Inspectors then called on him at his hotel to inform him of the reported flash. Roused from sleep, the airport manager told the police officers nothing could be done until first light at about 5.40am, and sent them away. But still concerned, the police officers arranged for a police patrol to be sent out to investigate. But in the dark with so little information to go on, nothing was found.

About an hour earlier, another Assistant Inspector of police, patrolling a section of the road to Mufulira in a Land Rover, had seen a sudden light in the sky in the direction of Ndola and gained an impression of a falling object. On reaching Mufulira and hearing an aircraft was overdue, he and two other police drove back along the road towards Ndola for about 30km, but could see nothing suspicious.

Low level aerial view of the accident site, looking east towards Ndola Airport. The swathe which the aircraft cut in the forest as it descended is unmistakable. (the former Federation of Rhodesia and Nyasaland)

Fears realised

At 9am, more than three hours after first light, the airport manager arrived for work to find that Salisbury FIC had declared the Distress Phase at 6.45am, requesting that two RRAF aircraft be made available to begin searching for the missing DC-6B north and south of Ndola Airport. To assist the air search, bearings were taken from where the police saw the flash of light.

The RRAF unit at Ndola was flying regular reconnaissance sorties that morning and instructions were radioed to pilots to look for any signs of a crashed aircraft. Canberra, Vampire and Provost aircraft were also detailed for the search effort as recommended by civil aviation authorities. At 3.10pm that afternoon, a RRAF pilot, flying a Percival Provost, came upon the fragmented and burnt out wreckage of the aircraft lying in a forest reserve only 15km to the west of Ndola Airport.

Heading almost in the direction of the airport, the DC-6B had cut a deep swath through the trees as it broke up, before being destroyed by fire. From the air, the wreckage appeared to have been almost totally consumed.

INVESTIGATION

Police and emergency services responded promptly as soon as they were informed of the whereabouts of the crash, rushing to the scene through the surrounding forest as quickly as possible. They were astonished to find that one man had somehow survived the crash. Badly burnt and with a broken ankle, his condition was critical after hours of exposure to the tropical sun. He was found to be one of the sergeant military bodyguards on the aircraft. All the other 15 occupants, including Mr Hammarskjold himself, had either been killed in the impact or died in the fire.

In view of the highly sensitive political aspects of the tragedy and its possible consequences, a

formal Board of Inquiry comprising senior officials of the Federation's Department of Civil Aviation was appointed at once to take responsibility for investigating the cause of the accident.

The Board comprised the Director of Civil Aviation, his Department's Senior Operations Officer, its Chief Inspector of Aircraft, and a RAF Wing Commander acting as Air Adviser to the British High Commissioner. Swedish civil aviation officials, representatives of ICAO, the International Federation of Airline Pilots, and Transair, the operator of the aircraft, were also invited to participate in the investigation.

Wreckage site examination

The forest reserve into which the aircraft had crashed consisted of trees up to 10m in height and between 35 and 60cm in diameter Beneath them was long grass, dry at the time of the year and easily fired.

The surrounding country was generally flat, with some small

hills in the vicinity. There was no significant change in the terrain between the site of the crash and the airport. The ground elevation of 4300ft AMSL at the crash site fell gently to 4200ft, rose again to a height which, from very low altitude, would have obscured the runway lights, then fell gently again to the runway threshold. Descending at a shallow angle on a heading of 105°T towards the airport, the DC-6B had cut an increasingly deep swath in the forest, breaking up as it went, before exploding into fire.

A survey of the swathe cut through the trees gave a clear indication of the heading of the aircraft at the time and showed it was descending at an angle of less than 5°. It struck trees while in a shallow turn to the left at normal approach speed. The wreckage trail was 245m in length, with no sign of fire until the last 120m, the main area of incineration being over the last 24m.

At the moment of impact with the trees, the engines were under power, the undercarriage was down and locked, and the flaps were extended 30°. Watches recovered from the wreckage established the time of the crash as 0.13am. This was consistent with the time the police saw the flash and glow in the sky in the general direction the aircraft appeared to be flying.

The intensity and extent of the fire left no doubt that there was plenty of fuel on board at the time, and there was no evidence of any pre-accident failure of the aircraft's controls or systems.

The flightdeck's three altimeters were all adjusted to the barometric setting provided by the Ndola tower controller. Detailed examination disclosed no abnormal condition not attributable to impact damage and fire.

Ndola approach facilities

The NDB instrument approach procedure for Ndola consists of initial approach at 6000 feet on a track of 280° until 30 seconds after the aircraft has passed the NDB. A procedure turn is then made to the right and, on completion of the turn, when established inbound to the NDB on a track of

100°, the aircraft descends to cross the NDB at 5000 feet before continuing the descent to the airport minima. The high intensity approach lighting at Ndola included a Visual Approach Slope Indicator System (VASIS).

It was usual for Transair's pilots to use approach charts published in the Jeppesen Manual. One decipherable loose leaf Jeppesen Manual was found in the wreckage, with the chart for the Ndola NDB approach missing from it. It was crew practice to remove the relevant chart from the manual while conducting an approach, placing it where it could be readily referred to by the pilot flying the approach. Amongst the wreckage of the DC-6B's flightdeck, the spring clip for this purpose on the captain's side had been damaged, and whether or not a chart had been attached to it could not be determined.

Firearms

In the wreckage, and on the bodies of the two military bodyguards who died in the crash and fire, a total of 201 live rounds, 342 spent bullets, and 362 empty cartridge cases were recovered. All were of 9mm calibre – the same as the small arms being carried in the aircraft. Both men were wearing ammunition pouches when they boarded the DC-6B at Leopoldville. The spent bullets recovered were examined microscopically, but none had been fired by a weapon. Rather, they had apparently been discharged in the heat of the wreckage fire.

A careful examination was made of the wreckage for any sign of the aircraft having been hit by a bullet or other projectile, but none was found. Nor was anything found in the wreckage to indicate that explosive damage had occurred in flight. In addition, 180 men carried out a search of a six square kilometre area of bush immediately to the northwest of the crash, over which the aircraft would have flown before it descended into the trees. Nothing was found that could be associated with the crash, and there was no sign of fire in the area.

The DC-6B had been slightly damaged by small arms fire directed at it from the ground during an earlier flight on the day of the Secretary-General's trip, the investigators learnt. But on the aircraft's return to Leopoldville, the only damage found was to an exhaust stub on one of the engines. The exhaust stub was replaced, normal pre-flight checks were carried out, including an examination of the interior of the aircraft, and it was refuelled for the Ndola flight. The DC-6B was fully serviceable when it left Leopoldville.

The victims

Post-mortem examinations carried out on the bodies of the 15 victims of the crash showed that nine, including Mr Hammarskjold, were killed instantly. Three of the bodies were too badly burnt to assess their injuries, but another three had sustained no fatal injuries apart from burns. From their positions in the wreckage it was evident they were rendered unconscious in the impact and were unable to escape.

The flight

It was evident that the captain was willing to compromise enroute safety standards for the sake of security. Operating at night over a long distance of the African interior without anyone, other than his crew, knowing of his route or intentions, he declined the precaution of leaving a flightplan or even a passenger manifest. He also conducted the flight in radio silence and with no apparent information on the en route weather, and did not make use of en route navigation aids that would have been available on request. Furthermore, he did not report the aircraft's presence in flight until he was satisfied it had cleared Congolese territory

Because of the secrecy and silence surrounding the DC-6B's movements, the investigators had difficulty in reconstructing the route followed by the aircraft, particularly for the portion of the flight between Leopoldville and the position at which it first reported its position at 10.35pm.

However, from the aircraft's known time intervals, the probability that the captain was navigating by dead reckoning, his

Low level aerial view of the main wreckage at the eastern end of the wreckage trail. Little remains of the aircraft's structure after the fire that followed the impact. (the former Federation of Rhodesia and Nyasaland)

explanation to Salisbury FIC at 10.35pm that he was avoiding Congolese territory, and the aircraft's positions in the latter part of the flight, it seemed most probable that the route flown would have been due east from Leopoldville to Lake Tanganyika. The aircraft then flew southwards down Lake Tanganyika to the position at which it first reported. At this point, the DC-6B would have been crossing the border between the Republic of the Congo and the Federation of Rhodesia and Nyasaland, and the captain probably considered radio silence was no longer necessary.

The total time interval for the DC-6B's flight from Leopoldville to Ndola suggested it would have flown a distance of about 1504nm (2787km). By contrast, OO-RJC's almost direct route to Ndola covered only 973nm (1803km).

Witness evidence

Cleared to descend from its cruising level to 6000ft at 11.57pm, it was apparent that the DC-6B began its descent at this time, reaching 6000ft on QNH by the time it was overhead Ndola at 00.10am. The aircraft's reference to "descending" at that point probably referred to its continuing descent from 6000 feet.

None of the witnesses in and around Ndola who heard and saw the DC-6B pass over the airport on a westerly heading noticed anything unusual in its flight. It was evident that the aircraft overflew Ndola airport at approximately the correct height (6000ft AMSL, 1840 feet above aerodrome level), heading towards the Ndola NDB 4km to the west of the airport, before beginning its approach to land.

Yet witness evidence generally described the aircraft as being lower than normal over the beacon area and beyond it, and it did not appear to be following the Ndola instrument approach procedure. Rather than passing over the airport precisely on track as it flew towards the NDB and beyond, it did so more than a kilometre to the north. And, from the sound of its engines, it then seemed to be lower than the normal instrument approach altitude, being heard at relatively low level over a farm 11km to the northwest of the airport. The normal procedure turn would not have taken it so far out, nor should the aircraft have sounded so low.

In hospital in Ndola, the surviving but badly burnt military bodyguard, although almost incoherent, told medical staff that the aircraft "blew up", apparently believing this occurred over the runway. "Then there was the crash," he said, "and there were lots of little explosions all around". He escaped through an emergency exit. Others in the aircraft "were just trapped".

Later he told them: "We were on the runway and there was an explosion", and "We were on the runway when Mr Hammarskjold said 'Go back', then there was an explosion. I was the only one that got out – all the others were trapped." Later again, when asked why they had not landed, he indicated that Mr Hammarskjold had changed his mind or said "Turn back". An explosion and a crash followed.

The survivor subsequently died as a result of his burns. His condition had been aggravated by exposure, in a shocked condition, during the six hours of darkness after the crash, followed by exposure to the sun for about 10 hours. Had his rescue been accomplished earlier, it was possible that his life could have been saved.

ANALYSIS

Mr Hammarskjold's apparent order to "go back"

The only indication of any change of plan to land at Ndola was the survivor's statement that Mr. Hammarskjold "changed his mind" or said "Turn back". But the investigation found nothing else whatever to support this evidence. Rather, what seemed probable was that, as the aircraft struck the tree tops, Mr Hammarskjold in alarm, shouted words such as "Go back" almost instinctively.

Sabotage

Examination of the wreckage and bodies revealed nothing to indicate any bomb had exploded in the aircraft. None of the bullets examined had been fired through any weapon barrel, and the many found were all of the type used in the firearms carried in the aircraft. They came from ammunition carried by the military bodyguards, which exploded in the fire.

If any projectile or rocket had hit the aircraft, there would have been an explosion. No witness spoke of hearing an explosion before the aircraft hit the trees. Furthermore, if the aircraft was hit by an explosive missile, some part of it, some part of the missile or some sign of fire, would have been found on the ground over which the aircraft passed just before it crashed.

The approach

Eyewitnesses evidence established that SE-BDY crossed Ndola Airport at about 6000ft on a heading close to 280°. The absence of a report from the aircraft on reaching 6000 feet on descent, as requested by the tower controller, might well have been because the aircraft had already descended to that altitude when the request was made. What was certain was that the aircraft began descending below 6000ft soon after it passed over the airport. The witness evidence also established that the aircraft then turned to the right. To reach the point where the accident occurred therefore, it was apparent that the crew continued their approach with a subsequent turn to the left.

Whether or not their decision was prompted by not having a Ndola approach chart on board the aircraft, the crew evidently elected to make a visual approach to the runway instead of the prescribed Ndola NDB non precision approach. The fact that it was a clear night, the runway and approach lights were set to maximum intensity, and they had been told there was no other traffic, could have influenced their decision.

When the DC-6B hit the trees, it was descending at an angle of less than 5°, a normal angle for an approach to land. The engines were under power, the undercarriage was down and locked, and 30° of flap was extended, a normal setting at that stage of an approach. The landing lights remained retracted, but the aircraft was not yet close enough to the runway to require them.

To the west of Ndola there was only bush, and after the aircraft passed over the lights of Ndola and began its descending turn to the right, there would have been only total darkness ahead – in aviation parlance a "black hole". If, in the course of its turn the aircraft descended too low, the slight rise in the ground in the direction of the airport would have obscured the runway lights as the aircraft was completing its turn back to a heading where those lights should have again become visible to the crew.

The investigators were unable to explain why the crew failed to recognise the dangerously low height of the aircraft in relation to the airport's elevation, and to that of the slightly higher bush terrain to the west over which they were turning.

Search and rescue action

The police report to the Ndola airport manager after 3.30am, of a flash and glow in the sky in the direction in which the aircraft disappeared, laid on him the responsibility for further action. His failure to initiate action as soon as possible after first light displayed an extraordinary lack of any sense of urgency.

The report came from a responsible police officer and was thought sufficiently important to justify a search in the dark by a road patrol to investigate the phenomena. But the distance of the crash site from the road and the thickness of the intervening bush effectively prevented the patrol from sighting the burning wreckage. The sudden light in the sky and the falling object which another police party sighted while on the road to Mufulira a little later, was probably an oxygen cylinder in the wreckage exploding in the heat of the fire. Again the intervening bush rendered their search along the road ineffective.

Although bush fires and lightning are commonplace at that time of the year, the coincidence of the flash and glow with the sudden loss of all contact with SE-BDY should have been warning enough that an emergency of some sort might have developed.

A report by the airport manager to Salisbury at first light that he was apprehensive for the safety of the Secretary-General's aircraft would have certainly produced

Ground view of the wreckage trail and the swathe cut in the forest, looking back in the direction from which the aircraft approached. (The former Federation of Rhodesia and Nyasaland).

the authority for an immediate search of the vicinity by an RRAF aircraft. The crash site might then have been found far earlier and the survivor rescued before exposure to the tropical sun aggravated his burns.

Despite Salisbury FIC's repeated teleprinter requests to Leopoldville during the night for information on the whereabouts of SE-BDY, made at the request of the Ndola airport manager when the aircraft first became overdue, no response came from Leopoldville FIC until 7.40am, when it reported it had no news of the aircraft.

The messages to Leopoldville during the night were apparently received by a Congolese national who did not understand English and needed assistance before he could process them. This involved further serious delays.

CONCLUSION

The investigators were forced to the conclusion that the pilots simply allowed the aircraft to descend too low while turning on to a final approach to the north and west of the airport, and that it struck the tree tops in the total darkness, crashing through them to the ground with disastrous consequences.

The irony of the accident was that, despite all the extensive and diversionary measures taken to

ensure the safety from interference of the Secretary-General's flight to Ndola, all were nullified in the end by a classic and simple error of judgement on the part of the DC-6B's crew.

Visual "black hole" night approaches in clear weather have been the undoing of countless aircraft, both large and small, since aeroplanes first began operating in the dark. The tragedy exemplified once again the truth that, however good the visibility for a night approach, it is far safer to make use of the approach aids that are available, than to trust visual judgement with its potential for many insidious illusions.

CHAPTER 17

Crew confusion aboard a chartered Constellation

As major American airlines re-equipped with turboprops and jets in the late 1950s and early 1960s, many of their former front line piston engined types were sold to small operators at a fraction of their original cost. Some of these operators lacked the resources, experience and professionalism to manage these complex, high performance aeroplanes safely. This was what overtook one Lockheed Constellation at Byrd Field, Virginia.

The US Army chartered a Lockheed L-049 Constellation from Imperial Airlines at Columbia Airport, North Carolina, in November 1961 to pick up a number of new recruits in preparation for their initial military training.

Previously trading as Regina Cargo Airlines, Imperial was then flying three Lockheed Constellations and one former military Curtis C-46 Commando on nonscheduled operations. The army charter was to collect recruits from Newark, New Jersey; Wilkes Barre, Pennsylvania; and Baltimore, Maryland, and fly them to Columbia, where their training would begin. The Constellation allocated to the trip, N2737A, had been part of Capital Airlines' fleet and had flown a total of 32,000 hours.

In command was 29 year old Captain Ronald Conway. Although he had qualified as a Constellation captain eight months earlier, he had a total of only 4500 hours ex-

perience, less than 300 of which were on the type. Acting as Conway's first officer, possibly because of the captain's lack of experience, was a more senior pilot, Captain James Greenlee, 45. With endorsements on C-46, DC-4, DC-6 and DC-7 aircraft as well as the L-049, he had flown nearly 18,000 hours, but his Constellation experience was barely more than Conway's. Flight Engineer William Poythress, 30, with 200 hours experience on L-049s; Student Flight Engineer Peter Clark; and Stewardess Linda Jones were the other members of the crew.

The Constellation departed for Newark at 3.15pm local time. Conway was in the captain's seat, Greenlee occupied the right hand control seat, and Peter Clark was at the flight engineer's console, with Poythress supervising him. But as the aircraft lifted off from Columbia, there was a sudden drop in the No 3 engine's fuel pressure.

"What are you going to do?" demanded Poythress as he saw the No 3 pressure gauge.

"I'm going to No 3 and No 4 crossfeed to assure positive pressure on the right side," replied Clark.

Clark opened the crossfeeds and fuel pressure was then maintained. When the Constellation reached its cruising altitude of 9500 feet and the engines were throttled back to cruising power, the flight engineers closed the crossfeeds again and the flight continued normally. Neither Poythress nor Clark mentioned the fluctuation in fuel pressure to the pilots.

The remainder of the flight to Newark was uneventful. The aircraft touched down at 5.30pm, taxied to the terminal, and shut down all four engines in preparation for boarding the first 26 of their army passengers.

At 6.20pm, the engines were started again and the aircraft taxied for departure for Wilkes Barre. This time, in preparation for take-off, Flight Engineer Poythress opened the No 3 and No 4 crossfeeds to avoid any repetition of the loss in fuel pressure.

The flight to Wilkes Barre, where they were scheduled to pick up another 31 recruits, took only 35 minutes, cruising at 4500 feet. After landing and taxiing to the tarmac, the crew shut down only the No 1 and No 2 engines while entry steps were wheeled to the main cabin door on the port side and the additional passengers filed aboard. Ten minutes later the port side engines were started again and, at 7.12pm, the Constellation departed for its next stop at Baltimore. Again the engineers opened the No 3 and No 4 crossfeeds for the takeoff and climb, and again the aircraft cruised at 4500 feet for the one hour flight.

At Baltimore the crew followed the same procedure, keeping the No 3 and No 4 engines idling while another 16 passengers came aboard through the main cabin door. Taxiing again for Columbia as soon as the additional passengers were seated, the aircraft had reached the run-up area when the Tower recalled it to the tarmac to pick up an additional recruit who had arrived late. The Constellation finally took off from Baltimore at 8.30pm, the engineers again opening the starboard side crossfeeds for the takeoff and climb.

Five minutes after takeoff, Greenlee lodged a flightplan to

An early model Lockheed L-749 operated by TWA, the launch customer for the high performance 1939 design that became the Constellation. Outwardly identical to the L-049 involved in the accident, the L-749 differed only in being fitted with long range fuel tanks and a heavier undercarriage for international operations.

Columbia by radio, reporting the Constellation would cruise at 218 knots at 4500 feet, that its estimated time interval was 130 minutes, and its endurance 330 minutes. It was Conway's intention to keep to the west of Washington DC to avoid its congested airspace, and to intercept Victor Airway 3, tracking via the Brooke Omni.

In cruising flight some time after the aircraft had passed the Brooke Omni, there was a sudden loss of power on the starboard side, the aircraft yawing to the right as the fuel pressure warning lights for No 3 and No 4 engines illuminated.

Student Flight Engineer Clark, at the engineer's console, shouted to Poythress, who immediately took over. By the time he had done so, the No 3 engine had stopped rotating and No 4 engine was surging between 1500 and 2000 rpm.

"You've got a fuel problem!" Conway called to the flight engineers.

Poythress opened all four crossfeed valves, checked that the fuel selectors were positioned for tank to engine feeding and turned on all four fuel boost pumps. "I'll try to restart No 3 and 4," he replied.

"Concentrate on No 4 – that's still running," Conway told him. "And feather No 3."

But the flight engineer found he was unable to restart No 4 engine. "I can't do any good with No 4 – I'll try No 3 and shut down No 4 instead," he said. Poythress then ordered the student engineer to go back aft into the passenger cabin and open the midships fuel crossfeed valve.

Clark returned to the flightdeck soon afterwards. "I need a screwdriver to get at that valve," he told Poythress.

A Lockheed L-749 in flight. This aircraft, PH-TFD, was one of seven 749A Constellations flown by KLM in the late 1940s and early 1950s. The L-049 Constellation N2737A operated by Imperial Airlines, was first owned by BOAC as G-AHEK, them became part of Capital Airlines' fleet in the US when BOAC re-equipped with Super Constellations. By the time of the accident at Byrd Field, it had flown a total of 32,000 hours.

terwards Poythress reported the temperatures on Nos 1 and 2 engines were holding normally.

By now it was 9.10pm and dark, and Conway told Greenlee to report their situation to Byrd Tower. He also advised Stewardess Jones of their engine problem and that they would be landing. She promptly relayed this to the passengers over the public address system. Because the landing was not expected to pose problems, the pilots did not ask the stewardess to give emergency evacuation instructions.

Replying to Greenlee's call, Byrd Tower transmitted that all runways were available and that the wind was northwest at 15 knots with gusts to 22 knots. The controller requested the Constellation to advise the runway chosen when on base leg, and asked if standby emergency equipment was required. When Greenlee replied that it was, Conway asked Greenlee to take over the controls so he could check the flight engineer's panel for himself.

The aircraft was now passing to the south of the city, heading towards the airport on its eastern outskirts, and Conway told the tower they would use Runway 33. The Constellation was maintaining altitude and had a "healthy airspeed," he added. Nearing the airport, the crew had begun the in-range checklist, when Greenlee suddenly exclaimed, "Let's land on this runway!" simultaneously reducing power, beginning a shallow left turn towards Runway 02, and selecting the undercarriage down.

Sighting the lighted Runway 02 in front of them, Conway thought they were too high and too fast for a straight-in approach and his gaze dropped to the undercarriage position lights below the glare shield. They still indicating red! "The gear isn't down!" he shouted.

"Don't open that valve," Greenlee interposed from the first officer's seat. "You've got good pressure on No 1 and 2; leave it!"

Again Clark did as he was told. Poythress in the meantime had no success in his attempts to restart No 3 engine. He finally turned to the captain again: "I've tried every procedure I know, but it's no good – there's no way we can get No 3 or No 4 to start. I think we'd better get the aircraft on the ground as soon as we can."

Conway agreed. By this time the Constellation was not far to the west of Richmond, Virginia, and he turned the aircraft east towards Richmond's Byrd Field. Checking Nos 3 and 4 propellers were feathered and the feathering checklist completed, he retrimmed the aircraft to achieve a satisfactory airspeed. Shortly af-

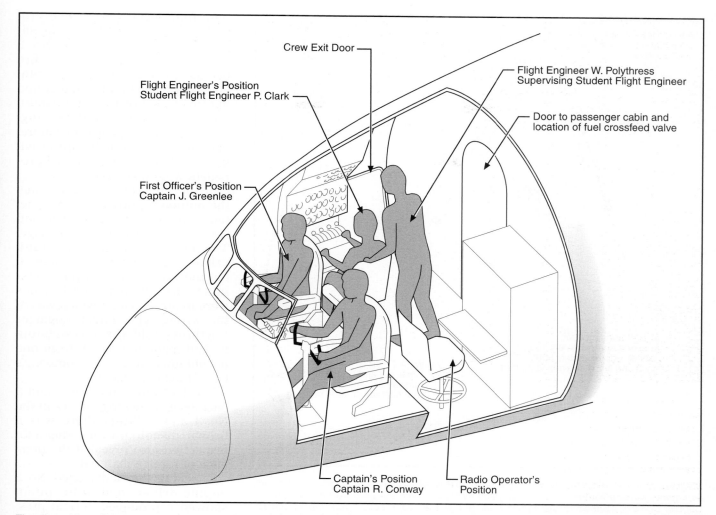

The disposition of the crew on the flightdeck of the ill-fated N2737 during the intended charter flight to Columbia, North Carolina. Accident investigators found that the crew lacked the overall knowledge and experience to safely operate an aircraft as complex as the Constellation. The aircraft's maintenance standards also left much to be desired. (Aero Illustrations)

Labels in figure:
- Crew Exit Door
- Flight Engineer W. Polythress Supervising Student Flight Engineer
- Flight Engineer's Position Student Flight Engineer P. Clark
- Door to passenger cabin and location of fuel crossfeed valve
- First Officer's Position Captain J. Greenlee
- Captain's Position Captain R. Conway
- Radio Operator's Position

Both pilots simultaneously called for full power on No 1 and 2 engines, Conway believing their airspeed and altitude were sufficient to make Runway 33, although this would require almost a 180° turn. Taking over the controls, Conway began the right turn, but quickly lost sight of the runway and was forced to hand control to Greenlee again. On the starboard side of the flightdeck, Greenlee was in a better position to see the runway out to the right. Conway then reached down and re-cycled the undercarriage, but there was no change in the indicator lamps.

Greenlee held the turn until Conway could see the runway, when he took the controls again. About this time, someone on the Constellation's flightdeck, presumably Greenlee, transmitted: "Tower, get everybody off – we're losing another one here and we can't get our gear down."

Poythress then confirmed they were losing No 1 engine, reporting it was progressively decreasing in power, and instructed Clark to be ready to pump the undercarriage down. Again without Conway's knowledge, the lever was selected down, and Clark began pumping.

As the aircraft turned on to final approach, it was well to the left of the runway centreline. But about a mile out from the runway threshold, now with two green lights on the instrument panel indicating two of the three landing legs were down, the Constellation's airspeed began to decay. Realising they would not make the runway, Conway pulled back on the control column. His last recollection of airspeed as the aircraft stalled into trees was an indication of between 90 and 95 knots.

The trees cushioned the ground impact to some extent, but the aircraft immediately caught fire and when Poythress opened the door to the cabin, the flightdeck filled with smoke. Poythress then opened the crew exit in the side of the flightdeck and jumped to the ground, while Conway opened the port side sliding window and escaped through it. Although Greenlee was behind Poythress, preparing to jump, the aircraft was engulfed in flames before he could do so. The fierce fire consumed the aircraft and Conway and Poythress were the only survivors.

Investigation

Examination of the accident site showed that the Constellation was banked to the right, descending at an angle of about 10°, when it first struck trees 50 feet above the ground. The initial impact severed

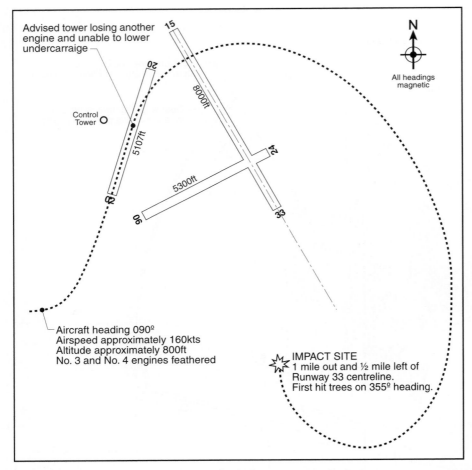

Within the diagram:

Advised tower losing another engine and unable to lower undercarriage

15

20

8000ft

Control Tower O

5107ft

N
All headings magnetic

5300ft

24

90

33

Aircraft heading 090º
Airspeed approximately 160kts
Altitude approximately 800ft
No. 3 and No. 4 engines feathered

IMPACT SITE
1 mile out and ½ mile left of
Runway 33 centreline.
First hit trees on 355º heading.

Diagram of the Constellation's night approach to Byrd Field, Richmond, for the intended emergency landing with Nos 3 and 4 engines feathered. With the wind from the northwest, Captain Conway planned to use Runway 33. But as they approached from the southwest, Captain Greenlee, the more senior pilot acting as first officer, made a sudden decision to land straight ahead on Runway 02. When the undercarriage failed to extend, the crew attempted to go round to reach Runway 33, but the No 1 engine, apparently overboosted, began failing also. The airspeed decayed during the turn on to final, and the Constellation stalled into trees, becoming engulfed in flames almost immediately. (Aero Illustrations)

both wing tips and the starboard tailplane and rudder, before the aircraft ploughed into a clump of bigger trees 30 metres further on. It came to an abrupt stop in a level attitude in another 35 metres with the fuselage broken open and the wings torn off.

Except for the tail section, the fuselage and most of the port wing were destroyed by fire. The starboard wing was only slightly affected, the fire being confined to a small section of the leading edge containing the No 4 fuel tank. There was no evidence of fire along the wreckage trail. The nose undercarriage was in the retracted position, but its uplock was released. The main undercarriage legs were both extended, with the undercarriage selector in the down position, and the flaps were retracted.

Fire destroyed the entire passenger cabin, apart from the seat frames. Only two forward seats were dislodged by impact, and only one seat belt buckle remained fastened. Indeed, the grouping of charred bodies in the wreckage showed most passengers had left their seats after the crash as they tried to escape. The largest group lay near the main cabin door, which was either jammed or held closed by trees and debris. Clark apparently went to the cabin immediately before the crash to assist Stewardess Jones, for both her and Clark's bodies were found with those of the passengers. There was no evidence of impact injuries and the cause of death in all cases was suffocation by carbon monoxide poisoning. No one had tried to escape through the over-wing exits.

All four engines, with their propellers, were torn from the nacelles at their firewalls, No 2 engine sustaining only slight fire damage in comparison to the others. No 1 engine had disintegrated internally as a result of the failure of its master rod and bearing. There was no evidence of failure, malfunction or inflight fire in engines 2, 3, and 4. Nos 3 and 4 propellers were feathered.

In the unburnt starboard wing, the outboard portion of No 3 fuel tank was free of fire damage and No 4 tank had little fire damage. The position of the fuel tank valves could not be determined, but the No 2 fuel boost pump was intact. Its pump motor brushes were in place, one of which was of the wrong type. Flight Engineer Poythress told the investigators he had made this brush from one he obtained from the company's Chief Flight Engineer.

The fuel filters for Nos 1 and 2 engines were destroyed, but in the No 3 and 4 filters there was a brown discolouration. Magnetic inspection also revealed the presence of foreign material.

Checking the undamaged No 2 engine-driven hydraulic pump showed it produced normal pressure, indicating that hydraulic pressure would have been available to the aircraft's primary system. The selector valve on the hydraulic hand pump on the flight-deck was in the position for emergency undercarriage operation. The hydraulic crossover valve was closed. This valve, when opened, permits pressure from the primary system to operate the entire secondary system, including the undercarriage and flaps. No evidence of malfunction was found in this valve or its electric motor.

The Constellation was serviced with 1800 US gallons of fuel before leaving Columbia, Greenlee instructing that both inboard tanks be filled and the outboard tanks fuelled to 800 gallons each. Two tankers were used and it was found that the tanker which fuelled the Nos 3 and 4 tanks contained contamination. Its filter assembly had rust in it, and two of its elements were not properly seated, allowing some unfiltered fuel to pass.

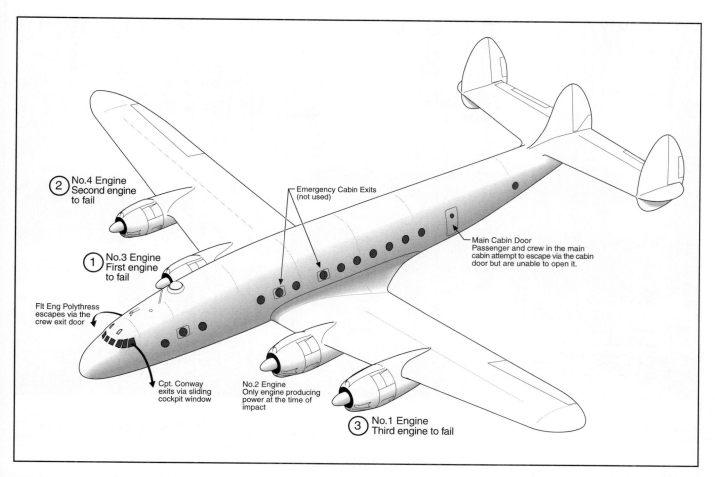

Although deceleration forces were not severe enough to cause serious injuries, only the captain and the flight engineer escaped the ferocity of the instantaneous fire that broke out on impact. The diagram shows their escape routes. The occupants of the passenger cabin were evidently unable to open the main cabin door in the short survival time available. No attempt was made to use the overwing emergency exits. (Aero Illustrations)

For some time before the accident, the FAA had been conducting inspections of Imperial Airway's operations and maintenance. There were discrepancies in the company's records and numerous errors in overhaul periods for aircraft components. In many cases, crews were not reporting aircraft faults in writing.

A further audit of Imperial Airlines after the accident revealed that company manuals were not current and, in some instances, were not approved by the FAA. Company policies were not reflected in the manuals and set down procedures were not being followed. Aircraft inspection periods were being exceeded, records were missing, and in some instances repairs were not signed off by a certificated maintenance engineer. Aircraft had been flown at times for as much as 70 hours with no flight log notations then, on the final flight be-

fore a periodic inspection, as many as 40 or 50 discrepancies would be recorded. In one case a flight was made with an unserviceability affecting the aircraft's airworthiness.

Analysis

Evidence given by Imperial's Chief Flight Engineer concerning maintenance on the Constellation was contradictory. First, he claimed he obtained two electrical brushes for the Nos 2 and 3 fuel boost pumps from another airline. One of the brushes had to be cut down to fit. The other brush, he said, was an approved type. He later qualified this statement, saying the second brush 'appeared' to be of a suitable type. After hearing evidence that denied he had been given two brushes, he again changed his statement, saying he had got the second brush from the student flight engineer.

The No 2 boost pump, fitted

with a brush of incorrect type, confirmed Poythress' claim that he adapted the brush. The investigators also believed this brush was the only brush obtained, and that no repair was made to the No 3 boost pump so as not to delay the flight.

The fluctuation in fuel pressure on No 3 engine during takeoff from Columbia was symptomatic of a boost pump failure, with the engine-driven fuel pump continuing to supply fuel. The student engineer responded by opening Nos 3 and 4 crossfeeds, and in this configuration, fuel from No 4 tank would be supplied to the crossfeed manifold under pressure from the No 4 boost pump.

Even though the No 3 tank selector valve remained open, no fuel could flow from this tank, because the higher pressure in the crossfeed manifold from the No 4 boost pump would hold a check valve closed between the manifold

The still smoking, burnt out wreckage of the Constellation amongst the trees into which it crashed, photographed on the morning after the accident. From the initial point of impact, the aircraft was brought to a stop in 65 metres. Only the tail assembly and the torn off starboard wing escaped destruction by fire. The victims' causes of death in all cases was suffocation by carbon monoxide. (Wide World Photos)

and the No 3 tank. Thus Nos 3 and 4 engines would both be running on No 4 tank for as long as the No 4 boost pump remained on.

Poythress said that for each takeoff, the crossfeeds were opened in anticipation of any further fluctuation in fuel pressure, and that the fuel system was returned to the normal tank-to-engine configuration at cruising altitude. But the investigators believed the greater part of the flight was conducted with the crossfeeds open and the boost pumps on. Using engine powers and rates of fuel consumption set out in the airline's operations manual, with Nos 3 and 4 engines on crossfeed from the No 4 tank for the greater part of the flight, it was calculated that the 800 gallons in this tank would have been exhausted at about the time the loss of power actually occurred.

The possibility of the engines being affected by fuel contamination was considered, but it was highly improbable to have resulted in a simultaneous loss of fuel pressure in two separate fuel systems without any warning. No

other aircraft serviced at Columbia reported trouble from fuel contamination. It was clear to the investigators that the sudden loss of power was not the result of any malfunction, but of incorrect fuel management, leading to fuel exhaustion.

Flight Engineer Poythress' efforts to restart the engines demonstrated a lack of knowledge of the aircraft, and an inability to diagnose the boost pump failure. Had he followed the correct procedures, there was no reason why Nos 3 and 4 engines would not have restarted. When the No 4 fuel tank ran dry, the No 4 fuel tank shutoff valve remained open, allowing No 4 boost pump to force air into the crossfeed manifold and on to the fuel lines of both engines. Because the No 3 boost pump was inoperative, the air in the lines would have had to be displaced by gravity and suction from No 3 engine-driven pump. Even so, the No 3 engine would have restarted had No 4 boost pump been turned off, and enough time allowed for No 3 engine-driven pump to prime.

Investigators also believed the engines would have started if the crossfeed valves had been closed. Opening the midships crossfeed valve would also have started the engines. This would have allowed fuel from Nos 1 and 2 tanks to be supplied to engines Nos 3 and 4 under boost pump pressure. Captain Conway told investigators he did not know the midships crossfeed valve had not been opened until after the accident.

When the Constellation first contacted Byrd Tower at 9.12pm, its Nos 3 and 4 engines were feathered and the crew were experiencing no problems in flying the aircraft on its two remaining engines. But when the Constellation had almost reached Byrd Field, Greenlee made his sudden decision to land almost straight ahead on Runway 02. Although the senior pilot, Greenlee had elected to act as first officer, yet when the emergency developed, he issued orders as captain. Confusion prevailed on the flightdeck as a result, Greenlee's spur of the moment decision a clear indication of this division of command.

His hasty attempt to lower the undercarriage was also ill considered. On the L-049, hydraulic power for the undercarriage comes from the secondary hydraulic system, supplied by Nos 3 and 4 engine-driven hydraulic pumps. With Nos 3 and 4 engines feathered, no hydraulic power was available from this system, and the undercarriage did not extend.

This particular Constellation however, was equipped with a hydraulic crossover valve which allowed hydraulic pressure from the primary system supplied by Nos 1 and 2 engine-driven pumps to be routed to the undercarriage. This valve and its electric motor were recovered from the wreckage in the closed position, and showed no evidence of malfunction. Moreover, the No 2 hydraulic pump was still operable. The investigators believed the crew did not open the hydraulic crossover valve, and indeed were unaware that the aircraft was equipped with the valve. Had the valve been opened, the undercarriage would have extended within 25 seconds.

When the undercarriage failed to extend, the attempt to land on Runway 02 had to be abandoned, and the pilots called for full power on Nos 1 and 2 engines. Conway then took over the controls again and began a right turn on to a downwind leg for Runway 33, but had to pass control back to Greenlee because only he could keep the runway in sight. From the location of the wreckage, it was evident the approach to Runway 33 was poorly judged, the turn being steepened on base leg in a vain attempt to avoid overshooting the centreline of the runway. But the increased rate of turn bled off the airspeed and the aircraft began to sink. Greenlee called for '...all the power you've got', but the No 1 engine, overboosted as a result, failed completely. With only one remaining engine still delivering power, it became impossible to maintain flying speed and the Constellation stalled into trees.

Few traumatic injuries occurred in the impact, but the cabin was breached in several places, allowing toxic smoke and flame to fill it almost at once. Estimates of how long the occupants could have remained conscious varied from as little as 30 seconds to as long as two minutes. Some at least should have been able to escape, but the jammed or blocked main door, the lack of any emergency briefing, the dense smoke, possibly shock and panic, and the rapidly increasing heat, obviously combined to prevent any from doing so, apart from the captain and the flight engineer.

Overall, the investigators concluded the crew were incapable of assuming responsibility for the Constellation's charter flight, and that the management of Imperial Airlines condoned not only substandard aircraft operations, but poor maintenance practices as well.

Cause

The National Transportation Safety Board attributed the cause of this accident to lack of command coordination and decision, lack of judgment, and lack of knowledge of the aircraft and its systems, leading to an emergency the crew were incapable of handling.

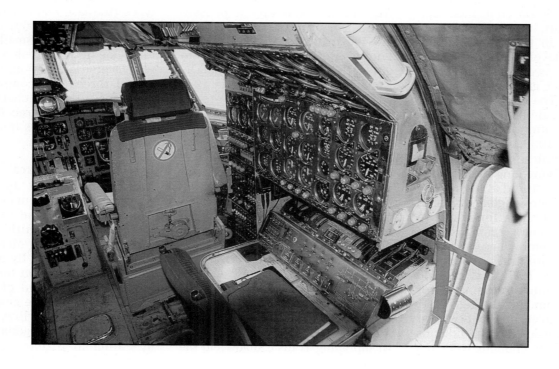

CHAPTER 18

The tragedy of the disappearing fuel

The basic aircraft type was exceptionally well proven. Yet within its fuel selection system there lurked an unrecognised pitfall with potential for disaster.

Holiday charters

The holiday charter business to the continent run by British Midland Airways was doing well in the mid 1960s. Based at East Midlands Airport, Castle Donington, Derbyshire in the UK, the company had developed from Derby Aviation, formed in 1953 at Derbyshire's earlier grass aerodrome at Burnaston. The company actually traced its beginnings to a prewar charter operation founded in Derbyshire in 1938. One of Derby Aviation's earliest contracts in the 1950s was flying new Avon jet engines, manufactured at the nearby Rolls-Royce aero engine works, to Toulouse in France for fitting to Caravelle jet liners coming off Sud Aviation's assembly line.

Castle Donington aerodrome, originally an RAF Station and home to a conversion unit for Bomber Command during WW2, was taken over in the post-war years by a consortium of Midlands city and county councils to be developed as a major civil airport. With a new runway, hangars, workshops and airport facilities, it opened as East Midlands Airport in April 1965.

Amongst the aircraft types British Midland Airways operated from East Midlands Airport were its three Canadair C-4 Argonauts. Basically a pressurised version of the Douglas DC-4 airframe, powered by liquid cooled Rolls-Royce Merlin engines, the type was developed by Canadair Ltd in Montreal in 1944 to meet the requirements of Trans Canada Airlines and the Royal Canadian Air Force.

The C-4 was fitted with Merlin engines for two reasons: The Merlin improved the performance of the aircraft over that of the Pratt & Whitney R2000 powered DC-4 and, under a British Commonwealth trade agreement at the time, the Merlins could be imported into Canada duty free, whereas Pratt & Whitney engines were subject to customs duty.

Canadair produced 70 C-4s up to the time production ceased at Montreal in mid 1949. In addition to supplying Trans Canada and the RCAF, the manufacturer received orders from BOAC and Canadian Pacific Air Lines. In Canada the C-4 was known as the Canadair North Star. But BOAC chose the equally imaginative name Argonaut for its fleet of C-4s.

In due course, as BOAC replaced its Canadair Argonauts with later types (the last was not withdrawn from service until 1960), they were sold to a variety of smaller operators. One of the British purchasers was Overseas Aviation, which acquired three. The company used them for a time in charter work, then in 1961 the three Argonauts were sold again, this time to British Midland Airways.

Return flight to Majorca

On Saturday night, June 3 1967, Argonaut G-ALHG, under charter from British Midland to the tour operator, Arrowsmith Holidays Ltd, took off from Manchester's Ringway Airport to fly a party of tourists to Palma, on the Spanish Mediterranean island of Majorca. The flight, under the command of Captain Harry Marlow, was uneventful and the Argonaut landed at Palma at 3.20am local time (2.20am GMT – Majorca is one hour ahead of GMT) on the Sunday morning.

In preparation for the return flight with the same crew, the aircraft was refuelled at Palma to the company's standard Palma-to-Manchester fuel load, which was considered ample in the existing weather conditions. Running 40 minutes behind schedule, Captain Marlow lodged a flightplan for Manchester, nominating Birmingham as an alternate. A capacity load of passengers whose summer holiday had come to an end – 77 adults and two children – boarded the Argonaut, and with First Officer Pollard flying the aircraft from the right hand seat, it took off just after 5am local time.

The other three members of the crew were Engineer Lloyd and Flight Attendants Taylor and Partleton. Lloyd was not a flight engineer, but was carried on the Argonaut to perform ground engineer duties during turnarounds at ports of call away from the company's base. Even so he occupied a jump seat on the flightdeck and assisted the pilots in flight where possible, particular in keeping the aircraft performance logs, as directed by the captain.

The homeward flight across France, the English Channel and over southeastern England towards Manchester was in all outward respects uneventful. At 8.56am GMT, nearly five hours after departure, the Argonaut, cruising at 6000ft, was a little over 10nm (19km) south of Manchester's Ringway Airport, and approaching the Congleton NDB.

It was a mild but showery summer's morning at Manchester, with a moderate westerly wind, and visibility reduced to about 1600 metres in rain and drizzle. At the airport, 14km almost due south of the city centre, there were three octas of cloud at 300ft, and seven octas at 400ft, with the sky completely overcast at 5000ft. The wind was from 270°T (due west) at 12kt (22km/h) and the QNH was 1025mb.

Runway 24 was in use, with its ILS operational. The Manchester Approach controller was vectoring aircraft normally by radar, but because of an improvement in the weather a short time before, the airport's Precision Approach Radar system had been briefly decommissioned for a minor technical adjustment.

The prototype Canadair C-4, developed in Montreal in 1944 for Trans Canada Airlines and the RCAF. A pressurised version of the DC-4, it was equipped with Rolls-Royce Merlin engines. BOAC and Canadian Pacific Air Lines also operated the C-4, a total 70 being produced. Known as the North Star in North America, it was called the Argonaut in Britain. The three Argonauts operated by British Midland Airways from 1961 were originally part of BOAC's fleet.

At 8.57am, when the Argonaut passed the Congleton NDB, the approach controller vectored it on to a northeasterly heading and cleared it to descend to 5000ft. On this heading the aircraft was skirting the western edge of the High Peak District between Manchester and Sheffield, 56km to the east. Two minutes later the controller instructed the aircraft to continue its descent to 3500ft, informed it that it was now 8nm (15km) east of the airport, and vectored it on to northwesterly headings to intercept the ILS localiser.

Engine problems

At 9.01am when the Argonaut was still well left of the centre line, the approach controller asked if they were receiving the ILS. Captain Marlow replied they were and would turn right a little. Two minutes later, seeing the aircraft 6nm (11km) from touchdown but still well to the left, the controller asked were they yet established on the ILS. When the crew failed to reply, he asked were they still receiving his transmissions. Captain Marlow then answered, "Hotel Golf is overshooting."

Instructing the aircraft to turn left on to 160°M and to climb to 2500 feet, the controller asked why. "We've a little bit of trouble with rpm – will advise you," the captain replied. He then asked for

The Canadair C-4 CF-TEL photographed during a European sales tour in 1947. The C-4 fuselage differed from that of the DC-4 in being pressurised and having square rather than circular cabin windows. Although the RR Merlin engines improved the cruising speed of the C-4 by up to 70kt (130km/h), the aircraft were a good deal noisier.

the heading to be repeated. But the controller, seeing the Argonaut had already turned 25° to the right instead of left, told it to continue turning right on to 020° and repeated his instruction to climb. A minute later, First Officer Pollard asked for the heading to be repeated yet again. By this time the Argonaut had broken through the overcast and, now visible from the ground, was flying below cloud in reasonable visibility.

At 9.05 the controller gave the aircraft its position as 7nm (13km) from the airport on a bearing of 040° and asked for its altitude. The reply, partly by the captain and partly by the first officer, was "Hotel Golf 1000". Realising for the first time the Argonaut was in serious trouble, the controller declared an emergency, told the aircraft to turn right immediately on to 180°M to intercept the localiser, and asked if they could maintain height.

Unable to maintain height

When Captain Marlow answered, "just about", the controller told them to continue the turn on to 200°M and to maintain as much height as possible. Moments later the captain transmitted: "unable to maintain height at the moment".

At this point, because of the Argonaut's low altitude, the controller lost radar contact and

asked the crew to report when they were established on the ILS. First Officer Pollard replied they had "the lights to our right" and were "at 800 feet, just maintaining height". The controller cleared the Argonaut to land, confirming the surface wind as 270° at 12kt.

With the time at 9.08, the airport's Precision Approach Radar was now operational again, and its controller informed the aircraft it was 6nm (11km) from touchdown. Captain Marlow asked for the distance to be repeated, and First Officer Pollard added they were "down to 500 feet". The terrain at this point is about 200ft AMSL, and with the aircraft about on the centreline of the ILS, it was heading directly towards the centre of Stockport, an industrial suburb on Manchester's southeastern outskirts.

A few seconds after 9.09am, witnesses in the streets of Stockport suddenly heard and caught sight of the Argonaut flying slowly at extremely low level just above the rooftops of the densely builtup area where they were standing. From the noise of the engines, it was obvious they were running at high power.

Impact

Moments later, after skirting a gasometer and a tall factory chimney, and just when it seemed the aircraft was about to crash into

tall blocks of flats that lay ahead of it, the sound of its engine ceased abruptly, and the big aircraft dropped heavily in an almost level attitude into an open area that lay between the buildings.

As it did so, the port wing struck a disused warehouse and an electricity substation, partly demolishing the building, setting two mains transformers on fire, and tearing the wing off at its root. Sliding fast over the ground, the aircraft almost instantly slammed into a single storey motor garage and workshop, missing its two petrol bowsers, but setting this building on fire also. This impact broke off the aircraft's nose section, tore a gaping hole in the side of the fuselage near the wing leading edge, and brought the wrecked aircraft, with its starboard wing and engines still attached, to a violent stop in only 15m. The tail remained projecting over the edge of the building. No intense fuel fire broke out immediately, but small flames appeared in several different places amongst the wreckage.

The site of the crash, in the middle of Stockport, was only about 100m from police headquarters and close to the town hall and hospital. Seeing the crash, a police motorcyclist radioed the station, then ran to the scene with other rescuers from nearby. They included members of a Salvation Army band that was forming up in a nearby street. They were joined almost at once by scores of police from their nearby headquarters. The small fires in the wreckage were insufficient to hamper rescuers, and their efforts began at once. Flight Attendant Julia Partleton, badly injured, lay on the ground outside the aircraft, apparently thrown from cabin when the fuselage was breached in the final impact

Reaching the victims through this break in the fuselage, rescuers found a confused heap of badly injured passengers in the forward section of the cabin. All were still strapped into their seats, which had come away from the cabin floor. Some were already dead, while severe leg injuries sustained by those who were still alive hampered efforts to free them. The rescuers also experienced difficulty releasing their seat belts.

Fire!

The rescuers were concentrating their efforts on the forward part of the cabin because the break in the fuselage made it the obvious place to start. Working feverishly for about 10 minutes, they had succeeded in rescuing 10 of the injured when suddenly there was a massive explosion in the starboard wing – fuel from the ruptured tanks had caught fire.

Flaring up fiercely, the flames quickly engulfed the fuselage, penetrating the forward section of the cabin and beating the rescuers back from where dead and injured still lay trapped. Rapidly intensifying, the fire then spread powerfully rearwards through the fuselage where many more dazed and injured passengers remained trapped. Rescuers had made no attempt in the short time available to open the emergency exits or the main rear cabin door. As a result, none of the occupants in the after part of the cabin escaped or could be rescued. The victims included Flight Attendant Taylor.

The first firefighting vehicle reached the scene from Stockport fire station just before the explosion, but as it was a water tender only, its efforts were largely ineffective. At least 30 more fire engines arrived soon afterwards from the Cheshire County Council brigade and the Manchester brigade, with foam tenders rushing from the Airport Fire Service. But all were too late to save the aircraft's occupants. As well as tackling the now massive aircraft conflagration, the fire crews had to deal urgently with fires in the electricity substation transformers and the burning garage to prevent the two 500 gallon (2275 litre) petrol tanks in the garage forecourt from exploding.

Meanwhile, beaten back by the flames from the main section of the fuselage, rescuers turned to the wreckage of the nose section which lay further forward, clear of the flames. Internally, it was a tangled mass of control cables, instrument wiring, and the flight-deck instruments and fittings, and

As originally designed, the C-4 provided seating for 40 first class or 62 economy class passengers. But the high density cabin layout adopted by British Midland Airways enabled the aircraft to seat 78.

rescuers had difficulty freeing the unconscious crew. Ambulance crews ultimately succeeded in getting them out, but although the captain had sustained only moderate head injuries, including a broken jaw, both the first officer and the engineer had been killed in the impact.

Police cordoned off the crash site almost immediately, but being a Sunday morning, sightseers began flocking to the scene almost at once. Within the hour, parked cars were blocking nearly every main road leading to it, and but for the police cordon, rescue and firefighting operations would have been severely hampered. Police later estimated that in the hours that followed the accident, no less than 10,000 people came to look at the scene. Even late in the afternoon, streets within half a mile of the accident site were still thronged with cars and pedestrians. Sightseers continued to come for several days afterwards.

INVESTIGATION

Inspectors from the Accident Investigation Branch of the Board of Trade found the Argonaut struck the ground more or less level in pitch, slightly starboard wing down, and yawed a little to the right. From eyewitness evidence, it was clear that the crew, when they saw an accident was inevita-

ble, deliberately cut the power and put the aircraft down on what was the only relatively open space in central Stockport.

Tall blocks of flats, the town hall, the police station, and Stockport hospital lay directly ahead in the direction of the airport, and the captain's split second decision meant that, despite horrendous casualties to his passengers and crew, no one on the ground in the heavily built up area was injured.

Wreckage examination

At the time of impact, the undercarriage was retracted, and the flaps set at 10°. Nos 1 and 2 engines were rotating under power at impact, but it could not be determined whether or not No 3 engine was doing so. The condition of its spark plugs indicated it was probably windmilling. No 4 propeller was feathered and its engine appeared to be undamaged.

It was evident from the positions of the radiator shutter actuators and the fact that the main fuel boost pumps were switched on, with each engine selected to its main fuel tank, that the crew were carrying out their approach checks when the emergency occurred. There was nothing to suggest any failure or malfunction of the aircraft or its systems had occurred before the crash.

BOAC's C-4 Argonaut, G-ALHD, soon after the aircraft entered the airline's service in late 1949. BOAC operated a total of 22 Argonauts. They were ordered as substitutes for the Avro Tudors the airline intended to introduce to its routes in the late 1940s.

G-ALHG, the Argonaut tragically destroyed at Stockport, Manchester, while being operated by British Midland Airways. This air-to-air picture was taken in Australia in the 1950s when the aircraft was in BOAC service.

The Rolls-Royce Merlin engines were removed from the wreckage and dismantled to determine whether there had been any pre-crash malfunction. None was found, and there was no evidence of overspeeding. The oil supply to all engines and propellers had been functioning normally.

The propellers were similarly examined to determine their blade angles at impact and for evidence of pre-crash defects. Again, none was found. Propellers Nos 1, 2, and 3 were in the flight fine position, and damage to No 4's blades supported the mechanical evidence that it was feathered.

The aircraft

Designed in the mid-forties, the Argonaut was built in Canada in 1949 and, after service with BOAC, was bought ultimately by British Midland. It was being properly maintained and its Certificate of Airworthiness and maintenance certificate were both valid.

BOAC used its Argonauts on long haul operations, at first with only 40 first class seats. Later the airline increased the seating to 54. But when Overseas Aviation acquired the Argonauts they were modified to carry 72 passengers. In 1962 British Midland further modified them to take 75 seats, and in 1964 the seating was increased to 78. In this final configu-ration the seating provided an average seat pitch of 79cm (31in). All the modifications had airworthiness approval from the Air Registration Board. There was no possibility that overloading contributed to the accident, and on the flight from Palma the aircraft was within its weight and centre of gravity limits.

The seats and their anchorages, stressed to 9g, complied with air safety requirements. But the main disintegrating force in the cabin appeared not to have been fore and aft deceleration, but vertical forces considerably greater than 9g. This caused the cabin floor to collapse, allowing the seats and their occupants to concertina forward.

Seat damage and passenger survival

The seats had two bracing bars between their rear uprights, about 23mm above the floor. While the inner bracing bar was massive, the bar nearer the passenger seated immediately behind was comparatively narrow in section. In the burnt out remains of 66 seats examined, this narrow rear bar was fractured in 38 instances, and bent forward in the other 28. This damage was caused by the legs of the passengers seated behind as the seating concertinaed during the violent deceleration of the crash.

Medical evidence indicated crash forces towards the rear of the aircraft were less than further forward, and that in all but the front section of the cabin, they were potentially survivable. While postmortem examination of the victims in the first nine rows of seats showed a preponderance of fatal deceleration injuries, examination of the bodies seated elsewhere consistently revealed mainly lower leg injuries, involving massive soft tissue damage, with fractures of the tibia and fibula. Clearly, most of these passengers should not have become fatalities. Their leg injuries were obviously the reason – they were unable to escape or could not be rescued before the fire took hold.

The main difficulty hindering their rescue was their inaccessibility in the short time available, and the rescuers' lack of familiarity with the aircraft's seat belt releases added to the delay. All taking part in the rescue effort when the flames beat them back were deeply moved by the horror of a situation they were powerless to avert.

The few passengers who did survive were, with one exception, seated on the starboard side of the forward section of the cabin. They survived only because, although they were in the cabin section subjected to the greatest deceleration, they were closest to the break in the fuselage and therefore accessible to the rescuers.

The crew

Captain Marlow, 41, trained in the wartime RAF and remained a RAF pilot until 1954 when he joined Skyways Ltd. Six months later he joined British Midland (then Derby Aviation) as a first officer. He became a captain on DC-3 and Miles Marathon aircraft in 1957. At the time of the accident he had flown more than 10,000 hours, 2000 of them in Argonauts.

First Officer Pollard, 21, was licensed as a pilot when he was only 17, and joined British Midland as second officer two years later in 1965. Within another two years he was flying as first officer on both Argonauts and Viscounts. He had more than 1000 hours experience and was regarded as a professional pilot of considerable promise.

There was no evidence that Captain Marlow or First Officer Pollard were unduly tired after what had been an uneventful tour of night duty in good weather. In particular, the recording of communications between the Argonaut and Air Traffic Control contained no suggestion they were suffering from fatigue.

Captain Marlow was first interviewed in hospital the day after the accident while still under sedation. Although still severely shocked, four of his remarks were of interest to the investigators:
• First Officer Pollard was flying the aircraft until the trouble started. Then the captain took over control.
• He couldn't hold the aircraft straight "even with rudder".
• He had been trying to find

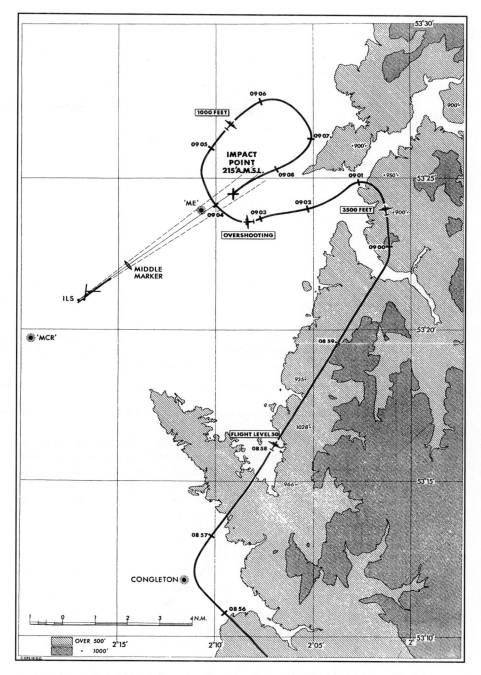

Diagram illustrating the latter stages of the Argonaut's flightpath as Manchester Approach Control vectored it to intercept Ringway Airport's ILS. The stage at which the aircraft attempted to go around when the two port engines failed, and its point of impact in the Manchester suburb of Stockport are indicated. (UK Board of Trade)

somewhere to "put the aircraft down".
• He asked the interviewing investigator, "Which engine was it?"

Captain Marlow's head injuries were afterwards accompanied by retrograde amnesia, as a result of which he could remember nothing about the last stages of the flight after passing the Congleton NDB.

Also interviewed in hospital, the surviving flight attendant, Julia Partleton, said that when the emergency developed, the "Fasten seat belt" and "No smoking" signs were on in preparation for landing. And Flight Attendant Taylor, who was further back in the cabin had remarked to her that the flaps had been lowered but then retracted again. She had noticed no abnormal engine noise before the impact.

Flight Data Recorder

The Argonaut was equipped with a early type FDR which recorded airspeed, altitude and heading. By

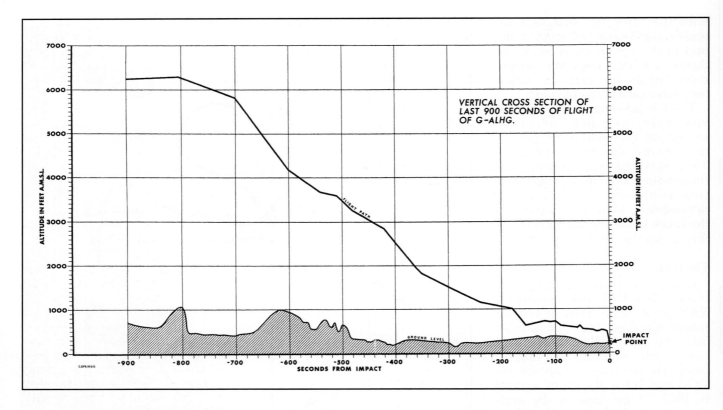

Profile of the Argonaut's flightpath in relation to ground level during its final 15 minutes of flight. (UK Board of Trade)

plotting the data from its undamaged recording tapes in graphical form, the investigators were able to reconstruct the last 15 minutes of the flight. (See diagrams).

The readout began with the aircraft in cruising flight at a constant speed and height. The height and speed then began to reduce as the Argonaut began the initial stages of a steady approach.

The changes in airspeed and altitude 495 seconds before impact were consistent with lowering 10° of flap, followed by a small increase in engine power. Between 415 and 405 seconds before impact, a sudden loss of height at 2000 fpm, with a corresponding increase in airspeed from 126 to 140 knots (233 to 259km/h), suggested that two engines failed within 20 seconds of each other.

By minus 375 seconds, the airspeed was falling again and the aircraft had begun turning right, continuing to do so although vectored to the left 50 seconds later. The aircraft's behaviour was now entirely consistent with its crew experiencing severe control difficulties. At minus 340 seconds there was an increase in power on the live engines, no doubt as the captain attempted to overshoot

and go round. But by this time the airspeed had fallen to only 116kt (215km/h), and the altitude to 1838ft. At minus 215 seconds, when the Argonaut's airspeed had further decayed to 111kt (206km/h) and it had lost height to 1287ft, engine power was further increased to maximum continuous.

The data recorded from this point on was in accord with the configuration in which the aircraft crashed, with one engine feathered, one windmilling, and the two live engines at maximum continuous power. This power situation was the only reasonable inference that could be drawn, and was consistent with the aircraft maintaining a constant heading at a speed of less than 110kt (204km/h) during its last 80 seconds of flight.

Handling

To assess the Argonaut's handling qualities in the configuration suggested by the FDR during the last seven minutes of flight, and to establish minimum control speeds in that configuration, the Air Registration Board's Chief Test Pilot, Captain D P Davies, carried out flight tests on a sister British Midland Airways aircraft, G-ALHY. The company's Chief Pilot, Cap-

tain S D Fenton, occupied the right hand control seat.

With the undercarriage retracted, up to 15° flap extended, No 3 engine windmilling and No 4 engine feathered, it was found that minimum control speeds at different power settings on the two live port engines were adversely affected by the extremely high rudder forces needed to maintain directional control. This was severely so at maximum continuous power on the live engines. Although full opposite rudder trim substantially reduced the rudder pedal forces required at higher speeds, the trim's apparent effectiveness progressively decreased as speed was reduced. At minimum control speeds, the rudder trim seemed to be of little assistance.

Even with only one starboard engine "failed", full opposite rudder trim was still required at low speeds. And with both starboard engines "failed" and the flaps retracted, it was impossible to maintain height, even with full power on the two port engines.

Because of the poor performance and handling qualities revealed by the flight tests, it was evident that, during the emergency that overtook G-ALHG, the

The wrecked Argonaut burns furiously after the fuel tanks in the starboard wing exploded. (The Times)

captain would have been wholly occupied in controlling the flight path. At the same time, the remaining workload would probably have exceeded the capability of the second pilot. The handling tests also showed that a short pilot, with his seat correctly adjusted for landing, would be unable to hold on full rudder in the circumstances. And unless the pilots undid their shoulder harnesses, they would have been unable to reach some of the fuel selectors and minor controls.

The general assessment of the flight tests was that the Argonaut was rather a heavy aeroplane to fly, but that as long as its engines were all running, there was no serious problem with its controls. However, because of its difficult control characteristics with one or more engines out, it would no longer be acceptable for certification as a new type transport aircraft.

The fuel system

In the absence of any evidence of engine or system malfunction, and the fact that the fuel on board the aircraft should have been entirely adequate for the trip, attention was turned to the aircraft's fuel system. It was significant that the double engine failure occurred during the approach checks, when the selection of each engine to its main fuel would be physically verified and the main fuel boost pumps switched on.

The Argonaut's fuel system, identical to that of the DC-4, comprised four main tanks and four auxiliaries. No 1 main and auxiliary tanks in the port wing supplied No 1 engine, while No 2 main and auxiliary tanks supplied No 2 engine. The arrangement was the same in the starboard wing, with No 3 main and auxiliary tanks supplying No 3 engine, and No 4 main and auxiliary tanks supplying No 4 engine. Electric boost pumps in the outlets of each tank, with cross feed lines, made up a complex fuel system that enabled any engine or combination of engines to be fed from any tank. A large number of selector combinations were thus possible.

The four levers controlling the tank selectors were mounted on the centre pedestal below the throttles on the captain's side, while the two levers controlling the crossfeed valves were in the corresponding position below the throttles on the first officer's side. It was difficult to reach the crossfeed selectors from the captain's seat, or the tank selectors from the first officer's seat. For a pilot wearing shoulder harness it was impossible.

Similar in design, the tank selector and crossfeed valves both had three positions. A tank selector lever in its fully forward position turned its respective main tank on and auxiliary tank off. In the selector's midway position, the main tank was off and the auxiliary

tank on. In the fully aft position, both tanks were off. With the crossfeed selectors fully forward, the crossfeed system was off. When both selectors were fully aft, "cross ship crossfeed" was provided. In their midway positions, the selectors provided inter engine crossfeed between the engines on the wing to which the selector related.

Fuel management

British Midland's standard fuel load for its Argonauts on the Manchester to Palma run was all main tanks full, and 100 gallons (455 litres) each in Nos 1 and 4 auxiliary tanks. No 2 and 3 auxiliary tanks were left empty.

Takeoff and climb were accomplished with booster pumps switched on and each main tank feeding its own engine. When settled down in the cruise, normally at between 8000 and 16,000 feet, the main tanks would be switched off and Nos 1 and 2 engines supplied from No 1 auxiliary tank, with Nos 3 and 4 engines fed from No 4 auxiliary. The booster pumps would then be switched off.

When the estimated time for the consumption of fuel from the auxiliaries had elapsed, all booster pumps would be switched on again, all main tanks selected, and the auxiliaries and cross feeds turned off. As soon as the fuel flow stabilised, the boosters would be switched off.

The injured captain is carried from the wreckage of the unburnt but severely damaged nose section of the aircraft. (The Times)

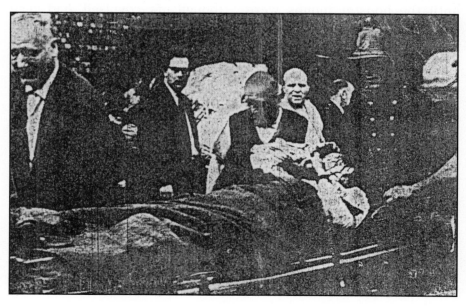

Aerial view of the crash site after the fires had been extinguished. The crew put the aircraft down in one of the few unoccupied spaces in central Stockport, narrowly avoiding houses, a block of flats, and factory buildings. (The Times)

For the remainder of the flight, each engine would be supplied from its own main tank, the whole system remaining unpressurised until the booster pumps were switched on again during the approach checks.

Inadvertent transfer

It was widely known at British Midland that, after Argonauts had been standing on the ground for a time, fuel could be found to have transferred from one tank to another. This was commonly ascribed to mishandling of the selectors on the ground, pilots and engineering staff believing that inadvertent fuel transfer in the air was impossible.

However, although there was no reference in the aircraft's flight or maintenance manuals to any possibility of inadvertent fuel trans-

fer in the air, examination of the fuel logs of British Midland's Argonauts in fact suggested that inadvertent fuel transfer in the air, though unrecognised, had been commonplace.

The tank selector and cross feed valves were "plug" cocks consisting of a casing in which there were three ports. A rotor within the casing contained passages which, by turning the rotor, could either be aligned with the ports or could shut them off. The ports shut off were sealed by a spring loaded carbon pad, with the selected rotor position maintained by detents on the outside of the casing.

But if the rotor happened to be only slightly off its fully closed position, the spring loaded carbon pads, impinging on the inner face of the casing, opened the ports to the space between the casing

and the rotor (see diagram). As a result, some fuel transfer could occur. For example, on the starboard crossfeed valve, the fuel line from No 4 tank selector, instead of being sealed off, could be partly open both to the port leading to No 3 selector, providing some inter engine crossfeed, and to the port leading to the other crossfeed valve, providing some cross ship feed.

The flightdeck selectors controlling the valves moved through an arc of only 80°, and although the method of selection was labelled, the three detent positions were not marked. The only identification that a valve had been correctly selected to any of its three positions was the feel of the detents.

Several highly experienced British Midland pilots were adamant

Firemen and emergency crews work on the burnt out wreckage. Note the crushed motor vehicles in the background that were parked in the demolished garage workshop – and the crowd of spectators on the rise overlooking the site. (The Times)

Another view of the wreckage and damage to surrounding buildings. The loss of life on board the Argonaut was horrific, but no one on the ground was even injured – an extraordinary outcome in the circumstances of the accident. The crush of sightseers that flocked to the scene as news of the disaster spread became a serious problem to the police. (Wide World Photos)

that, though the midway detent was easily found, the detents at the forward and aft positions could not be felt. In flight, they customarily pushed or pulled the selector as far as it would go. Some pilots did not even know there were detents at the end travel positions. One British Midland pilot was unable to feel the detents at the end positions during flight even though he purposely tried to do so. And an Accident Investigation Branch test pilot, flying with only his lap strap fastened, found when moving the crossfeed selector from midway to the forward off position, that he was tending to leave it 10° short of closed. Several other senior pilots also failed to get the crossfeed selectors correctly into position while flying the aircraft.

On the other hand, engineers from both British Midland and the Accident Investigation Branch were able to feel the positive engagement of the detents in all three positions. It was clear that, although presenting no problem to a maintenance engineer who was free to move around the flightdeck while exercising the selectors on the ground, the position of the tank and crossfeed selectors made it impossible for pilots wearing shoulder harness to feel the detents in the fully forward position.

In flight therefore, it was possible for a selector, ostensibly moved to its closed position, to remain "cracked" slightly open.

Ground tests

Engine tests were carried out on a sister Argonaut on the ground to determine whether an undetected fuel transfer could have contributed to the accident. With the tank selectors to Nos 1, 2 and 3 main and auxiliary tanks all closed off, No 4 main tank and its booster pump was selected on, and the crossfeed selectors "cracked". In this condition, all four engines ran normally at 30 inches of manifold pressure, and continued to do so even when No 4 booster pump was switched off.

Next, all four engines were run off their respective main tanks with booster pumps on and the crossfeed selectors "cracked". When No 4 main tank ran dry, No 4 engine stopped almost at once. With all main tank booster pumps left on, No 3 engine was then selected to its empty No 3 auxiliary tank, and the auxiliary tank booster pump switched on. Again all three engines continued to run at 30 inches of manifold pressure. But when the throttles were opened above 40 inches towards rated power, No 3 engine, instead of accelerating, stopped.

Previous Incidents

In the light of the tests, examination of British Midland's Argonaut fuel logs revealed previous incidents of inadvertent fuel transfer in flight that had not been diagnosed:

• On two occasions in flight, while drawing fuel from Nos 1 and 4 auxiliary tanks, each containing 200 gallons (909 litres), with their booster pumps running and inter engine crossfeeds selected, the tanks ran dry after 50 minutes. The missing fuel was found to have transferred itself to Nos 1 and 4 main tanks. A maintenance engineer who afterwards made a full check of the fuel selection system of the aircraft concerned, could find no discrepancies. With hindsight, it was evident the selectors had been slightly out of position in flight, but when the engineer checked them on the ground, he correctly positioned them in their detents.

• A significant fuel transfer incident had taken place in the Argonaut involved in the accident only a week earlier, when it was making a previous return flight to Palma. On that occasion also, the aircraft took off from Manchester with the standard fuel load for the Palma run – main tanks full and 100 gallons (455 litres) each in Nos 1 and 4 auxiliaries. After an hour, the crew switched from mains to auxiliaries, and an hour later again switched back to the mains. But about four and a half hours into the flight, with nearly an hour still to run to Palma, the first officer became concerned that the No 4 main fuel gauge was indicating less than an hour's fuel.

He asked the captain if he should crossfeed from No 3 main tank for a time, as this was showing a much higher reading. But the captain said he'd been told No 4 gauge was under reading, and that, with the main tanks full when they took off, there should be enough fuel remaining in each to reach Palma.

As the aircraft neared the destination, the first officer, still concerned about the No 4 tank's now very low reading, asked the maintenance engineer travelling on the flightdeck to watch the fuel pressure gauge for No 4 engine and let him know if it started to fall.

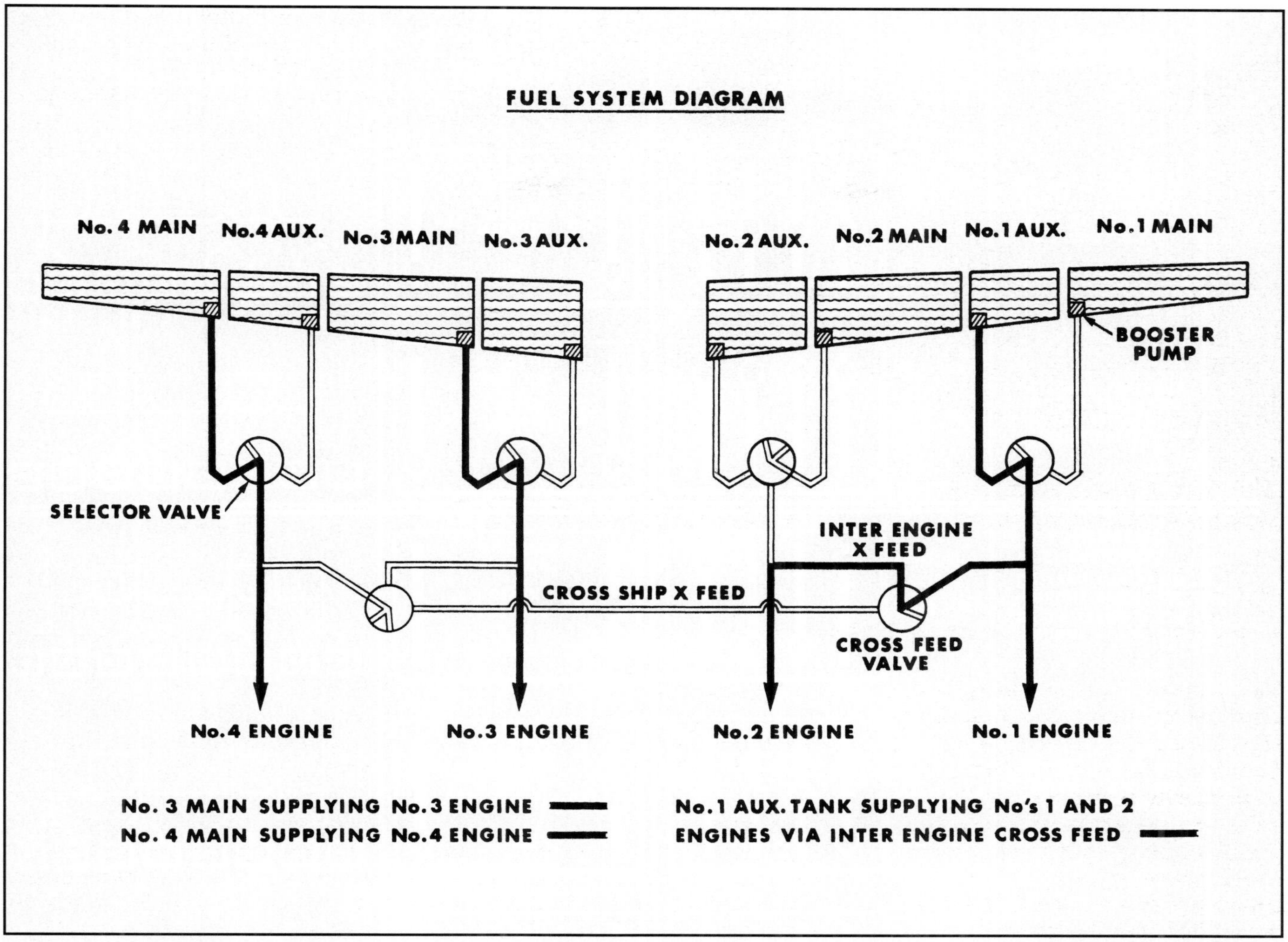

FUEL SYSTEM DIAGRAM

No. 4 MAIN   No.4 AUX.   No.3 MAIN   No.3 AUX.   No.2 AUX.   No.2 MAIN   No.1 AUX.   No.1 MAIN

BOOSTER PUMP

SELECTOR VALVE

INTER ENGINE X FEED

CROSS SHIP X FEED

CROSS FEED VALVE

No. 4 ENGINE   No.3 ENGINE   No.2 ENGINE   No.1 ENGINE

No. 3 MAIN SUPPLYING No.3 ENGINE ━━━
No. 4 MAIN SUPPLYING No.4 ENGINE ━━━

No.1 AUX. TANK SUPPLYING No's 1 AND 2
ENGINES VIA INTER ENGINE CROSS FEED ━━━

Schematic diagram of the Argonaut's eight tank fuel system. The system is similar to that of the DC-4. (UK Board of Trade)

When the Argonaut was on final approach, nearing the runway threshold, the first officer misunderstood a gesture by the engineer to mean that the No 4 fuel pressure was falling. He at once moved the starboard crossfeed selector lever to the inter engine position, but could not reach across to close the No 4 main tank selector without interfering with the captain's handling of the throttles during this critical stage of the approach to land. His crossfeed selection caused the No 4 gauge indication to both increase and fluctuate, and after a few seconds the No 3 fuel pressure gauge indication also began fluctuating.

At the end of the landing run the first officer told the captain he had opened the crossfeed. He closed it again while the captain taxied in on all four engines and the first officer monitored the fuel pressures. They did not fluctuate

and the captain remained convinced there was still plenty of fuel in all the main tanks.

After the engines were shut down, the first officer asked the engineer to note the fuel quantities required to fill each main tank. The figures recorded were in litres, and the first officer, converting them to gallons, worked out that on shut down, the No 4 main tank contained only an alarming 14 gallons (64 litres). After checking the total amount of fuel, he concluded there was some mistake in the figures – the result of his calculations just did not seem realistic. But it did not occur to him to work out the fuel quantities added to the other three main tanks.

On the return flight to Manchester, the first officer kept a careful watch on the fuel system, but saw no abnormalities other than what he believed was a substantial under reading of the No 4 main tank contents gauge.

Late that night, when the aircraft returned to its base at East Midlands Airport, the presumed defect was listed for corrective action by the company's maintenance staff. But unfortunately, not a word of what had happened on the approach to Palma, nor of the extraordinary result of the first officer's fuel calculation, reached the company's chief pilot or flight safety officer.

ANALYSIS

The crew evidently began their approach checks about 9.01am, when the approach controller told the Argonaut it was still well left of the centre line, and the captain replied he would turn right a little. The crew had just extended 15° of flap for the approach when the No 4 engine suddenly lost power.

The approach checks include

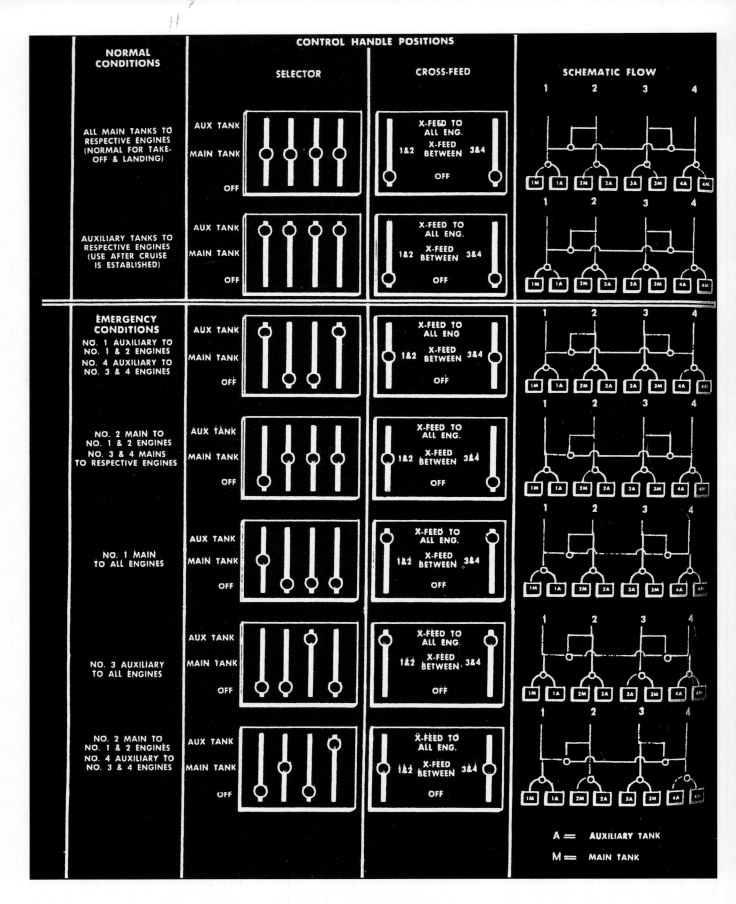

Diagram illustrating the operation of the Argonaut's fuel tank selectors and crossfeed selectors. The complexity of the system and the large number of possible combinations posed an understandable dilemma for the crew when two engines failed from fuel starvation at a critical stage of their approach to Manchester Airport.

ensuring the main fuel tanks are selected on, and the crossfeeds off. If until that moment No 4 engine, with the contents of its main tank already exhausted, was being fed through a "cracked" crossfeed selector from another tank, the crew's drill would have fully closed this selector, resulting in fuel starvation of the No 4 engine almost at once.

The crew feathered the propeller, but almost immediately experienced difficulty holding the aircraft straight and, as the approach controller asked if they were established on the ILS, No 3 engine also failed.

Although the investigators were unable to finally determine why this second engine failed, one possibility was that, when No 4 failed, the crew misidentified it as No 3 and feathered its propeller, only to find their action had not eased the handling problem and the aircraft was continuing to lose height.

But the crew might not have immediately recognised this misidentification, and while the captain continued to be fully occupied fighting the heavy controls, the first officer would have had to determine the problem, then restart No 3 engine and shut down No 4. To do so, he would among other actions, have had to undo his harness to reach the main fuel selectors. It seemed possible to the investigators that power was not restored to the No 3 engine in time to prevent the accident, simply because of the high flightdeck workload involved. Such a possibility would also make sense of Captain Marlow's question while under sedation in hospital, "Which engine was it?"

The other possibility was that No 3 main tank had also run dry because of inadvertent fuel transfer and the engine was feeding from another tank through a "cracked" crossfeed selector. So that when the crossfeed and tank selectors were checked during the approach drill, its fuel was also cut off.

This could explain why only 15 seconds elapsed between the failure of No 4 and No 3 engines, and why in the minutes before the crash, the crew were unable to restore power to either engine. It

The flightdeck of the Argonaut. The fuel selector and crossfeed selector levers, immediately in front of the two sets of throttles, are partly obscured by the centre pedestal and barely visible in this picture.

also seemed possible that the crew might not have recognised that a second engine ceased to deliver power soon after they feathered No 4.

At the height and position of the Argonaut at the time of the emergency, it would have been possible for it to reach the runway. But not until the aircraft, still 7nm (13km) from the runway, had begun going round and was flying a reciprocal heading only 600ft above the ground, did the controller realise the gravity of the situation. By that time, an accident of some sort was inevitable.

Although in the event the captain's decision to go round proved disastrous, it was clear from the radio transmissions that, faced by a sudden wholly unexpected situation, he reasonably decided to try to sort it out, rather than attempt an immediate emergency landing with both engines out on the same side. It was probably at this stage that the flaps were retracted from 15° to 10°.

Engine failure recognition

The Argonaut's instrumentation was typical of the heavy piston engined, pressurised transport aeroplanes of its era, with engine rpm, manifold pressure, fuel flow, fuel pressure, oil temperature and oil pressure gauges all indicated on dual pointer instruments, each serving two port or two starboard engines. RPM, manifold pressure and fuel flow were indicated by concentric pointers for each engine. But experience has shown that multi-pointer instruments are open to misinterpretation, particularly if the pointers are oscillating when an engine fails.

Engine failure in a multiengined aeroplane fitted with supercharged piston engines and constant speed propellers can in any case be difficult to recognise, especially at low cruising power – the constant speed unit maintains the rpm, while the supercharger maintains the manifold pressure. The only reliable instrument indication that the engine is not delivering power is the fuel pressure gauge, coupled with the flowmeter. Captain Marlow's question in hospital, "Which engine was it", suggested that the multipointer instrumentation could, to a small extent, have contributed to the accident.

The fuel transfer mystery

The reputed inaccuracy of the Argonaut's fuel gauges helped to mask any evidence of inadvertent

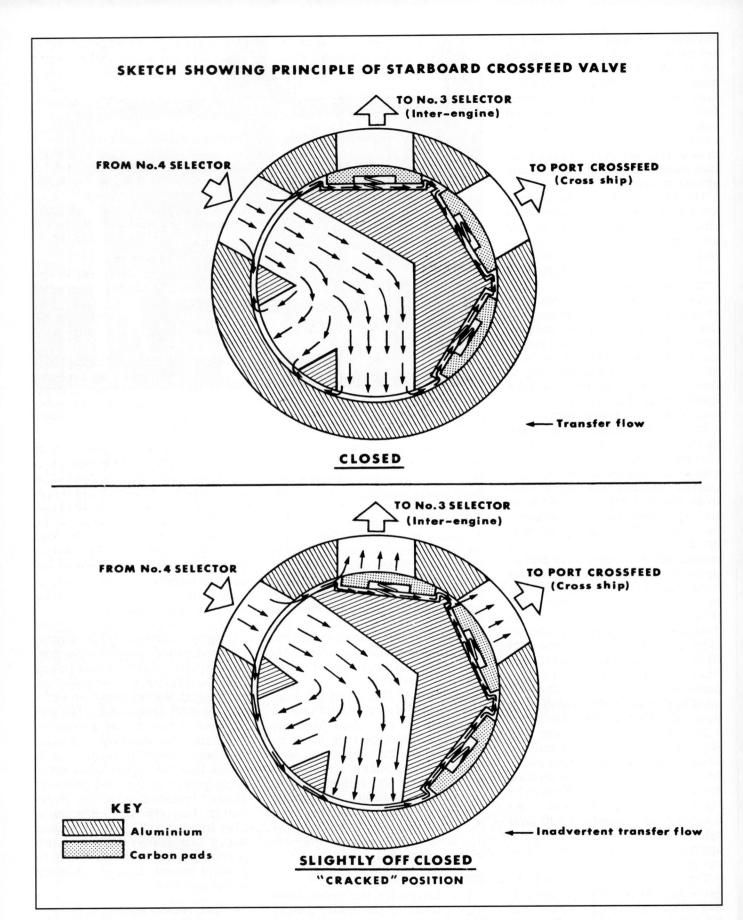

SKETCH SHOWING PRINCIPLE OF STARBOARD CROSSFEED VALVE

TO No. 3 SELECTOR
(Inter-engine)

FROM No. 4 SELECTOR

TO PORT CROSSFEED
(Cross ship)

← Transfer flow

CLOSED

TO No. 3 SELECTOR
(Inter-engine)

FROM No. 4 SELECTOR

TO PORT CROSSFEED
(Cross ship)

KEY

Aluminium

Carbon pads

← Inadvertent transfer flow

SLIGHTLY OFF CLOSED
"CRACKED" POSITION

Schematic diagram illustrating the way in which a "cracked" selector valve can allow fuel to flow to selector positions intended to be shut off. The starboard crossfeed valve is shown as an example. (UK Board of Trade)

tank to tank fuel transfer occurring during flight, something all British Midland pilots and engineers firmly believed it was impossible. But the tests showed this belief to be wholly without foundation, no one appreciating the difference between the ease of finding the selector detents while on the ground, and the difficulty of doing so by pilots strapped into their seats in the air. No warning of the problem was contained in any technical literature on the aeroplane.

The failure of the captain or the first officer to report what had happened at Palma the week before the accident was unfortunate. Had they done so, the incident could have revealed the risk of inadvertent fuel transfer in flight and a warning could have been given to Argonaut pilots. Armed with this information, Captain Marlow might have been in a better position to cope with the emergency that overtook the same aircraft only five days later.

During the investigation it was learnt that both Douglas and Canadair knew that if the fuel selectors were "cracked" as little as 10° from their detents, all three ports would be open. But despite all the years that the basic DC-4 design had been in worldwide operation, until the tests that fol-

lowed the Stockport accident, neither Douglas nor Canadair appreciated the high rates of flow that could take place when the selectors were "cracked" between 10° and 15°. Had they done so, a warning would doubtless have been included in the aircraft type's flight manual. As it was, no steps were taken to inform operators of this design characteristic and its implications.

Other British Isles operators of DC-4 and Argonaut aircraft, including BOAC and Aer Lingus, had found from experience in 1953 and 1954 that inadvertent transfer was quite possible. But neither the British Air Registration Board nor the Accident Investigation Branch realised it could occur on any significant scale. Had British Midland been informed of the possibility however, the tragedy at Stockport might have been averted.

British Midland and the Air Registration Board subsequently agreed on a drill to ensure that fuel selections were correctly made during flight, by turning on the relevant booster pumps and observing the resulting fuel pressure gauge indications. And because of the poor performance and difficult control characteristics of the Argonaut with one or more engines out, as demonstrated by the flight tests, and the

resulting high flightdeck workload, the Air Registration Board also required that Argonaut flightcrews in future include a third pilot or a qualified flight engineer.

CAUSE

The immediate cause of the accident was a loss of power in both engines on the starboard side, resulting in control problems which prevented the pilot from maintaining height on the available power with one propeller windmilling.

Contributory causes

• Failure of the designers of the fuel system to warn operators of the danger of inadvertent fuel transfer during a long flight if the selectors were not correctly positioned in their detents.

• Failure of British Midland Airways to recognise, from evidence available from previous incidents and Argonauts fuel logs, the possibility of inadvertent fuel transfer in the air.

• Failure of other operators of DC-4s and Argonauts whose experience had revealed the possibility of inadvertent fuel transfer in flight, to inform the Air Registration Board and the Accident Investigation Branch, in order that this information could be communicated to other operators of the aircraft types.

Below: The Argonaut involved in the accident at Stockport, Manchester, when being operated by BOAC in earlier years.

CHAPTER 19

Total electrical failure – loss of control

Disorientation in cloud – long the bane of inexperienced VFR pilots – claims an experienced Viscount crew, demonstrating the phenomenon is no respecter of persons.

London to Central Europe

British Eagle Airways's Viscount service from London Heathrow to the historic city of Innsbruck in the Austrian Alps on August 9, 1968, was scheduled for departure at 9.30am.

Designated Flight EA802, it was under the command of Captain Edward Dawdy and was expected to take a little over two and a half hours. The crew comprised First Officer Garry Holland and two flight attendants. Both Dawdy, 43, and Holland, 32, were experienced Viscount pilots, Dawdy being a company training captain for the type. The Viscount 700 allocated to the trip, G-ATFN *City of Truro*, was configured to seat 59 passengers, but the number booked on this flight was 44.

The flight planned route was in controlled airspace throughout, on established airways via Frankfurt, Nurnberg, Munich, thence to Innsbruck. The beautiful old city, elevation 1880 feet, is situated in a picturesque valley surrounded by the towering snow covered mountains of the Austrian Alps.

The weather forecast for the route indicated that conditions would be fine, particularly over the latter portion of the flight, but overcast with four to six eighths of alto-stratus and alto-cumulus between 7000 and 16,000 feet. In the event however, the development of a severe storm in the vicinity of Heathrow shortly before 9.30am forced the company to delay the aircraft's departure pending an improvement in local conditions.

While they waited at the airport, Dawdy and Holland learnt that the weather over much of their proposed route was also deteriorating. Under the influence of a stationary front lying across the route, the sky was becoming completely overcast by cloud with a base of between only 700 and 1000 feet, with tops extending to about 16,000 feet. Beyond Munich, visibility was reported as reducing almost to ground level.

But nearly an hour later, conditions at London Airport had improved sufficiently for the flight to proceed, the Viscount finally lifting off from Heathrow at 10.37am GMT. With a planned cruising airspeed of 264kt (489km/h), its estimated time of arrival at Innsbruck was now 1.17pm, and it was carrying sufficient fuel for five hours flying.

Radar vectored out of the Heathrow control zone and over southeastern England, the Viscount reported passing over Dover at 11.02am, climbing through Flight Level 175 (17,500 feet). It reached its cruising level of FL210 (21,000 feet) 10 minutes later, the flight then apparently proceeding normally in all respects, making successive routine position reports to European air traffic controllers at Brussels, Frankfurt and Munich.

Entering Munich ATC's airspace and passing its position to Munich at 12.52pm as over Allersberg, the Viscount advised it was estimating its next reporting point at the "Mike" NDB, 31nm (57km) southeast of Allersberg at 1.02pm. The Viscount's radar return was now visible on the Munich controllers' medium range radar screens and, at 1.02pm, Munich Radar informed the aircraft it was now passing the "Mike" NDB, and cleared it at the same time to descend to FL120 (12,000 feet) in preparation for its approach to Innsbruck.

Loss of contact

The Viscount did not acknowledge this transmission, nor did it reply to further calls the controllers then made to it. Even so, the Munich controllers continued to watch the aircraft's progress on radar until it was about 13nm (24km) to the south of the "Mike" NDB. It then faded from their screens.

Nothing more was heard of the aircraft at Munich ATC, and it did not arrive over Innsbruck at 1.17pm as expected. But at 1.29pm, 12 minutes after its ETA Innsbruck, people on the ground in and around the village of Langenbruk, seven nautical miles (13km) north of the "Mike" NDB, heard the sound of turbine aircraft engines approaching. Their scream increased in intensity above or in the overcast cloud, culminating in a crescendo akin to the sound of a propeller driven aircraft performing aerobatics, when there was a sudden loud bang. Moments later they were awe-struck to see a four-engined airliner descend out of the cloudbase, diving in a turn at high speed towards the ground. Its dive unchecked in any way, it plunged with disintegrating impact into the side of the substantial embankment carrying the busy four-lane Munich-Nurnberg autobahn, exploding in a fireball.

The momentum of the high speed impact carried most of the fragmented wreckage up and over the embankment, scattering burning fuel and components across the autobahn itself. Some of the flying debris struck and injured a bystander, as well as

Viscount G-ARDW, one of a number of the type operated by British Eagle Airways during the 1960s.

damaging a car that happened to be passing at the critical moment on the north-bound carriageway. The mind-numbing, instantaneous disintegration of the aircraft precluded all possibility of survival, all 48 people on board dying in the impact.

INVESTIGATION

Investigators from the German Office of Civil Aeronautics who arrived at the scene later in the day found that although the Viscount struck the ground on a northerly heading, its final descent had followed a curving flightpath to the left from a easterly heading. At the initial point

of impact on the side of the embankment, depressions in the ground made by the four engines and the underside of the fuselage were clearly recognisable.

From these marks, together with the fact that the aircraft passed over a powerline near the autobahn that crossed the final descent path, it was evident that the Viscount had dived into the ground at angle of at least 12.5°.

On the ground, some 2000m back along the curving final flight path, both outer wings were found lying near one another. Scattered around this area, and further along the flightpath for a distance of nearly 400m, were smaller

The planned route of British Eagle's Flight EA802 to Innsbruck in the Austrian alps. The company's Viscount 700 G-ATFN, City of Truro, carrying a crew of four and 44 passengers, disappeared from Munich air traffic control's radar screens three minutes after the controllers lost radio contact with the aircraft. Up to that time it had been cruising normally at 21,000 feet, making all routine position reports. (Aero Illustrations)

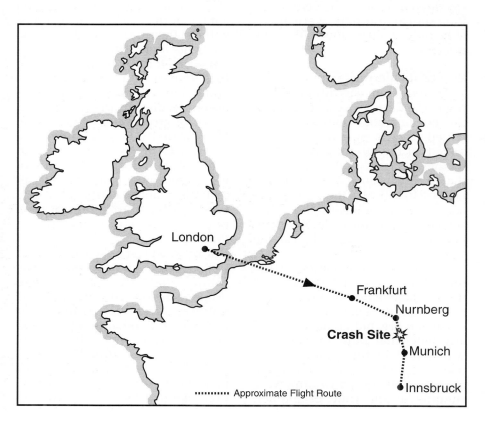

pieces of wing wreckage. Further still along the flightpath, sections of the port elevator and elevator anti-balance tab were also found, lying about 400m and 500m respectively short of the crash site. It was obvious that all this wreckage had broken away from the aircraft in flight.

Detailed examination of the burnt and fragmented main wreckage showed both wings had fractured symmetrically immediately outboard of the two outer engines. The wing failures evidently occurred simultaneously as a result of overstressing during an attempt to recover from a high speed dive, probably at an airspeed in excess of 310 knots. There was no evidence of metal fatigue in any of the fractures in the wings and elevators, and no indication of any malfunction in the aileron controls before the failure of the wings, nor in the elevator and rudder controls before impact. At the time of the crash, both the undercarriage and the flaps were retracted.

Examination of the engines showed that all four were operating up to the moment of impact, but it was not possible to determine with certainty how much power they were developing. Even so, there was some evidence that their power outputs were probably only a little above the idle range.

Electrical failure

The Viscount was fitted with a flight data recorder and despite the considerable damage it sustained, it was possible to determine that the aircraft's DC supply to the inverters had failed while the aircraft was cruising at Flight Level 210 (21,000 feet) on headings corresponding to the route segment from the Allersberg reporting point to Munich, via the "Mike" NDB.

A thorough examination of the aircraft's electrical system was not possible because of the extensive damage sustained in the crash and fire, but no indication of any electrical fault or overload was found in the many components examined. Yet although the aircraft's four DC generators were running at the time of impact,

both AC inverters, normally energised by the aircraft's batteries, were stationary. Similarly, none of the aircraft's radio communications equipment, radio navigational aids or electrically powered flight instruments were being energised. In addition, the electrically powered gyros of each of the aircraft's two artificial horizons, gyro compasses, and turn and bank indicators, were stationary at the time of impact.

The aircraft's certificate of maintenance was valid and all mandatory airworthiness requirements current at the time had been complied with. However, a modification of the means of reconnecting the generators in flight, involving the addition of an auxiliary reset switch, which had been recommended by the manufacturer nearly 10 years before, had not been incorporated in this Viscount.

The hours logged by the engines, propellers and auxiliary equipment were all within specified limits at the time of the accident, but a total of 12 electrical faults had been recorded in the aircraft's technical log during the preceding five months, the last only three days before the accident. As well, the aircraft's four DC generators had tripped out on a number of occasions, sometimes without their corresponding warning lights illuminating.

It seemed likely to the investigators that a similar occurrence could have begun the chain of events leading to the accident. A series of ground tests were therefore carried out on another Viscount 700 of the same type, to establish how long such a loss of generator power would take to affect the voltage of the electrical system while normal inflight electrical loads continued to be drawn.

With power supplied only from the aircraft's batteries, it was found that the DC voltage dropped below 20 volts after 31 minutes. The VHF transmitter failed after 33 minutes, and the inverter warning light illuminated after 39 minutes. After 43 minutes, the DC voltage dropped below nine volts. According to information supplied by Vickers, the air-

craft's manufacturer, a minimum of 16 volts would be required to reconnect the generators in this aircraft, because it was not fitted with the auxiliary reset switch recommended 10 years earlier.

Instrument response

Tests were also carried out to determine for how long the artificial horizons and turn and bank indicators would have continued to operate after the electrical supply failed. From the time the power was disconnected, the artificial horizons continued to show the bank attitude for five minutes with not more than a two degree error. Ten minutes after the loss of power, the error increased to about 10 degrees. After that, the readings became progressively less reliable.

The pitch indication remained normal for about 13 minutes after power was disconnected, and the gyros ran down and stopped completely after about 15 minutes.

In Viscount 700 aircraft, the artificial horizons are energised from the AC inverters and further tests showed that normal readings from the artificial horizons could be obtained with the inverter input voltage as low as 9.6 volts. Below this figure, the power supply "off" warning appeared on the instrument, and when the input voltage dropped below 5.5 volts, the readings became unstable.

The tests of the turn and bank indicators showed that the accuracy of the turn needle remained within permissible limits until the DC voltage reduced to 17 volts. Indications in the correct sense continued down to a minimum voltage of 3.5 volts, when the gyro stopped rotating altogether. From the time normal voltage power was disconnected from the instrument, it took about 34 seconds for the gyro to run down to a standstill.

ANALYSIS

Analysing the accumulated evidence, the German investigators concluded that, some time between when the aircraft passed over the Allersberg reporting point and it reached the "Mike" NDB, the VHF transmitter failed. The fact the aircraft's transponder was selected to the emergency "communication failure" code,

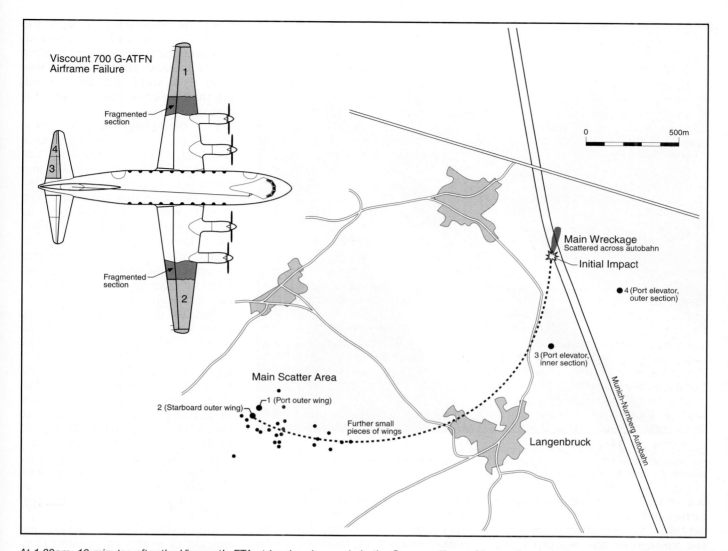

Viscount 700 G-ATFN
Airframe Failure

Fragmented section

Fragmented section

1

2

4

3

Main Scatter Area

2 (Starboard outer wing)

1 (Port outer wing)

Further small pieces of wings

Langenbruck

3 (Port elevator, inner section)

4 (Port elevator, outer section)

Main Wreckage
Scattered across autobahn

Initial Impact

Munich-Nuremberg Autobahn

0   500m

At 1.29pm, 12 minutes after the Viscount's ETA at Innsbruck, people in the German village of Langenbruck, half way between Nurnberg and Munich, were horrified to hear and see a four engined airliner plunge from low cloud in a screaming dive, exploding as it hit the embankment of Munich-Nuremberg autobahn. A loud bang, undoubtedly the outer wings failing in overload, preceded the aircraft's emergence from the cloud. This diagram of the final flightpath shows (1 and 2) where its outer wing sections fell, (3 and 4) where the two pieces of the port elevator were found, and the aircraft's point of impact against the autobahn embankment. (Aero Illustrations)

showed that the crew knew it had failed and were taking the required action.

Because there was no evidence of any fault in the VHF equipment itself, it could only be assumed that the radio failure was the result of the loss of electrical power. The flight data record showed a rapid fall in the DC voltage being supplied to the AC inverters which could only have resulted from the inverters being powered from the batteries alone. As the generators were still being driven by the engines when the aircraft crashed, and there were no indications of electrical failure in the busbar terminals, it could only he concluded that the generators had become disconnected from the main busbar.

A number of faults in this Viscount's electrical system had been recorded during the preceding five months and, as the generators had tripped out unexpectedly on other occasions as well, it seemed likely that, at the various times these previous faults were remedied, their true cause was not established.

With the generators disconnected from the main busbar, the Viscount's entire electrical system would be supplied only by the batteries, and as a result of this heavy current drain, the battery voltage would drop continuously until it failed.

To what extent the crew realised the aircraft's electrical system was failing when their VHF transmitter radio ceased to oper-

ate could not be determined. It was most unlikely that the pilots would have failed to notice the four generator warning lights on the instrument panel, so the investigators were doubtful that the warning lights had illuminated to indicate the generator failure.

The fact that the DC generators were disconnected would also have been indicated by the readings of the aircraft's four ammeters. But as these were mounted on the left hand side of the flightdeck behind the pilots' seats, the crew would hardly have been keeping these instruments under constant surveillance, particularly as the generator warning lights were so readily observable on the instrument panel. A further means of checking the electrical system

Low level aerial view of the fragmented and burnt wreckage of the Viscount, scattered across the divided Munich-Nuremberg autobahn. The initial point of impact is at the left of the picture. All 48 occupants were killed instantly.

was on the overhead instrument panel where, by selecting a switch, it was possible to measure the voltage of the batteries and the voltage being produced by the generators.

There could be no doubt however, that if the DC supply failure

had been recognised by the crew at the time, they would have immediately switched off all non-essential equipment, some of which would have been consuming heavy current. Had this been done, there would have been sufficient remaining power available

from the batteries to supply the navigation and radio equipment, essential for a descent and landing at the nearest airport. But it was clear from the flight data recording that the crew did not take this action.

The other actions the crew would have undoubtedly taken, had they recognised the failure in time, would have been to try and reconnect the generators. However, because this particular Viscount was not modified as recommended by the manufacturer, there was only one way in which this could be done, and this reconnection system would not have functioned once the DC voltage had dropped below 16 volts.

Because this system also would have been inoperative with an unremedied defect in the voltage control circuit, the investigators were doubtful whether any attempt could have been successful. In any case, because a minimum of 20 volts was required to operate the VHF transmitter. It would probably have been too late to reconnect the generators only one minute after the aircraft passed the "Mike" NDB – already the battery voltage would have dropped too low.

Reconstructing the likely sequence of events, it seemed that, when the radio failure occurred, the crew, in accordance with the regulations, selected the relevant transponder emergency code and continued their flight towards Innsbruck at Flight Level 210.

They probably did not abandon this intention until they realised their radio navigation aids had also failed. From the weather information previously supplied to them, they would have known that a descent in visual meteorological conditions would not be possible at Innsbruck. They also would have realised they had insufficient range to reach any other airport where a visual descent might have been possible.

Firemen and investigators from the German Office of Civil Aeronautics examine wreckage on the side of the autobahn embankment. The only piece recognisable is the Viscount's fin and rudder carrying the airline's logo.

The investigators therefore believed that the crew, after turning back from the mountainous terrain ahead of them around and to the south of Innsbruck, probably decided to descend while they still had a reasonably accurate idea of their position. Unfortunately however, the weather in the area of their descent was a good deal worse than forecast, with cloud extending from 14,000 and 16,000 feet down to a base of between only 700 and 1000 feet above the ground.

From the flight data record and other evidence of the investigation, the aircraft's battery voltage would have dropped below the minimum required for reliable indications of the artificial horizons and turn and bank indicators within only 10 minutes of the aircraft passing the "Mike" NDB.

The only flying instruments then available to the crew would then have been the slip indicators, the emergency compass, the altimeters, the vertical speed indicators and the airspeed indicators, provided of course that these pitot static instruments had not been affected by pitot icing after the electrically powered pitot heaters ceased to function.

As a result, the crew would have been without any means of determining the attitude of the aircraft during their prolonged efforts to maintain control while they descended in cloud. Indeed, to an increasing degree, the failing flying instruments could have given dangerously erroneous and misleading indications. The inevitable result would have been a progressive loss of control, leading to the application of severe structural loadings on the airframe, which finally exceeded its ultimate strength.

From a reconstruction of the Viscount's final flightpath, and the cloud base in the vicinity of the accident, there could be no doubt that the outer wing sections failed and broke off while the aircraft was still in cloud. The loud report heard by witnesses on the ground, shortly before the aircraft plunged from the base of the overlying cloud, was undoubtedly the sound of the wings fracturing as the crew vainly attempted to recover control. From this point onwards, it was impossible for the crew to maintain any control of the aircraft.

CAUSE

The accident was the result of the aircraft's electrical power supply failing in cruising flight, possibly without the generator warning lights illuminating. During the intentional descent that followed, which had to be carried out on instruments because of the weather, the vital instruments for indicating the aircraft's flight attitude showed increasingly inaccurate readings and failed completely after the gyros stopped rotating.

Under these conditions, uncontrolled flight attitudes were unavoidable, during which the aircraft was subjected to severe structural loadings. These loads exceeded the ultimate load and led to structural failure. It was not possible to determine with certainty why the electrical system failed.

CHAPTER 20

Catastrophic Corrosion

For passengers boarding a Vickers Vanguard at London Heathrow, the fine October morning seemed to herald the promise of good weather for their European skiing holiday. But an undetected patch of corrosion in the aircraft's tail had sealed their fate as effectively as any time bomb.

Salzberg in the Austrian snow-fields was the destination for British European Airway's Flight 706 from London on Monday, October 2 1971.

It was to be flown by G-APEC, one of the company's 139 passenger Vickers Vanguards. In service with BEA for the past decade, the medium range turboprop, powered by four Rolls-Royce Tyne engines, had been designed specifically for the company's European network.

In command of the morning's flight was 40 year old Captain E T Probert, with nearly 10,000 hours flying experience, almost 2000 of them on Vanguards. His flightcrew consisted of First Officer J M Davies, 38, with well over 3000 hours, and a more junior third pilot, Second Officer B J Barnes, 27, who had over 2000 hours, most of them accumulated as a Vanguard crew member. Also on the flight-deck for the trip was a BEA Viscount pilot, Captain G Partridge, travelling on the aircraft to gain first hand experience of Salzburg's ATC procedures.

The weather over southern England and the Low Countries that morning was fine and almost cloudless, with only a light south-easterly breeze. A layer of haze, reducing ground visibility to about four kilometres in places, lay over the London area, but above 3000 feet the air was clear with some bands of cirrus cloud at 25,000 to 30,000 feet.

Only 55 passengers had boarded the aircraft at London's Heathrow Airport by the scheduled departure time of 9.15am, promising a relatively light morning's work for the four flight attendants on duty in the cabin during the two hour flight. Pushing back from the terminal on time, the Vanguard was cleared to taxi for Runway 28L, finally lifting off from Heathrow in sunshine at 9.34am with a "Dover One" standard instrument departure clearance.

This route took the aircraft southeast over the Epsom NDB, thence eastwards via the Biggin Hill and Detling VORs, and at 9.54am, after a period of radar vectoring by London ATC, the Vanguard reported over the Dover VOR, climbing through 14,000 feet. A short time later, halfway across the English Channel on track for Belgium, air traffic control responsibility for the Vanguard was handed over to Brussels Control.

The crew called Brussels ATC on 131.1 Mhz: "Good morning Brussels, Bealine (company designation for BEA aircraft) 706 is passing 18 (18,000ft) for 190 (19,000ft), and estimating Wulpen at 04 (10.04am)." Brussels Control replied: "706, cleared Salzburg Green One (airway route), maintain Flight Level 190 on reaching."

The Wulpen VOR is situated seven kilometres inland from the Belgian coast, 18km southwest of the coastal city of Ostende, and 11km from the French border. At 10.05am, after passing over the VOR, the crew called Brussels again: "Brussels, Bealine 706. Wulpen 04 (10.04am), we're now level at 190 (19,000ft), estimating Mackel (next NDB reporting point

The turboprop Vickers Vanguard, ordered by British European Airways in 1956 following the outstanding success of the Vickers Viscount. Designed for the airline's medium range European routes, and powered by Rolls-Royce Tyne engines giving it a cruising speed of 363kt (673km/h), the type entered BEA service in late 1960.

in West Flanders, 31nm/57km further along the airway) at 10 (10.10am)."

This proved be the last normal transmission from the Vanguard. Just over five minutes later, 46 seconds after 10.09am, with no previous warning, two crew voices transmitted almost simultaneously and frantically, "We are going down...706...we are going down."

This was followed by a series of Mayday calls by both voices, and amid fragmented and garbled transmissions, accompanied by a rising propeller whine and increasing aerodynamic noise, the words, "we are going down vertically" and "Bealine 706...out of control," could be made out.

As the transmission continued over the next 54 seconds, there were also blowing and crunching noises, the words "no rudder", other weak and unreadable speech, and finally the words, "ah...this is it".

The transmission then ceased abruptly, after which a number of calls by Brussels Control to the Vanguard remained unanswered.

At this time, a number of country people in and around the villages Kanegem and Aarsele in West Flanders, just north of the road connecting the towns of Tielt and Deynze, heard a high pitched whining noise above them that was steadily increasing in volume.

Looking up into the clear sky, they were aghast to see a large four engined aircraft in a screaming, high speed dive. As it dived vertically towards the ground, they saw the aircraft was slowly rotating to the right about its longitudinal axis.

As this picture of a BEA Vanguard and Viscount (background) shows, the Vanguard was a considerably bigger aircraft, seating up to 139 passengers. But as in the case of Lockheed's Electra, the design was overtaken by the advent of the new medium range jets. Only 44 were built, 20 of which were bought by BEA.

As they watched, scarcely able to believe their eyes, the aircraft's frightening plummet continued unchecked, and it finally plunged with enormous impact into an open field, close to where a small creek crossed the Tielt-Deynze road. There was a huge fiery explosion as it did so, scattering fragmented metal in all directions over a radius of about 300 metres. One of the flying pieces of wreckage struck a car that happened to be passing on the road, slightly injuring one of its occupants.

Local people who rushed to the crash found there was nothing they could do. Apart from a vast amount of fragmented wreckage scattered around a deep impact crater, little appeared to remain of

the aircraft. Fire was burning fiercely within the crater and there was a strong smell of burning kerosene.

Investigation

Investigators from the Belgium Administration de l'Aeronautique (Aeronautics Administration) arrived at the accident site later in the morning, and were joined as soon as possible afterwards by three British air accident investigators from London.

They found that the Vanguard had crashed in a flat, grass covered field with soft clay sub-soil, close to a small creek bordered by a line of trees. The enormous impact had dug a main crater some six metres deep, and with

A BEA Vickers Vanguard approaching to land. Note the large flap area, which gave the aircraft the flexible handling characteristics desirable at some European airports.

the aircraft in an almost vertical diving attitude, the wings had each dug impact trenches on either side of the crater, so that the frontal area of the entire aircraft had been deeply imprinted in the soft ground.

Scattered around the main impact crater were pieces of disintegrated structure, while fragmented wreckage, mainly from the fuselage and empennage, and consisting for the most part of myriads of pieces of aircraft skin, lay all around. The remains of the wings, engines, and a large part of the fuselage, all in a disintegrated state, were embedded in the soft ground.

Fire had erupted on impact. There was evidence of severe burning inside the crater and of localised patches of fire damage amongst the scattered wreckage, where burning fuel, splashed from the disintegrating wing tanks as the aircraft struck the ground, had spread the fire.

Vanguard G-APEB, delivered to BEA immediately before the aircraft involved in the accident. Vickers' only other airline customer for the Vanguard was Trans Canada Airlines, which bought 23.

The fuselage, including the flightdeck and passenger cabin, was almost totally destroyed by fragmentation. The few pieces that remained were mainly from the tail area and included a portion of lower fuselage structure to which the rear pressure bulkhead was attached.

At the time of impact, the undercarriage and flaps were retracted and all four engines were under power. Pieces of equipment and structure from the flightdeck were identified, including the remains of the centre control pedestal, but no useful evidence as to the position of any other controls could be determined. Parts of all the doors, hatches and detachable panels on the pressurised fuselage were also identified, establishing that they were in place when the aircraft crashed. There was nothing amongst the wreckage to suggest that a bomb explosion had led to the accident.

It was found however, that the outer two thirds of both tailplanes and the port elevator, together with the whole of the starboard elevator, were missing from the aircraft when it struck the ground. Major pieces of both port and starboard tailplanes and elevators were found several kilometres from the main wreckage area, and their distribution on the ground was consistent with the aircraft's heading and the wind direction at the time control was lost.

A wind drift plot, constructed from the positions of the separated pieces and upper wind data, indicated that all these components had separated from the aircraft at a height of not less than 18,000 feet.

The Vanguard was equipped with a six parameter Plessey-Davall flight data recorder, mounted in the tail cone. Its cassette was recovered from amongst the scattered wreckage on the surface of the ground. Although the outer case had suffered some impact damage, the cassette had not been exposed to fire.

A printout of the data on the recorder showed that the aircraft had conformed to ATC instructions and levelled out at about 19,000 feet, six and a quarter minutes before the recorder stopped.

During this brief period of cruising flight, the airspeed increased from 210 knots to 250 knots (389-463km/h), where it remained throughout the last minute of the recording.

No unusual pitch or roll angles or acceleration levels were evident during this time, and the aileron and elevator channels of the autopilot were engaged. The recording terminated while the aircraft was in steady cruising flight at an altitude of 18,930 feet.

The recorded heading and airspeed data were used to produce a plot of the aircraft's ground track, which showed the flight recorder had stopped abruptly when the aircraft was about three kilometres to the west of the crash site.

During the last half second of the recording, the characteristics of the recording signal became highly abnormal. Even so, the remaining recorded data was still valid and showed no diversion from the previously established flightpath. The autopilot elevator and aileron channels were still engaged at the end of the recording.

In an attempt to establish the precise nature of this recording signal decay, the investigation team conducted a number of laboratory tests. They found that the type of signal deterioration experienced could occur as it did only if the power and data supplies from the processing unit to the recorder itself were interrupted in a particular sequence.

This required firstly, the separation of servo data signals, followed by that of the 115V power supply. It was also necessary that, during these separations, the two wires actually transmitting the flight data should remain intact. On Vanguard aircraft, the cable loom carrying these electrical supplies and signals passes through the rear pressure bulkhead.

The location of the accident near the villages of Kanegem and Aarsele in West Flanders, Belgium. The Vanguard impacted alongside a creek just north of a main road connecting the towns of Tielt and Deynze. Pieces of the tailplane and elevators were found scattered two to three kilometres to the north of the crash site. Their distribution, together with the aircraft's heading and the wind direction, indicated they had separated at about the Vanguard's cruising level. (Aero Illustrations)

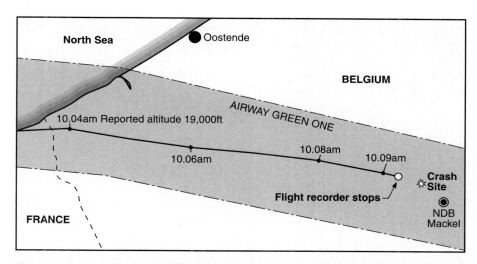

The air route being flown by G-APEC at the time of the rear bulkhead fracture. The 11 year old turboprop, carrying a crew of eight and 55 passengers, was enroute from London to Salzberg, Austria, in fine and almost cloudless conditions. It had reached its cruising level of 19,000ft only five minutes earlier. (Aero Illustrations)

Examination of the recovered loom of wires indicated that separation of the servo and power supply wires had occurred there in a manner consistent with the sequence required.

After the investigators completed their inspection of the wreckage at the accident site, some of the less fragmented pieces were taken to the Belgium Government's Administration de l'Aeronautique research establishment at Haren for more detailed examination. Any attempt to "reconstruct" the flightdeck and passenger cabin was out of the question because

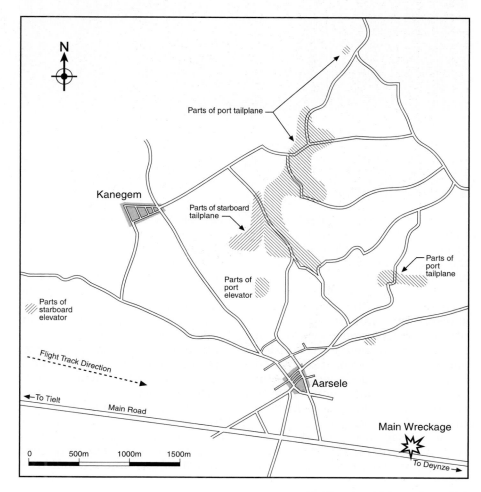

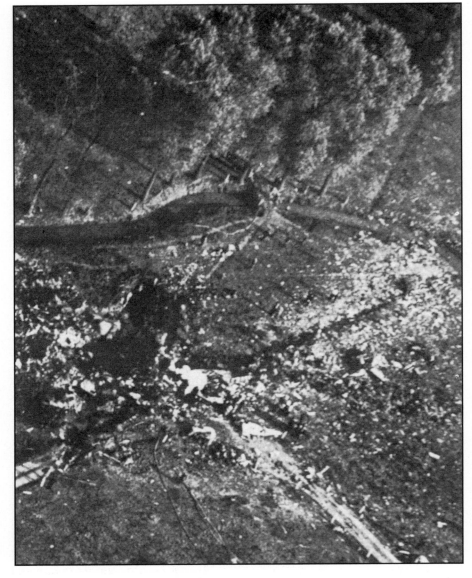

Low level aerial photograph of the fragmented wreckage beside the creek. The Vanguard's impact was so vertical and violent that, as well as a crater six metres deep, the frontal shape of the wings was deeply imprinted in the soft ground. Wreckage was flung 300 metres in all directions, one piece striking a passing car. The few remaining larger pieces included some lower fuselage structure to which the rear pressure bulkhead was attached. Fire burnt fiercely in the main impact crater after the crash.

of the devastating destruction they had sustained, but this type of investigation was possible with the less fragmented rear fuselage and empennage.

As it progressed, this "reconstruction" of the tail section showed that, with the exception of the tailplane and elevators, all the damage sustained was consistent with the near vertical attitude of the aircraft at impact. The fin and rudder had been grossly crushed and broken up, as had the fuselage dorsal structure.

The fuselage frame to which the rear pressure bulkhead was attached was broken into three main pieces, and the bulkhead itself crushed and torn into many pieces. The tail cone, with its access panel, was attached and in position at the time of the crash. The flying control linkages in the fuselage aft of the rear freight hold showed no evidence of inflight defect or malfunction.

But the skin, rib, and spar structures of both tailplanes showed a type of separation which could not be attributed to any external force. Both upper skins had been lifted and detached between the rear and front spars by either separation of the rivets, or pulling through of the countersunk rivet heads. The separation of the top skin appeared to have originated at the rear spar, where rivet impressions in the skin showed that movement of the skin occurred before any distortion of the spar took place.

Similar evidence was found on the under surface of the top skin in the region of the centre spar. Towards the tailplane roots, the upper skin had been peeled and torn from the structure.

The separation of the tailplanes and elevators from the aircraft appeared to have begun with the detachment of the upper skin, followed by rearward and downward separation of the front outboard spar sections, accompanied by a breakup of the lower skin and rear spar.

The appearance of the separated upper skin strongly suggested that internal pressure was responsible. Tests were therefore conducted to determine the behaviour of the tailplane assembly when internally pressurised.

For this purpose, another BEA Vanguard was modified to test the effect of a simulated rear pressure bulkhead rupture at a high cabin differential pressure. This included fitting a metal petal valve of appropriate cross sectional area to the bulkhead. It was calculated that the differential pressure in the cabin of G-APEC at the time its tail assembly failed was 5.75lb/sq in and, in an attempt to approximate the loads that could have acted on the aircraft's tailplanes if the rear pressure bulkhead had suddenly failed, it was decided to use a cabin differential pressure of 6.25lb/sq in on the ground to simulate a bulkhead failure at an altitude of 19,000 feet.

The tests involved increasing the cabin differential pressure to 6.25lb/sq in, then opening the petal valve to simulate the bulkhead failure. Within 0.12 seconds, the pressure differential in the tailcone reached a maximum of 5.5lb/sq in and, 0.03 seconds later it reached 4.12lb/sq in inside the tailplane.

At this point there was a sudden pressure fluctuation in the starboard outboard tailplane as severe distortion disrupted its upper skin. The worst damage was

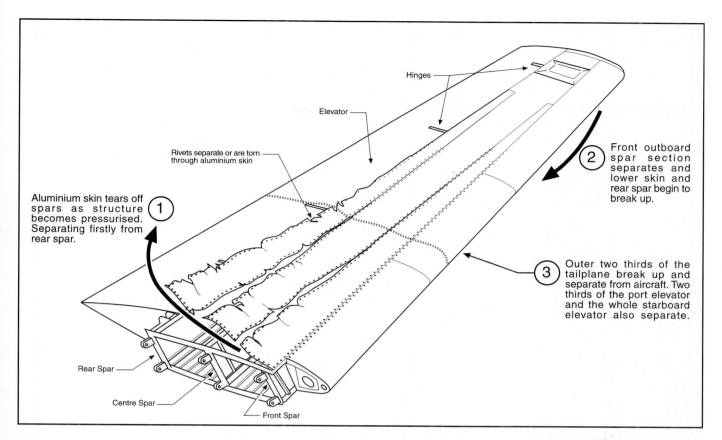

"Reconstruction" of the less fragmented pieces of the aircraft's tail at Belgium's Administration de l'Aeronautique showed the upper skins of both tailplanes had lifted between the rear and front spars, probably as a result of internal pressure, leading to separation of the tailplanes and elevators from the aircraft. Tests confirmed the damage was caused by internal pressurisation. (Aero Illustrations)

Diagram labels:

Hinges

Elevator

Rivets separate or are torn through aluminium skin

① Aluminium skin tears off spars as structure becomes pressurised. Separating firstly from rear spar.

② Front outboard spar section separates and lower skin and rear spar begin to break up.

③ Outer two thirds of the tailplane break up and separate from aircraft. Two thirds of the port elevator and the whole starboard elevator also separate.

Rear Spar

Centre Spar

Front Spar

---

across the chord of the tailplane at an elevator hinge rib, where rivet heads pulled through the skin. The skin was also distorted between the centre and rear spars. Internally, there were extensive failures of cleat-to-stringer rivets.

To determine what structural damage or failure could have occurred in flight to cause an internal pressurisation of the tailplane structure, a "reconstruction" of the crushed and torn rear pressure bulkhead was also undertaken.

The Vanguard's fuselage structure at the frame to which the rear pressure bulkhead is attached comprised a fuselage skin plating joint with doubler, the rear pressure bulkhead itself with a doubler plate bonded to its periphery, and the fuselage frame itself (see sectional diagram). The complete joint thus comprised six layers of metal riveted together.

The pressure bulkhead extended rearward in the form of a dome, built up of aluminium alloy sheet, with doubler plates at the joints. The whole of the frame joint was liberally coated with polysulphide sealant on top of the finishing paint, leaving no untreated edges, but the coating was not extended to cover the edge of the fuselage skin doubler plating.

The reconstruction established that corrosion had occurred at the base of the pressure bulkhead, beneath the peripheral doubler plate bonded to its forward face. For a distance of 48cm, roughly about the centreline, the bond was completely delaminated and the bulkhead metal had corroded away.

From the ends of the corroded area at each side, tears ran upwards and outwards, then upwards and inwards, across the lower centre panels of the bulkhead, terminating at the central hub fitting. (See diagram). The effect of the tears was to separate the lower quarter of the bulkhead containing the glands and seals through which pass the electrical services and flying controls, from the remainder, except for about 15cm of metal at the central hub fitting.

Close examination of the fracture faces of the tears on both sides of the corroded area showed that they had initially progressed gradually, possibly over more than 14 pressurisation cycles of the aircraft. By the time the tears had extended about 60mm however, a critical point was reached where the overall structural strength of the pressure bulkhead was no longer able to withstand the cabin pressure differential and, under this air pressure, the tears suddenly progressed, effectively breaching the bulkhead and allowing the pressure to extend into the tailcone and thence into the tailplane. Apart from impact damage, all the tears in the bulkhead had occurred before the aircraft struck the ground.

A second area of corrosion was found when the remains of the bulkhead plating were removed from the fuselage frame. This was located on and beneath the bracket attaching a radial bracing member to the frame and the fuselage structure on the lower starboard side. But the corrosion had

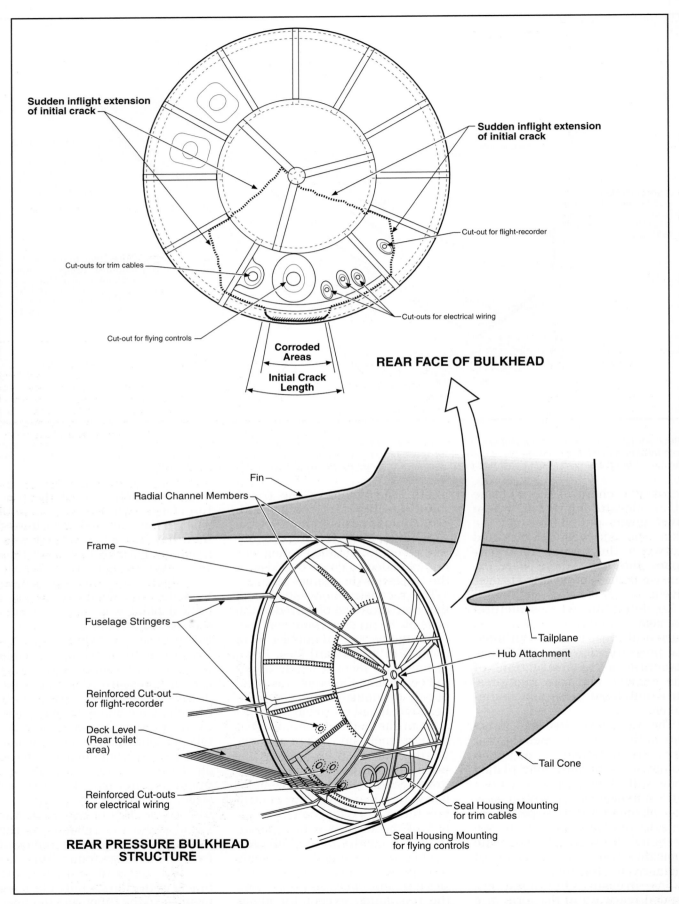

Sudden inflight extension of initial crack

Sudden inflight extension of initial crack

Cut-out for flight-recorder

Cut-outs for trim cables

Cut-outs for electrical wiring

Cut-out for flying controls

Corroded Areas

Initial Crack Length

REAR FACE OF BULKHEAD

Fin

Radial Channel Members

Frame

Fuselage Stringers

Reinforced Cut-out for flight-recorder

Deck Level (Rear toilet area)

Reinforced Cut-outs for electrical wiring

Hub Attachment

Tailplane

Tail Cone

Seal Housing Mounting for trim cables

Seal Housing Mounting for flying controls

REAR PRESSURE BULKHEAD STRUCTURE

A "reconstruction" of the crushed rear pressure bulkhead was also undertaken to determine what could have caused pressurisation of the tailplane. Cracks in the bulkhead, extending from an area of corrosion at its base, had suddenly progressed as tears, allowing cabin pressure into the tailcone and tailplane. (Aero Illustrations)

not yet progressed to the point where any crack had appeared in the bulkhead or frame structure.

No other area of corrosion was found either on the rear bulkhead itself or in the frame joint nor, superficially, was there any evidence of contaminating liquids. But on the fuselage frame immediately behind this bulkhead frame, there was a series of "tide marks" suggesting that liquid had been trapped between the rear of the bulkhead and this frame to a depth of several inches on at least 12 occasions.

The Vanguard's maintenance records also showed that an accumulation of fluid had been found in the tail cone on a number of occasions in the more recent service life of the aircraft. Since its last major inspection, eight entries, extending over a period of nearly nine months, had been made indicating that water, ice or hydraulic fluid was present in the tail cone and that the seal of the tail cone access panel required attention.

Shortly before this, one entry indicated a spillage of fluid in the rear toilet. Six months before the accident, there was a further entry concerning seepage from the rear toilet container.

In Vanguard aircraft, the fuselage space behind the pressure bulkhead is drained by pipes venting to the atmosphere. In the wreckage of G-APEC, the drain immediately behind the bulkhead adjacent to the "tide marks" was blocked by dried mud similar to that from which the wreckage was retrieved, and its pre-impact condition could not he determined. But the drain hole in the fuselage frame to which the bulkhead is attached, located at the lower centre, was found blocked by the polysulphide sealant, painted on its forward face. Surface corrosion of four square cm in area was found on the rear face of the frame, 15cm from the blocked drain.

The documented history of the aircraft showed that it was constructed by Vickers Armstrong at Weybridge in late 1959, but was not delivered to BEA until January 1961, by which time it had flown only 89 hours. It then remained in

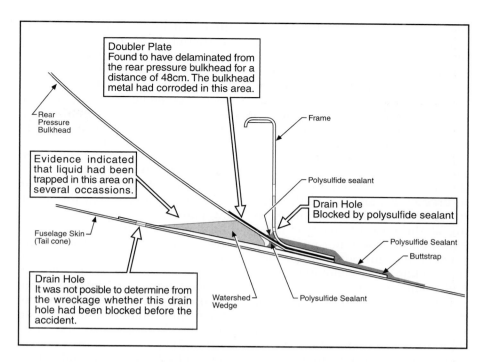

Sectional drawing of the Vanguard's lower rear fuselage structure, where the base of the pressure bulkhead attached to the tail cone. The space behind the pressure bulkhead drained to atmosphere, but the drain hole in the fuselage frame to which the bulkhead was attached was found blocked by sealant. Marks showed that liquid had been trapped behind the bulkhead many times during the 21,700 hours and nearly 11 years that the Vanguard had been in BEA service. Maintenance records confirmed that water, ice, hydraulic fluid and spillage from the rear toilet fluid had been found in the tail cone on a number of occasions. (Aero Illustrations)

continual service with BEA until the time of the accident, flying a total of nearly 21,700 hours.

Vanguard aircraft maintenance schedules required various inspections of the rear fuselage area, including the rear pressure bulkhead, for cleanliness, condition and the presence of corrosion, but only at major checks was the removal of soundproofing material below floor level required. No corrosion was reported when G-APEC was given a major check 18 months before the accident. Because it was not possible to adequately check the rear pressure bulkhead lap joints below floor level by visual means, a radiographic examination of this area was also carried out on G-APEC.

But during the investigation, a further examination of the photographic plates taken at that time showed one plate was of such poor quality that the radiographic inspection of the area it covered was of little value. No repeat radiograph was made of the section concerned, which was where the second area of severe corrosion was found after the accident.

Analysis

It was clear from the Vanguard's radio transmissions and flight recorder readout, that its operation was normal and without incident from the time of its takeoff from Heathrow to the point where the recorder ceased to function. Throughout this time, the aircraft followed its planned track and the crew responded promptly to ATC instructions.

Because the flight recorder stopped in level flight at cruising altitude, and there was reasonable accord between the last position plotted from the recorder data and the wind drift plot of the tailplane wreckage, there was no reason to doubt that it was the rupture of the rear pressure bulkhead that caused the flight recorder to cease functioning.

The investigation showed conclusively that the sudden failure of the rear pressure bulkhead began the sequence of structural disintegration that led to the accident. The rapid inflation of the tailcone and empennage by pressurised air from the cabin imposed a high differential pressure across the tailplane skin, causing its upper panels to become detached. Aerodynamic loads then caused a rapid breakup and separation of both tailplanes and elevators. The loss of the horizontal tail surfaces in cruising flight then caused the aircraft to pitch violently nosedown, with no possibility of recovery from the resulting dive.

During a number of flights immediately before the trip on which the accident occurred, the volume of pressurised air passing through the small tears that were developing at the base of the rear pressure bulkhead was not enough to prevent the aircraft's pressurisation system from maintaining normal cabin pressure.

The severe corrosion at the joint between the fuselage skin and the rear pressure bulkhead had been there for some time before the accident. It was doubtful whether the corrosion could have been seen from the rear during regular 400 hourly aircraft inspections because it was concealed within the joint, and the convergence of the bulkhead and fuselage structure restricted access to it.

By the time the tears had progressed into uncorroded metal on the bulkhead, at least one would have become visible from the rear, but the time from when it progressed to this extent until the final rupture of the bulkhead was relatively short, probably around 14 pressurisation cycles.

The aircraft's maintenance schedule assumed that the bonding paint and sealing around the bulkhead would remain effective, and provided for visual inspections only at relatively long intervals. As the investigation showed however, delamination, accompanied by corrosion, between the bonded doubler plate and the front face of the pressure bulkhead, could become severe before any visual indication was apparent.

The radiographic examination of the lower portion of the rear pressure bulkhead lap joint, made some time before the accident, did not detect the corrosion with the inspection technique then in use. The complex structure of the pressure bulkhead added to the difficulty of interpreting the photographic detail.

Because the extent of the problem at this bonded joint was not appreciated, no effective technique had been devised for its inspection. After the accident however, improved techniques, together with a modification to improve access for such inspections, were introduced.

Where hidden areas exist in an aircraft, corrosion is more likely to develop with increased age, and it is essential that inspection techniques effectively detect any such corrosion at its onset.

Cause

The accident resulted from the rupture of the rear pressure bulkhead, which led to the separation of both tailplanes in flight, causing the aircraft to dive into the ground.

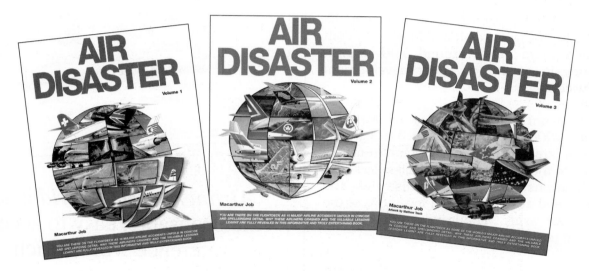

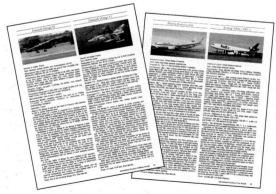
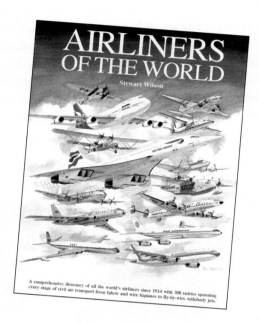